THE SUCCESS AND CONFIDENCE MANUAL

BY

LEONARD LOVE MATLICK

TABLE OF CONTENTS

HOW MUCH IS YOUR FUTURE WORTH?

Is your future worth $1000? Is your future worth $500? Is your future worth the cost of this book?

Then you can't afford to miss this opportunity to learn new ways to get ahead that will change your life forever.

The Success and Confidence Manual is highly concentrated to introduce you to methods that have been used since the beginning of time.

WHAT YOU WILL LEARN

1.   Success and Confidence Right Now!

2.   How to become a Smooth Talker

3.   How to Cover Your Butt at All Times

4.   How to Lie Effectively

These first steps will help you succeed now, RIGHT NOW, to get what you want….A well paying job when there isn't any jobs to get, confidence when you are talking to your boss or even with the opposite sex, a brand new career with sometimes a meteoric rise to the top!

If you've been downsized or laid off, never fear, the success and Confidence Manual is here.

This Manual teaches you methods, so that you'll never be laid off again.

Income Protection for YOU!

This manual is written by Leonard Love Matlick, a personal success trainer who will plan your career and advancement. This manual is too good to miss!

Buy this now! Today! You will learn thing to make you confident and succeed beyond your wildest imagination!

So, how much is your future worth? Only you can decide that. But we can help, we want the best for you. What have you got to lose? The price of this book? NO! Only your future.

CHAPTER 1

SUCCESS AND CONFIDENCE RIGHT NOW!

Hello, my name is Leonard Love Matlick, and I'm going to show you how to gain Success and Confidence right now.

Success and advancement is often based on **"behind the scenes"** maneuvering, rather than on competence or seniority. Specifically, those who want to succeed need to win favor with their superiors, join the company's social activities, and become an integral part of their company's work culture.

Today, you climb up the ladder, not on your skills, but on the strength of your demeanor and a failure to make observable mistakes. Sounds fairly strait forward, but to actually learn these traits is a required skill that many business courses left out in favor of more traditional advice. Why even parents ignored it!

This program is for anyone who wants to start or jump start their career or life using unconventional but tried and true methods. If you are stuck in a rut and don't know how to gain success and confidence, I will show you step-by-step exactly what you must do in order to obtain it. I will show you how to plan, create, and implement things that will generate confidence and success and a new life for you. All you need is desire. You know that you were destined for great things. **SO DO SOMETHING ABOUT IT!! START RIGHT NOW! START RIGHT HERE!**

So, let me tell you what I'm going to talk about, and I use plain language and I'll give you concrete tools, so it's very focused, to make you confident and succeed **RIGHT NOW – TODAY!**

First, I'll show you **HOW TO BECOME A SMOOTH TALKER**. How to let it ooze out of you like an oil leak. But, I'll show it to you in very practical terms. You'll discover that there is a whole world of difference between talking and "smooth talking". Vocal techniques and skill not withstanding, I'll show you how to practically apply them. And make no mistake about it, these are the techniques that smooth talkers use to ensure their success, and they are **SOO** easy, you can use them too. Smooth talking is going to be the foundation of your success and I'll show you how it works. You'll also find out what to say and how to say it. Without thinking, by rote, without fuss, without muss. You'll preface everything by first smooth talking. You've heard of "Jive talking", well this is smooth talking.

And I'm going to talk very bluntly about **HOW TO COVER YOUR BUTT AT ALL TIMES (CYA)**. This is also one of the most important things that you'll ever have to know. Today, it seems that you have to spend more time and be more adept at covering yourself than in actually doing the work. Nobody ever remembers how quickly you did something, only if there was a mistake and who's to blame. Nobody will come to save you either, so you must always cover yourself. And I'll show you how and who you can turn to and what you can use for protection.

We'll discuss why you should lie to get ahead. **HOW TO LIE EFFECTIVELY**. This is very important and we'll discuss that in depth. You must excel in borderline lies and manipulations to create the right circumstances for your advancement. However, social niceties aren't lies. And in the following chapters I'll show you how to do that also as well as many other things.

Previously, the rules for this was only whispered or discussed in executive washrooms. How would it sound publicly to say that one person got promoted over another because he kept his superiors better informed (**a** smooth **talker**), went to every company function (**a brown noser),**and clearly saw and heard the obvious at hand (**a backstabber).** Clearly, those who are ambitious seem to be on a different level than the average person who thinks that this type of training is just a bunch of bull (**and maybe it is).** But in this economy, whatever works, works, and **THIS WORKS!** Just look around and see if it doesn't.

And it doesn't matter if it's a technical field like say engineering or computers, or it's manual labor, say on the loading dock, or even if it's sales or a teaching position. Smooth talking does get you ahead anywhere. And fast! It's a fact – **smooth talking does work!**

And you know that for yourself. Just look around where you work and you can readily see that smooth talkers (**b.s.ers**) abound, not only there, but in politics, in school, everywhere. So then the question is, **why can't you?**

I'm an engineer by trade, so it was much more difficult for me than for most. Wherever I went, the person who knew absolutely nothing, even in a **technical field like engineering, I mean they did not even know the right time of day, but they knew how to b.s., how to gladhand, how to kiss ass, how to cover their butt, how to be a social butterfly, how to grandstand, they were getting promoted faster and kept their job even in a massive layoff.**

And it didn't matter what company I went to or in what state; I have worked everywhere, on the West Coast, on the East Coast, down South , in the Mid-West, they, the b.s.ers, would get ahead all of the time. So, being an engineer and a very logical person, I started to see if I could write down what were their traits. Could I profile them? How did they do this. I mean, there isn't a school like a Dale Carnagie course for b.s.ers (**I wish there was**), so how did they learn all this stuff. I wanted to see if I could find them anywhere. Could I spot a b.s.er. Was there a way to find them in a crowd?

So, could I put together a profile or a composite of a b.s.er and use this as a way to easily find them. And do you know what? After so many years of watching them (**almost 30 years**) , I was able to pinpoint them. I could spot them anywhere, they are so obvious. I got so good at spotting them that I found them everywhere I went. They are all over. **You know that**! But then I wanted to see if they would all react the same way, if they would all do the same predictable thing like all bsers. And do you know what? **They did! They did!!!**

Now, most of them did not know what they were doing, they probably weren't conscious of doing it, but they all had certain traits and characteristics common to all bsers. And it didn't matter if it was a man or a woman, it didn't matter if they were young or old, latino, black, asian or white, fat or thin, handsome or plain, it didn't matter, it was the same! It was the **SAME**!!!

Do you remember that famous phrase about bsing, the one that goes,

"If you can't dazzle them with brilliance, then baffle then with bullshit!"

Well, it's true! But I say forget brilliance altogether, concentrate on bullshit only. The person who can talk well and a lot, to any person, on any subject, is always liked and will get ahead faster than the person who is more knowledgeable or even the one who does more. This is true in almost every facet of life – at home, at work, in politics, business, the arts; good bull throwers always seem to make it to the top everywhere. Bullshit it seems, nowadays is being considered by many to be the logical replacement for natural born or acquired talents.

I don't know why this exists, but it sure does and throughout history has been a standard success formula. Why even Napoleon had said,

(In a very French accent)**"Be a posier, that's the way to succeed!"**

"Sacre bleu!" (A posier is a poser- an actor)

And he certainly did. How many times have you been in a bar or at a party and listened to a guy or a gal with a silver tongue who holds court for hours and keeps everybody's attention. He says,

"I'm the greatest!"

And no one says that he's not. He's the sharpest dresser there, he's super friendly, he's a ladies man, he's always telling jokes, he's sure that he's got his act together; in fact he's always considered by others to be a **"winner".** But if you got right down to basics and took him apart piece by piece, you'll find that in reality he's just a good bull thrower, **a "bullshit artist."**

Now being tagged as that today, doesn't carry with it the banal connotation of what it did. Years ago if you said that you were the greatest, the standard answer was uncontrollable laughter. Today, however, when someone says that, nobody questions it. They won't ask you to prove it for fear of offending you or calling you a liar or even being thought stupid. Like the Emperor's new clothes, nobody will admit that you're naked. (**Thank God!)**

Fortunately, anyone can learn how to get ahead with using this type of method. It doesn't take talent or training, and the few basics are very easily learned. And the best part is that it's open to all and there's no limitation as to age or sex. Why even mediocre workers will learn how to easily vault over those who possess even some iota of knowledge. **That's how great this is!!!**

And, I know, you're probably saying, yeah, it's true, but I can't bring myself to do that – to b.s.

You say that you can't stand them. **I agree.** Now, before we go any farther, let me say right now that I hate b.s.ers,brownnosers, backstabbers and the like. If this was a perfect world with all of my education and training, I'd be at the top of my profession. But this isn't a perfect world. And they, the bsers are the ones in power. Their methods do work! And if you'll just bear with me, I'll prove to you and show you that you can be one of us (**like the Marines) – the few, the proud (salute!) the scoundrels!**

But, you're also probably saying, how can I talk about b.s.ing, something that is so banal, something that is so trivial, something that is so crass. But that is what getting ahead is really about isn't it? Getting so lowdown where nobody else is. Forget all the bull about taking the **"high"** road, about being above all of this and working your butt off and getting education and training and seniority. **That is all bull!!** It's like that old Scottish ditti,

"You take the high road and I'll take the low road, and I'll be in Scotland before you!"

It's true! Even back then, 500 years ago they knew, take the low road! And how about the limbo – How low can you go. Or politics – that's about as low as you can go. They all tell you to get low. But b.s.ing is not inborn nor is it difficult to learn. And none of the methods that I'm going to describe are really hard. It is just how far are you willing to go in order to get ahead. And how far is that ? **As far as you want to go!**

Now we all know what the 3r's are, don't we-'readin','ritin',and 'rithmatic'. All high academic illuminating subjects and you're to be congratulated, all of you. Yes, you've done very well indeed. No, really. You can read, you can write, and you can do your checkbook. But you're here and that means to me that the 3 r's have not gotten you where your parents and your teachers promised it would take you. Like me, they told you to excel in school and in business and it would take you as far as you wanted to go. Now we all know that is a bunch of b.s. Don't we? Don't we?

The 3 b's however, can take you very high, much higher than the 3 r's. I'm talking about the banal arts. You've all heard about Harry Potter and the Magic Arts. Well this is similar but, this is real and not imaginary. Banality then is the key to success. **No, hear me out! The 3 b's are bsing, backstabbing and brownnosing**. And what we will learn here are their modern variations such as grandstanding, gladhanding, showboating, posturing, smoothtalking, scapegoating and most important of all, how to cover your ass. Yes, your backside, that good ole CYA. Most important.

So then, simply put, bsing is the quickest way to get ahead without possessing too much knowledge or luck. All it takes is a single minded desire to move forward at any cost and the willingness to do things that you thought you'd never lower yourself to do in order to accomplish it. Once you can accept this, doing the rest is easy. **Really!**

Now, none of what I am going to describe should be difficult to accomplish. You should be able to start right now, here, wherever you are. The methods that bsers use are the same everywhere and while it does take some getting used to at first, it can be learned fairly easily. It's a big job to be a bullshit artist, but I'm going to show you how to do it, so that it will seem like a piece of cake.

Realize that this is an actual school, but you won't get credit for it on your resume. But you will be able to use it for the rest of your life and that's what really counts. So, if anybody rudely asks you,

"Where did you learn to kiss ass like that?"

You just say,

"Right here!"

CHAPTER 2

HOW TO BECOME A SMOOTH TALKER

Smooth talking is your key to poise, popularity and success. Mastering it will increase your personal and social effectiveness, so in reality, you talk your way to success. But smooth talking is more than starting conversations, it's more than mingling, and even more than shmoozing, it is when you get right down to it ...**MAGIC!**

Smooth talkers have the **"gift of gab"**. These people are admired because they have the ability to enter a strange room and start to talk to others without the slightest hesitation. To some it's an inate ability, to those of us who know it, it's an acquired skill, and like other skills, it can be learned and perfected.

All it takes is the determination to do it. So what are you waiting for? But hear this, and hear it well, doing this will not make you Mr. or Ms. Popularity overnight. You have to do that on your own. **But even this is easy!**

As a general rule for smooth talking, you should feel as if the thing that you're doing is so stupid and so obvious that any fool can find you out. And most important, you've got to play act and think that you're getting away with it. The key here is to **FAKE IT UNTIL YOU MAKE IT!** That should be your motto, **fake it until you make it**. If you don't give yourself away, no one will find out. And if they do, all you do is laugh like you're agreeing with them, like it's a big joke or they caught you in a little white lie. Now think back, every time that you caught a smooth talker in a lie, he laughs right? **Do the same!!**

Of course you would always make up phony but logical sounding reasons for not doing something and this is essentially what smooth talking is really about. Never, repeat never, tell the truth or your real reasons for doing something. Be oily, be greasy, sidestep issues, actually bullshit your way out of the truth by use of bander or bluff, talking in circles or riddles; in plain language – double talk.

Sometimes a flurry of words one right after another will suffice, other times, use of exaggerated words or phrases deliberately affected will turn the trick for you. Then, and this is very important, you must embellish things when you do or say something. Make it more than it actually is. Say what you did was the greatest, say what you have is the best. Make your problems bigger than everybody else's. No wasteful boasting, but it starts to set up a showmanship style in the way that you talk.

Just speak in a loud, distinct voice and don't mumble. Talk slow and deliberately, like those men on TV soap operas do. Actually read a soap opera script if you have to, but don't speak in such a low voice that people keep having to say,

"What did ya say?"

or

"Pardon?"

You must also spend a considerable amount of time in chatting with others or in visiting other people. Be charming and sociable to all, especially those that you want to impress. But don't wait for them to invite you, always include yourself; barge right in if you have to. Then say anything that comes to mind, even if it's dumb or childish.

ESPECIALLY IF IT'S DUMB OR CHILDISH!!

Be spontaneous and talk about anything, it doesn't matter – the weather, sports, or travel. For instance, if you mention sports, know all of the scores of the local teams, even if you don't like sports. A lot of people are really into that and you can quickly get into a conversation if someone asks,

"What was the score of the Dallas game?"

And it doesn't matter if you don't know. Adlib. Say, "I only saw the first half." (Nobody is going to question you.)

Or you can **START** a conversation by saying,

"How about those Jets, huh?"

Make up about the game as you go along as if you were a TV sportscaster.

"What a play that was in the end zone. Wow!

He made some great catch!"

Nobody cares if you missed the fourth quarter. Just keep on talking. Talk about the same thing over and over again, and always have a story to tell. For example, if someone says something about the problems that he's having with his car (**and we all have problems like this**) you start a story about it.

"It's funny you should mention that...

And then tell the same story 25 times. Most people are too conscientious to say that they've heard it before. And in case that they do, they'll probably joke about it.

"Oh there he goes again, talking about his car."

After that, the best thing to do is always try to impress and awe people. Collect accomplishments and display them prominently. You got an award from the town for taking out the garbage 2000 times. Brag constantly about it and your accomplishments to anyone that you see. Call them by name and bring them over, and, if no one comes near, start yelling as loud as you can,

"C'MERE! C'MERE!!" to anyone who passes bye.

It doesn't matter if it's the neighbor's kid or some being that just arrived from another planet, like E.T. – just impress them. You should strive to give the impression that you only go for the best, whatever is the "**good stuff**".

And above all, always give the impression that you do things just because you **WANT** to and not because you **HAVE** to.

**"I play racquetball at 2 in the morning. I don't
need to reserve a court THEN."**

So just keep on bending their ear. Talk a lot, because nobody ever really listens to what you are saying anyway. They are just too concerned with themselves and their own lives. **Capitalize on this!** If a person makes a general statement on any stupidity like,

"Rain doesn't come from clouds – it comes
from all those space ships defecating."

You say,

"Oh, you're SOO right."

or

"I agree."

or

"I can't believe that somebody is so perseptive."

or

"It's refreshing to see that you are so well informed."

Remember, always ask them about themselves and what they're doing. Act like an interviewer and be moderately amazed at what they are saying.

"Unreal! You don't mean to say that you act-u-ally…"

or

"Wow! You climbed Mt. Everest in your BARE FEET!"

Just keep making them feel that they should have been made famous for it.

"They really should have named a street for you."

or

"Your picture should be on the cover of Time."

Make everyone feel that your whole interest in life is **THEM!** That you care only about **THEM!** That everything on this earth should go to **THEM!** That everything that they say are pearls of wisdom and that you are awaiting on their **EVERY** word! That's how it should always sound. Once you pick out a person, zero in on them to the exclusion of others. **(their turn will come as soon as you get to them!)** Now, since everybody likes to be included in a conversation, draw them in. Call them by name and ask them what they think.

"Hey, Joe, c'mere. I know that you know a lot about…"

or

Let's say that you're talking about playing tennis with someone. Pick somebody else out nearby and say about him so that he can just overhear it,

"I bet that Joe is a REAL tennis player."

Or if the subject is women, say,

"I bet that Jim there is a REAL ladies man."

So here's the truth. You must always complement or flatter someone shamelessly. You've got to actually snow them to get them to think that you're their friend, their bosom buddy. And to be really effective, you've got to get close to them. So go ahead – stand right on top of 'em. **Put your arm around them!** Shake hands like a politician does, with both of your hands clasped over theirs.

Then always say that what you have or what you do is **INFERIOR** to what somebody else does or has.

"Mine's okay, but yours is GREAT! No seriously, where did you get it?"

or

"I've always admired the best and you are IT! YOU ARE!"

Also do this. Be informal with others when talking about your family as if they know them well. For instance, call your mother and father,

"My mom"

or

"My dad"

When talking to others about your parents. Never say "My mother or my father."

And when telling about your brother or sister, say,

"Well Bill did......."

or

"You know how Suzie is....."

Whether they ever met them or not. Smooth talkers have their own language too.

In addition, try to do things unexpected, so that people will laugh. Don't be afraid to do things others are too inhibited to do. **Of course this is after you first sneak that it's safe to do!**

Become known as a comedian; joke a lot. Steal jokes from others and from TV shows and then claim them as your own. But never admit to the joke not being yours or give any impression that you are not the next greatest comedian to ever walk the face of the earth.

And to be a good talker, you must always be in the best of fashion and be the best dressed person wherever you go or whatever you do. Even if you're just going to work on your car or around your house, be super-hip and uninhibited in your clothes. Always wear what's **"in"** and not out. Not only in clothes, but in records, cars, language. If everybody is wearing a certain type of sunglasses at the beach and just standing around looking bored stiff, then you do the same. If everybody drives a Porshe, then you do it too. If everybody...., whatever, **YOU** do it. Individualists do not make it. **Me too ism does.**

Not only must you give the impression that you are the greatest gift to the world, but you must always give the **RIGHT** answers whether you believe it or not. For instance, if somebody out of the blue say, do you believe in kissing ass, you say, **NEVER!** In a really indignant attitude. Say,

"HOW DARE YOU!! The very thought of it indeed."

You should always say what is right, what is moral, what is proper, what is legal, what is expected, what is lawful, or else someone will turn it against you. **(He said!)** Be careful of what issues you talk about and to whom. And even if you do, **THEY** will say the same wonderful things behind your back about bullshit artists that you used to. Like,

"Money talks, bullshit walks!"

But don't ever listen to them. Here's the real truth, in this world it's bullshit that talks, and talks and talks.

CHAPTER 3

HOW TO COVER YOUR BUTT AT ALL TIMES (CYA)

Today, it seems that you have to spend more time and be more adept at covering yourself than in actually doing the work. You always have to stand and defend yourself and think fast on your feet. Nobody ever remembers how quickly you did something, only if there was a mistake and who's to blame. Even if it's 3 months or 3 years ago. They'll just as quickly forget the kudos you got for staying up to all hours at night or came in early or worked thru lunch and dinner just to get the job out on time. And God forbid it's not exactly right and **"THEY"** are the first ones to jump down your throat.

"YOU DID IT! IT WAS YOU!!!" They'll shout at you.

And it doesn't matter if you didn't have the right information or that you were rushed into doing it. Nobody will come to save you either, it is only you, and you can't count on anyone else, so you must always cover yourself. Who can you turn to or what can you use for protection? Where is there a tree to hide behind? Where is your safety?

First, look for an excuse, any excuse will do, to save your hide. Can you blame it on anyone? Pin the blame on another person or another department. Say that it was all because of the extra work and that's why. Take a closer look. Was there an addendum to it? If there was, latch onto that , or onto anything you can. But save your own hide, because no one else will. Say to yourself,

"Better you than me."

If someone pins you down on why you didn't get your work done, always pin it on someone else. Say,

"I would've finished it with plenty of time to spare

but Joe Blow held me up. I've been waiting for some VITAL information from him, that is ABSOLUTELY NECESSARY for me to finish my work, and you know how slow he is…

Well….so that's why. But I tried, I really did."

And then proceed to talk about the **"big picture"** of the job again. Get him away from your part of it, so he forgets what he came over for. If anybody else asks, say it's because all of these other people and all of these other departments are **NOT DOING THEIR WORK** and that's why and they're holding you up.

"If only Jim Shmoe would have done what he was

supposed to, we could have finished yesterday.

Now, because of him, we can't finish until next year.

At the earliest!"

And then in an afterthought, say,

"Come to think of it, maybe next century! That's how

far behind we are thanks to HIM!!!"

Then if anybody asks you if you completed your work or your part of the job, don't answer with a yes or no, say,

"It's in the works."

And then say as if in an afterthought,

"I'm still waiting for some VITAL information from that idiot George!"

And then start talking them to death. If it's your boss or some higher up who is asking you about your work, always lead them away from it. **LEAD THEM AWAY!!!**

Just start talking about anything, the weather, sports, or other people, but you **MUST** get them away from your work or knowledge of it.

So purposely ask a question that you already know the answer to in order to start a conversation with your boss or higher ups on anything.

"Do paper clips come in large sizes?"

Then tell a story about how, in the last place that you worked in, that you had to **ACTUALLY BEND** the paper clips to size and it was incredibly **HARD**, so **HARD** in fact, that if it wasn't for **YOU**, that the paper clips this company uses and the whole industry, even the **WHOLE WORLD**, wouldn't come in large sizes.

Wow! I really am the best! I really am!!

Get him to agree that you really are. ("Yes, you really are the best paper clipper that I've ever seen")

And use this excuse for everything – a mistake that you did, or if somebody asks who told you to do something – always put the blame on someone who left. If they are not there, who's to say it's not so. If you know that you made the mistake (**NEVER!!!-YOU DON'T MAKE MISTAKES!!!**), try to sweep it under the carpet. Destroy any original work that puts you at fault. This way, if they can't find it, they can't lay any blame on you, now can they.

Question:" I can't seem to find that original copy of the

Schmuck report. Do you know where it is?"

LIE!!!!! Your answer is: "**I NEVER saw it.**"

Here's another good one to try; make a file disappear. But not just the file, make the whole file cabinet or hard drive disappear. This way if anyone blames you on anything say,

"Don't blame me. You know the files that were stolen.

The proof was in there. And I don't have a copy. That's

why I can't document it."

Nobody can say differently, now can they?

Here's a trick that I learned that you can use to also save yourself. Have a very sloppy signature. If you can't distinguish it at all, then you're really going to have a meteoric rise to the top. The more scrawled the better.

Start by using your left hand to write if you're a righty and vice versa if you're a lefty. Then try to copy it with your writing hand. Then make it worse; pronounced worse. Look at higher ups signatures and try to emulate their signature. Most will have a big first letter and then a wavy line to represent the rest of their name. Try for this. That way, nobody can pin you down about signing something. If you can't make it out, neither can anyone else, so you can't be blamed. You can always say,

"That's not my signature."

It can be very effective sometimes when you're at fault and somebody finds out.

Don't be rushed into doing your work. Nobody ever remembers that that they rushed you; only if you made a mistake, and then they will blow it all out of proportion. They will always forget that they gave you kudos because you stayed up to 3AM to get it out, and then came back at 4AM to do more work. And it doesn't matter if it was 4 months or 4 years ago. **"THEY"** will be the first ones to jump down your throat again and again, until you gag. So always say,

"I will try to get it out as fast as I can, but I'm working for Mr. Idiot (the big boss) and we must adhere to the schedule that he put as a priority."

But don't ever say, that they should go ask him to put their work ahead of his. Just leave the hint that you're working on **HIS** favorite project.

"Mr. Idiot has said that this HAS to go out today; It's a must"

So always backcheck your work, always check your work too, because nobody else will, who has your best interests at heart.

Now, let's say that you have to go to a meeting. Never go into a meeting without protection. Cover your ass at all times. If somebody says,

"Who did it?"

You calmly proceed to pull out your papers and prove that **HE** did. **PASS THE BUCK!!!** Don't let it stop to even rest for a minute by you. Not even for a second. Not for any amount of time. Pass it on. Immediately pounce on them.

"What do you mean MY FAULT!!! IT'S YOUR FAULT AND YOUR WHOLE DEPARTMENTS FAULT!!!"

The purpose of meetings are not to exchange information. They are to exert domination, to find fault, to pin the blame on someone. Always go in there on the offensive. **ATTACK!!**

If someone makes a positive statement, say,

"Not necessarily."

If someone makes a negative statement, say,

"Why not?"

Armed with these two phrases and just repeating them can get you through any meeting without knowing anything at all.

Your opposition may say,

"Well why not?"

And you just lean forward adamantly and say,

"YES! WHY NOT?"

Your opposition will then have to give possible reasons for why not and you just say,

"EXACTLY!" as you lean back into your chair.

Always try to control the meeting. Don't let anyone else get even a chance to speak. Constantly interrupt them.

"One more thing…"

or

"Just a minute, let me say….."

or

"This is important…."

Every 2 seconds **DO NOT** let anybody else get a chance to speak! **EVER!!! EVER!!**

Say,

"Let me just tell you about this…."

or

"Look at this…."

or

"Before you begin…."

or the best,

"WAIT!! YOU HAVEN'T SEEN THIS…."

And then always talk over what people are saying, Just talk **LOUD A LOT!!**

"This is not a trivial thing that I'm talking about…."

or

"Can I also add a little item to what I was just talking about. Listen to this."

or

"WAIT!! HEAR ME OUT!!!

This is what they say of every tyrant, that he has his own agenda. It's not true!

HIS AGENDA (YOURS) IS THE AGENDA!!

This is the way it should always come across.

Also, it's a very good idea to make up an agenda and circulate this to everybody at the meeting before the meeting starts. This way if somebody should bring something unexpected up, you can simply say,

"Well, it's not on the agenda – let's go through this stuff first and then if we have time we'll take that up."

But remember at the end of the meeting **NOT** to bring it up.

However if he does bring it up say,

"I'm late for another meeting. Let's put it on the schedule."

There are also certain phrases which you should use at meetings,

"I'm glad you picked that up- it's significant. Very significant." (to a mistake that someone found)

or

"That's not my initials – who signed my initials- find out- it's very important." (to a document that you signed that's putting you at fault)

or

If somebody says, **(and this is especially good)**

"That's the way we've always done it."

Or asks a question,

"How did we do it in the past?"

You just answer,

"That's no criterion." (It gives you the upper hand, like you only care for what is he best way to do something) and then say,

"What's the matter with you! We are responsible for doing it the right way! The correct way!"

Now if they attempt to respond, cut them off!

"I'm surprised at you." (And then don't say anything, but continue to stare at them)

Now if somebody asks **YOU** a question that you don't know the answer to, make up a plausible excuse,

"I just got on the job."

And then, always agree with someone, anyone, at meetings,

"OK, alright….we'll do that."

Even if they talk about 40 or 50 items, just agree with each point.

"Yes, yes, I'll do it."

or

"OK ,ok. We'll do it."

or

"I'll take care of it." (Whatever **IT** is.)

or

"Yup, I'll fly to the Moon."

or

"Yes, we'll do a 5 year job in 5 minutes. Absolutely!!"

And then don't do any of it! **NOT ONE IOTA!** This way at the next meeting you call him and say,

"Oh, I just didn't have time. I've been on 30 different jobs."

Always use an even number, it sounds better.

And again, promise them, again, and again,

"You can count on me....I'LL DEFINITELY DO IT!"

But NEVER do it!

If someone should ask for specific information, say,

"Let me get back to you."

or

"I'll definitely get back to you."

And again, NEVER DO!

Also, if somebody should say,

"What about.......?"

You say,

"Oh, we don't have time for that now, let's take it up at the next meeting."

And then forget to schedule the next meeting.

Oh, and one more thing about meetings. Always, always, use this phrase at the end of a meeting,

"Did you get what you needed?"

Follow up to any question asked you, **ESPECIALLY** if you didn't know the answer.

And also say to nobody in particular as you're getting up to leave,

"I think that we got a lot accomplished."

Especially if **NOTHING** was accomplished.

Then, you must write everything down. Write it down. Even the most unimportant item.

People will forget, so write it down.

WRITE IT DOWN! WRITE IT DOWN! WRITE IT DOWN!! WRITE IT DOWN!!!

Say, **"Do you remember this?"**

And if you think that I am overstressing this, you are very right- **I AM!!**

You have to cover yourself at all times. Put down the date, the time, the person who gave you this information or the statement that they made. If you can't write it down, try to remember it until you can write it down. And then memo them to death with what you were told. Say,

"Jim, I just want to put down on paper what you said. It was……….."

And then memo everybody that's within the closest million miles on what "Jim" said.

And that's all you should ever do all day long – write memos to others or yourself, write memos to your boss and his boss, the Vice-President, the President, the CEO anybody!

Even go out of your way as to write memos to those who have absolutely nothing whatsoever to do with your job or even your company. Or even this continent. Forget about getting the work out – this is much more important. I would suggest that at least every fifteen minutes throughout the day, you should write a memo to someone. Some of these should be about complaining what was not done (**the coffee pot was not cleaned!!),** some grandstanding about what you did (**I emptied the garbage pail 100 times),** even some backstabbing about your co-workers (**Jim forgot to shut the lights and when I came in at 3AM to do some extra work, well, is he paying the electric bill?) (more on this later).**

Also, you should collect and assemble any and all documents to prove your point.

Maintain an extensive file system for all that you need – other peoples memos, letters, calculations, business cards, tapes of recorded conversations (**YES!**) whatever….even the smallest piece of paper that you hurridly copied down what they said is vitally important.

And I would strongly suggest keeping this evidence in a vault or fire-proof box for a minimum of 10 years or until everybody else leaves the company or dies.

But no matter how diligent you are in doing this, others will corner you at the most inopportune moment and you won't be able to pull out your proof that fast.

They will plot and plan and set up an ambush just to do you in.

"Good, he's away from his desk – Now let's get him!"

But, don't worry – play the game like they do and you'll do just fine. It really doesn't matter if it's right or wrong as long as you can outsmart them. Simply do this on your feet even as the person is talking to you. See what you can turn that they're saying to your advantage. Do like a lawyer would and pick up on small inconsequential points and blow them all out of proportion.

"WAIT A MINUTE! WAIT A JUST DARN MINUTE!!

"The paper that you're showing me is all wrong! The margin is off by 1 millionth of an inch – incredible!!"

Then listen to what their saying and again pick up on minor points; pick up on everything in your defense. Don't be a nice guy and let it pass or just take it, because **"THEY"** won't. I would even suggest that you take a course at a law school in debating semantics.

That's how important picking upon small points is the only protection that you have is **YOU!!** So use your mouth to cover yourself. For instance, always use the words,

"Not my job."

When anybody asks you why you didn't do something or why didn't you take the responsibility. Always know what the limits of your job or responsibility is and don't take anything extra on without the credit for the work. Say,

"I'd love to help your project make its date,

but Mr. Jones has me doing a special project also."

Another thing, never, **NEVER!** Make snap decisions. Even if it is the easiest answer you can give, **NEVER DO IT!!!** Here's why. You just came inside, and somebody asks you a very simple question,

"Is it sunny outside?"

DON'T DO IT!!!

Don't give an answer that even it appears harmless will just only get you into trouble. Because let's say it's your boss who just asked you if it was sunny outside, and you told him it was. Well guess what. There was a sudden thunderstorm and your boss is going out without an umbrella and he is going to get soaking wet, all because you just told him that it was sunny outside!

Always make up an answer.

"I haven't been outside, I'll get back to you and find out."

Even if you've just walked in. Always say that ,

"I'll get back to you."

or

"I can't give you an answer on that since I don't have my papers with me." (that always sound good)

And always add,

"I'll get back to you."

And then **NEVER DO! DELAY! DELAY! DELAY!!**

Don't answer any questions. If you do this all day, nobody can trip you up.

Also, don't give an answer until **THEY** give **YOU** everything first. Let them first give you all material, paperwork, answers **BEFORE** ever giving them the time of day. Just simply don't give an answer. Always say, "We'll go back to the office (or file room) and take a look at it. We can't give you an answer right off the top."

Now, anybody who can write their name can be good at memo writing and it's such an easy subject to master. The first thing is never let anything pass your desk without commenting on it . Even if it's just the scores of the company softball game, write something like.,

"Great game! You guys should turn pro!"

or

"Better luck next time. It wasn't fair –they cheated!"

In addition, you have to give the impression of a true winning type person at all times and the only way that is accomplished is to sneak that it's safe first. So learn to be sneaky. Wait. Always, always make sure that it's safe before you do anything- even leaving your work area. Who's watching you go? Is the boss counting the number of times that you go to the bathroom or to the water fountain? Check around first. Every few minutes gaze around to see who's watching you. Somebody will be, I guarantee it. If you are on the way up, somebody is **ALWAYS** watching you. Don't leave it to chance.

But, even if not one person is watching you, it sets up a feeling of being sneaky. So check around first before you attempt to do something.

Then, always look busy in case anybody should glance over to you. You've got to be working or at least appear to be. It doesn't matter if you're just erasing what you just put down, but make it appear that you're always working. **NEVER SIT BACK AND RELAX!**

Also, make a lot of noise to prove to everybody that you're working. If your boss can hear you, he knows without watching you that you're busy. So get a noisy pen or computer or keep sharpening pencils all day or move quickly or open and close desk drawers or make your chair squeak or put your pen down hard so that it makes a noise or slam something into the wall or staple pages very loudly, etc. But be **VERY NOISY!**

People are strange – if you're noisy, it means to them that you're working; if you're quiet, it means that you're not. And you must **ALWAYS** give the impression that you're very busy, so busy in fact that you're loaded with work, say aloud,**" I've got 30 jobs going out at the SAME TIME!!"**

I would also suggest very strongly that you work during lunchtime. At least until everyone leaves and then start again when everybody start coming back. This makes you look like you've worked thru lunch.

Staple pages together. And again, make a lot of noise. Staple it very loudly. But lift the stapler and the paper high in the air, about face level if you're sitting down. This looks good and it looks like you're working. And by the way, you really don't have to be working on company projects, far from it; only let it appear that way. You can write out bills, write letters, read magazines, etc. and it works. It really works.

WATCH OUT THOUGH!!

There may be some people who eat in during lunch too. Don't let them come over to you to see what you're doing. Let's say that you're writing something personal and somebody comes over and says,

"Can't get your work done, huh?"

LIE!!! Say as **LOUD** as you can so that the next century can hear you.

"NO!!! THEY'VE REALLY PILED THE WORK ON ME.

I HAVE NO HELP TO GET IT OUT. SAY, BY THE WAY, IF YOU'RE JUST STANDING AROUND DOING YOUR USUAL NOTHING, HOW ABOUT GIVING ME A HAND?"

Or something to that effect. But zing it to them, because they're trying to zing it to you. Or you can use the old standard,

"NO!!! THIS IS A RUSH JOB. THEY'RE COUNTING ON ME TO GET IT OUT!"

And then there's the good,

"WELL, IF YOU MUST KNOW NOSY, I'M DOING A SURVEY ON YOUR DEPARTMENT FOR THE PRESIDENT!!"

This usually shuts them up and /or gets them worried. Like, are **THEY** in that report and how come **YOU** have been given the job.

Then don't say anything else or feel that you have to. But continue to write or do whatever that you're doing. Now, some type of people will continue to press on and say,

"Well, what are you doing?"

STARE AT THEM!! Slowly- very slowly! Eyes stern, focused on them. Then keep denying. **DENY! DENY! DENY! LIE!!** Joke about it.

"Ha,ha. Can't pull the wool over your eyes, can I?"

But don't ever say what you're doing. Keep fending off and eventually they will give it up. And if they don't – simply walk away. Say,

"I'd love to talk but I gotta go take a piss!" (More on fending off embarrassing direct questions later)

Now, what I am going to say may sound stupid, but it is very good training on how to do less work and get paid for it. You have to be able to sleep on the job without getting caught. And not only that, it is excellent training on other things, i.e. not being at work and being paid for it, or of doing other stuff on company time or even how to get away with certain things. There are tricks to every business.

First, get a pair of very dark sunglasses, the darker the better; tell them that you need it for the glare. So when you want to take a quick snooze, put these glasses on. If your boss comes near, you just take them off, stand up quickly and say,

"I was just coming in to see you."

or

"I'm glad that you stopped by. I've been wanting to speak to you about the problem with….."

The more tricks that you know, the better you'll be at it. So always cover your ass at all times. Ask yourself,

"Am I covered?

The answer must always be yes. **IT HAD BETTER BE YES!!!**

CHAPTER 4

HOW TO LIE EFFECTIVELY

Being truthful in this day and age puts an individual at a distinct disadvantage. You must excel in borderline lies and manipulations to create the right circumstances to your advancement. However, social niceties aren't lies. People expect you to be polite and tactful. And lies are an easy way out of awkward situations.

It's really very easy to lie. You have to constantly smile, train your voice to sound real sincere and mellow, and talk like you're talking to an infant.

And most people lie. They lie about what they have, or how great their children are doing in school, or what a fantastic deal they just got or how much they make or the title of their job, or even what they did in the war.

"Yeah, I was the chief special operative **behind enemy lines in the past two wars**."

Some need to cover up something done or not done, others lie or mislead , or deceive to make themselves better in the eyes of colleagues, and some lie to evade questioning. Whatever you choose to lie is up to you, but you have to work out your lies and whom you are telling lies to and for what purpose.

In fact, our society is so lie oriented that we reward only those who can lie well – actors, writers, lawyers, politicians – people who lie for a living. These people make fantastic sums of money for just not telling the truth.

And this is not unusual. Most people **WANT** to believe a lie; the truth is never really flattering.

Whichever you choose to lie is up to you. But a lie has to accomplish two things – impress someone by sounding plausible and be hard to prove. So when you lie, lie well. From your own experience you can tell when a person is lying through his teeth or when it is possible. So learn to become a professional at it. Work at lying. Let lying become a part of your everyday life. Don't tell people things that you don't want to. Purposely give out misleading information to trick people so that it will take them longer to find out things. Do you remember that old saying,

"Ask me no questions and I'll tell you no lies."

It's true. But if you're confronted in a lie, deny everything.

DENY! DENY! DENY!!

Never admit that you lied. Blame it on somebody else. This is especially good. So just act like a politician. Keep the act up; never admit that you lied even if they prove that you did. Keep denying! The first one who gives in **LOSES!!!**

So boldface lie. If someone says that it's too cold in here say,

"Well, I was raised in northern Minnesota – I'm used to the cold here – it doesn't bother me."

Then if you don't know how to do something, never admit that you don't.

LIE!

Never say that you don't know how to do it. Say,

"Well, you don't seem to understand the problem."

Or use double talk to get out of it,

"It's not a factor of not knowing, it has more involved procedures then just to be associated with simplistic answers or complex questions."

It's like when somebody asks you to say that they're not there when a phone call is for them,

"I'm not there."

That's what you should do all of the time. Lie, but with a straight face. Simply don't answer the truth by rote.

LIE!!

Go out of your way to lie. It's like when you order something from a store and they say,

"It's on the truck."

When it hasn't even been shipped.

Or a bill unpaid.

"The check's in the mail."

Which happens to be the two biggest lies in the world. The next biggest lie is the male one,

"I won't come in your mouth."

You should start a program of lying regularly to get what you want. First little white lies and then work up to bigger things. Say, do you want to do something that's illegal or immoral and you need a place to do it in? No problem.

LIE!

Very few places will let you if you give the real reason for it, so never tell the truth. Do you want to have a bachelor party or an orgy, or run a porno studio? Rent a hotel room and say that it's for the**," Independent Investment Club**", and you'll be having about a dozen or so people. Have them put down the time and room number on the marques or calendar of events. This way a hotel detective won't bother you. How else are you gonna get whatever you want going if you tell the truth.

So unless you are trying to impress someone with what you do, don't tell others what you do for a living. Let people guess and if they ask, say,

"I'm a mercenary."

or

"I'm a jigalo."

or

"I'm a stud."

Then, always lie about your age. Tell different people different ages. You should cater your age to what they think you are. This sets up a feeling of being a contemporary. So if someone says that their 25, you say that you're 26. Or if they say that their 35, you say that you're 38. Usually, there is a 10 year difference that you can get away with.

Now, if something is socially embarrassing to you, make up a lie. Don't tell the truth. It's like the childless couple who got tired after 10 years of explaining why they didn't have children to relatives, co-workers, or acquaintances. So anytime this couple met somebody new who asked them,

"So how many kids do you have?"

Instead of saying none, and then having to give reasons why they didn't have children, they said,

"Nine, and one on the way!"

Lying is ingrained in our culture. It's like a manufacturing plant which got an award for the fewest equipment breakdowns. It's not that their equipment was superior or that their maintenance people were better, or even that their equipment never broke down. They listed all of the breakdowns as normal maintenance, instead of breakdowns and then they went around bragging about it. So sure they got an award. (For **LYING!**) This is how you should lie. Bend the truth to your own advantage

Look at stories of famous events and people. Everyone can recall the movie or TV story about an historical event, but that's about as far from the truth as you can get. The story makes it easier to remember, the actual thing was boring, the story is bigger than life. Yet most people look to Hollywood for its version of history. The reason for saying this is that people want to hear lies. Very few times will people shout,

"Liar, liar, pants 're on fire; nose's as long as a telephone wire."

And rarely will they ask you to submit to a polygraph test, or truth serum, so what are you waiting for!

START LYING!!

Let's say that a female co-worker arrives at work in the most hideous blazer with a lapel that is emblazoned with dog shit. And this person then asks you,

"Hi love. How do you like my new outfit?"

Just say,

"You look simply mah-velous!"

And then fawn all over her, like where did she get it and how well the dog shit goes with her complexion. **ANYTHING! LIE!** She **WANTS** to hear it!

Now there are plenty of good lies, and not the golf ball sitting high on the grass for an easy swing type either. These good lies are anything that will benefit you. Telling a lie to a co-worker that will make them like you more is a good lie. Complementing people when there is no real reason for it is a good lie. In fact, almost anything that you do, not to tell the truth to advance yourself is a good lie. A very good lie.

An artful liar is almost difficult to catch.

So how do you learn to become good at it. For one thing, stay calm. Don't blush or squirm. Don't let your voice become higher pitched or louder. Again, stay calm. If you don't give yourself away no one will ever find out. And if they do just laugh, like they caught you in a little white lie, but never agree that you lied.

DENY! DENY! DENY!!! Remember?

If you don't have or can't earn awards, diplomas, licenses, etc. then buy them or have them made up. It looks nice on a wall and it impresses most people. Especially people with simple minds. And since most of the people that you are trying to impress are of this type, you should do very well indeed in this arena. Go to rummage sales, garage sales, flea markets, etc. or even better – printers!

You will quickly find a dishonest one. Tell him that it's a joke that you're playing on someone. And then also for a price, photos can be retouched and retaken to show proof of **YOUR** accomplishments. There are always amateur photographers who want to make some extra money. And again, tell them that you're playing a joke on someone.

Let's say that you're giving your boss a line of bull about the war and you want to impress him and prove that you were in combat, say a fighter pilot. The Air Force recruitment posters show pilots either sitting in their plane or in front of them. Steal one! They can be retouched on your home computer to show **YOU** in the cockpit. Or old combat photos can be retouched. Even medals or combat citations can be phonied up for a price, if it means that much to you. Army and Navy surplus stores, sell loads of medals. I know of one guy who printed up a phony Congressional Medal of Honor and also the picture of the President awarding it to him. It all depends on how much this means to you, as to the extent that you go. However, Medal of Honor winners are too easily traced, because their numbers are too few and their deeds too courageous.

Now, if I were telling about **MY** combat experience, I would say that I won the Silver Star, the Bronze Star with **FOUR** oak clusters and maybe throw in the Distinguished Service Medal or the Navy Cross. It sounds just as heroic as the Medal of Honor and it's harder to prove. (General Douglas Macarther kept awarding himself medals for non-combat experience) You can also say that you were recommended for the Medal of Honor but all of the other members of your squadron or platoon were killed and there was nobody left to report your exploits.

Or let's say that you're telling some guy what a great athlete you were. Cut out a picture of a guy pole vaulting in the Olympics and say that it was you. **IT WAS YOU!!** (at least tell him it was you. **Wasn't it?**)

Or let's say that you want to prove that you're a macho man. Cut out a picture of a guy on a motorcycle in a motorcycle race from a bike magazine.

Then frame it. Say it's you (**IT IS YOU!!**) At least say this to him. Or do the same with a picture with a guy in a triathalon race. Who's to say it's not you with the helmet on?

Mark Twain had a good saying about lying:

"There are lies, there are damn good lies, and then there are statistics."

Which means statistics lie. Or do they? Research done on lying says that most people do lie 62% of the time, or more than 2/3 of the time. So every 2 out of 3 times someone speaks to you , is a lie! Use this to your advantage. Push ahead, since they are all liars too. Most people will tell the truth only 38% of the time. Only once out of three times.

USE THIS TO YOUR ADVANTAGE!!

For instance, be honest only when it is in your interest. Don't tell people things that you don't want to – lie or make up a plausible story.

LIE!

a.   No, I can't help you.

LIE!

b.   No, I don't know how.

LIE!

c.   No, I can't do it.

Select from any of the above answers and let them guess if it's the real reason or a lie.

Liars are everywhere and everyone at some time or another has told a little white lie. But to become good at kissing ass you must do this all of the time. This is not to be confused with being a pathological liar, which is a sickness, but again to use it to further your career.

For instance, if you don't have a college degree or an advanced degree –

LIE!!

Say that you graduated from a college where the records were destroyed. Like Cornell University, whose records were burnt. Or how about those foreigners who always say that they graduated from a college in Vienna or Czechoslavakia or Russia or some other country where the records were destroyed during the war. It sounds good and nobody can prove you wrong.

Just remember to work out your lies. Remember who you told and what. Ad- lib as much as possible beyond the original lie. **You have an absolute right to lie to evade a question that is none of the other person's business.**

And you can always tell them,

"Would I lie to you?"

CHAPTER 5

GLADHANDING –HOW TO BE A POLITICIAN

Gladhanding is the single most important quality that you have to learn in order to make it to the top. Smooth talking is fine and you have to master that too, but if you can learn gladhanding, you will be well on your way to becoming a real success.

And it's soo easy! Always be the **FIRST** to introduce yourself,

"Hi, I'm George Wonderful…….."

as you extend a warm handshake and try to put them at ease with a winning smile and then try to talk them to death about any subject under the sun.

"Say, do you eat food? Well, so do I and you're not going to believe this, but……."

So always be the first to talk, the first to break the ice in a conversation, the first to crack a joke, and again **ALWAYS** be the first to smile. Smile before you start to say hello. Smile as you move or walk or talk or even before you go to the bathroom. But smile broadly. Let them see those teeth; let your whole face light up. Beam. Radiate a glow. Open your eyes very wide. But don't have a faceless smile that you wear all of the time. Flash it on and off as you need it and make it look like this is really sincere and that you're not just doing it for effect. Are you?

OF COURSE NOT!

You're just trying to be like a good ol' boy, jus' bein' friendly and not like some smooth talking politician out looking for votes. This is the way it should always come across. Sincere friendliness.

And it's so easy that there isn't anyone reading this who can't become good at it very quickly. To begin with, just smile before you do anything. **SMILE!** C'mon, you **CAN** do it.

Smile, God damn you!!

However, if you're not the daring type, you can get around this until you get some courage. Now, this is not as hard as it seems; it just takes guts and practice. Plenty of practice. Start by listening to others. If somebody is talking to you or anybody else on the most idiotic thing in the universe,

Do floors resent being walked on. (And by the way, yes they do!!)

You say,

"Interesting."

or

"That's interesting – I never knew that."

No matter what he continues to say, just keep repeating that, interjecting,

"Interesting."

Every few minutes. Then nod your head yes in agreement and lean towards them as if you are waiting on their every word. Agree with them, to the point of it sounding sickening.

"You're SOOOOOOOOO right!!"

And then tell them what they want to hear,

"You ARE a genius! It's true! Everybody, and I do mean everybody here knows it."

But you have to keep from laughing or cracking up. If you don't give yourself away, they will think that you're really interested in them. I have found a simple trick on how to do this, and I'm doing it right now. I dig my fingernails into my palm. This causes extreme pain. And you stay focused. **But it does definitely work!!**

Now, if they don't talk to you, don't worry. Purposely lie or ask a question that you know the answer to just to get a conversation going.

"Excuse me, but....is this the 5th floor?" (when it's the 6th)

or

if there are people near you, simply drag them into the conversation to get it started. Stare at them very intently until they have to acknowledge you. Make them say (**WHAT?**) and then say,

"How do you feel about it?"

or

"Jim, is that right?"

or the best,

**"Al, I know that you're an expert in the field,
what's your opinion on all of this?"**

Or, if you see someone standing in a store, you say,

"You get a gold star." (for standing there)

And you can also purposely start a conversation by agreeing with whatever was said,

"Yes, that IS true. Isn't it Jim?"

or if that doesn't get them to nibble then call the person by name and say,

"Hey Al, this month is flying by, isn't it?"

or

"WOW! Today's the 21st already. Where did this month go?"

You can also set someone up purposely by making any statement of fact said aloud.

This works very well with strangers. Let's say that you're eating something or trying something new, say aloud to nobody in particular, but turn and face anyone, and point to what you're eating,

"This is great, REALLY great!!"

And then simply introduce yourself,

"Hi! I'm George Wonderful!"

as you extend your hand. (**Always extend your hand**)

Then, there are basics for shaking hands. They are:

Always move your hand toward the other person at a slight angle (maybe 10 degrees or 15 degrees) and with the thumb raised up. Then as you start to shake hands the base of your thumb should touch the other person first, before you wrap your fingers eagerly around their palm. Next, squeeze it with a fair amount of firmness. You don't have to squeeze it to death or crush them. Then pump the other person's hand 2 or 3 times and let go.

LET GO!!

A handshake should be a strong steady bone crusher, not a wet noodle. It should be firm and also respectful. But to learn glad-handing properly you must learn to shake hands really well. And yes, they even have their own style of how to shake hands. It's not like some fraternal organization greeting, but it sets up something. You shake hands so that you wind up with your palm facing upwards. Like you're asking for a handout. And then you cover it with your other hand.

Psychologically, this means a person is submitting to you. Insurance salesmen are great for this one. It sets up a sale even before they say anything. However, if someone should do it to you, grab his wrist and turn it sideways to straighten it out. Then you can shake hands. This says something immediately to him that you know this trick and are not going to submit to him. It takes the pressure off of the sale and in this case if you don't have the upper hand.

So after you've broken the ice what do you say? Simple. Always make them talk. Pull it out from them like a dentist does a tooth. Always encourage a person to talk by saying,

"And what else?"

or

"Jim, what do you think that meant?"

or ask a question prompted by curiosity,

"Moses, can you tell me how to part the sea?"

Another trick a glad-hander uses is to repeat the person's name 5 or 10 times in the first minute of conversation. This demonstrates that you know who they are and it also reinforces their name on your subconscious. These first few steps are very important and you must master the principles. A glad-hander must have no likes or dislikes. Just agree with each person whether you personally like it or not. If somebody says that he loves a certain type of food, you say that you love it too.

"I love pizza with every topping on it, especially kidney beans," he says. You say,

"Me too. I didn't know anyone else liked kidney bean pizza."

If somebody else says that he hates a certain type of food, you say that you hate it also.

"Ugh! How could anybody eat kidney bean pizza." He says.

You say,

"Gross! You're right- that's disgusting!"

Become like a sponge; absorbing whatever they say, and then squeezing it dry. Always take everything in around you, but in the same way, let everything out. Have no emotions like anger or sorrow; no feelings, only determination.

I say this so you can get along with anybody, the prime prerequisite for gladhanding, smooth talking, or anything else for that matter, even ass kissing. Be a people pleaser and get along with everyone. Remember, b.s.ers and glad-handers are the ones who get ahead in this world, for that sole reason; they please people.

Politics are short for polite; and to master the banal arts, you must be polite.

You must purposely get people to love you and think that you are their friend, their bosom buddy.

Now, just starting conversations won't make you good at glad-handing and won't even make you a b.s.er or glad-hander. To really become popular you should also compliment people on the most mundane things like filing or making copies.

"You did a very thorough job."

or

"You put a great deal of effort into this. I can see why you are so highly considered."

But always make the praise specific, say,

"You really stapled those pages perfectly"

or

"Wow! Those 3-hole punches you did were just right. Thank you for being so exact."

And also don't forget to give the person compliments to their face.

"You are amazingly punctual."

Then smile and nod your head yes as you tell them that. So always keep coming back to compliments in a pinch. Build up the person's ego and worth.

"My you have an excellent memory. That's some tremendous asset."

Again, give the person a handsome self-image that they want to live up to. We all want to accept praise readily; capitalize on this. They'll never think that you're snowing them; **REALLY!!**

Next, cultivate a certain, **"look"** Like you are a lot of fun to be with. Now again, this is not as hard as it first seems. Try to spend a considerable amount of time in chatting with others or in visiting other people's work areas. Get to be known as **"Mr. Personality"** or the man with the **"Silver Tongue"**. You can accomplish this easily enough. Try to say something, especially funny to make people laugh. Always crack a joke or tell a story. Become known as a raconteur of stories. Now don't say that you can't – you must certainly can!

Simply maintain a card file of jokes, stores and put downs. You should be able to easily steal these from others or from TV shows. Any late- night talk show like the Tonight Show with Jay Leno or David Letterman or Jon

Stewart will give you a wealth of stories, and if you can't find them elsewhere, then look at Playboy or Reader's Digest. But don't just lift the joke out of there. Rephrase it to add more of your own mannerisms to it. Relate your story or joke to your audience. When you steal a joke, make sure that you don't say that you took it from wherever you got it. Just tell the joke and don't worry if somebody heard it before. And never, **NEVER** announce,

"I'm gonna tell a joke."

or use the standard joke opening such as,

"Did you hear the one about……"

You immediately warn people that a joke is coming and they mentally think**, "it better be good**." Try to disguise your jokes to make it sound like it came from you, and not tip them off that a joke is coming. Sneak into the story or the joke. Make it like you are telling a story and then lead them into the joke. Humor is just a tool to help you serve your purpose. And what is your purpose? **Simply to get ahead.** Always keep that in mind before you do anything.

If you get good a stealing material, then try your hand at writing jokes. You should be able to write at least 10 jokes a day. It doesn't matter if they're any good or not- it will still get some reaction or comment from people even if it's terrible. Even if you don't get the giant laughs like a stand-up comic would, so what?

You should also do things unexpected so that people will laugh. Don't be afraid to do things that others are too inhibited to do. **After you first sneak that it's safe to do of course.**

Let's say that you're at work. Break up an office routine that won't get you into trouble. Make it look like you're above the rules of everyday behavior. For instance, get a long tube that they use to roll up blueprints and blow into it to sound like a fog horn. This is good at quitting time or if everybody is engrossed in their work. Pretend that you're a little child and doing infantile things.

Then, you should try to become a good impersonator of voices, both ethnic and personalities in your office or circle of friends. And again, this is not hard to learn. It just takes practice. A lot of practice. Simply stand in front of a mirror and mouth those peoples accents or quirks. You will soon get very good at it.

Now here is something that is very important. Ordinary things keep happening all of the time. Simply things that happen every day in your life, such as going to the store, at work, at home, etc. Rehearse material for places that you'll be at or for people that you know that you'll meet. And I'm not talking about jokes or stories, but of conversations with different people. For instance,

Things to say to a neighbor (man, woman),

"How do you manage to keep your lawn (house) looking so great?"

Things to say at a party (to a stranger)

"I can tell. You've had your picture in the paper, haven't you?"

Things to say in a store,

"Excuse me, is this the 5th floor?" (especially if it isn't)

Or ask questions that you purposely know the answer to or ask if they could help you with information. For instance, to a man with tools or to a woman with housewares,

"I'm really terrible with pots and pans, could you help me?"

or

"Tell me , what does a drill do?"

Things to say to the opposite sex,

"What do you have on? You smell GREAT!"

You can do better than these – a lot better. So do this now, right now. Make up 10 things to say to a person right now. It doesn't matter. Be gutsy – go ahead, try it now. **RIGHT NOW!** Say anything spontaneous that comes to mind – even if it's stupid or cutsee sounding.

ESPECIALLY IF IT'S STUPID OR CUTSEE SOUNDING!!!

The other person isn't going to say anything except maybe to laugh or agree with you.

So what can you use to say something? What are people talking about? Are they talking about what's on TV? Or are they talking about the latest trouble spot in the world.

TALK ABOUT IT!!

Also look for something to pick up on. Let's say that you're on line for a movie or tickets or even in the supermarket. Think of anything else, and then talk about this to nobody in particular,

"The lines are unbelievable."

It works better if there are very few people on line. Then pause, for a laugh or comment, and then say jokingly,

"What are we doing this for?"

And again, pause and then continue like a stand-up comic would,

"But seriously…"

And then talk about your job and how much you have to do and how wonderful a person you are, and if you can't think of anything else, then talk about this:

What's **"hot"** right now? Or **"in"**?

Talk about the latest fad whether you like it or not.

What's new?

Did anybody find a better way to do things?

Or did somebody just discover a new way to have **SEX**?

TALK ABOUT IT!!

Do you remember the film" The Music Man?" In it Robert Preston's character, a con man who has just gotten into town, asks his friend, what's the latest thing going on in town. And the answer was, a pool hall. That became, if you've ever seen the film, an intro into the wrongs of young

people playing pool, and how he now could sell them musical instruments in a band. A boy's band to prevent them from playing pool.

Do this now. Talk to the next 5 people that you see. Say anything that comes to mind, anything. And if you can't think of something – count, **ALOUD!**

"ONE! TWO! THREE!!"

People may or may not ask what you are talking about. Whether they do or don't, you just say to nobody in particular,

"I'm counting spaces."

If that doesn't get some reaction, then continue to say,

"Did you ever see on a computer, the space bar. Well it's the same here. There are people and then there are spaces. I'm counting the spaces."

That should get some reaction. At least if they start shaking their heads in disbelief or laugh silently to themselves, you continue to say,

"No, really it's true. Don't you think that there are more people than spaces?"

Then, make up things to say to a stranger (man, woman)

"Hi! How are you doing?"

But make your **HI!** sound emphatic. Like you haven't seen them in a long while or that you're truly glad to see them. Even if they don't know you from Adam, lie – make them feel good by showing that they are a long lost friend.

Also jazz up your good mornings. Say,

"GOOD morning!" instead of the perfunctory,

"morning"

What can you use to say something? What's in the news? If the headline is about foreign trade say,

"Buy American!!"

that's always good to stir up national pride.

You can always start a conversation with someone if they have a bumper sticker that says,

"I love...... (New York, Virginia)"

or

You can start a conversation with someone if they have a cat or dog. Say,

"Are they good with kids?"

You will endear them to you if they think that you interested in their family or hobbies.

Another thing to do is make a new person feel welcome. If existing cliques don't welcome or a new co-worker or neighbor or whatever, then **YOU** do it. It will make the person love you.

Go right over and introduce yourself, and make them feel welcome. Introduce them to others. Always try to break the ice. If someone walks in alone, in an empty place, make some nonsense statement.

"The way you marched in here, you must be in band."

Or say anything, but make them feel at ease. That they can count on you as a port in a storm or as a friend. They won't forget you or that you made them feel welcome. And you would want the same thing done for you.

You have to try to have a following of people; ones who look up to you, whom you can count on, those who will form **YOUR** clique. The way to do this is to slowly get people on your side. Start with little things first. For instance, you will have an easier time of getting people to listen to you if you don't rush to get on a line. Like a coffee line or a lunch line. Wait until everybody else is already on the line. This way you will have plenty of people to talk to and it shows that you don't rush for mundane things like standing on a line. **You're above all that aren't you?** At least always try to give that impression.

And speaking of impressions, try to baffle people when you're writing too. Use words that baffle people but are actually words. Look in a dictionary and pick out words that could be construed as no such word or those that look misspelled. How about,

"commingling"

It actually means to blend harmoniously, but if you said it, it would sound like you're tongue tied, and even better, if you saw it in a report you would say, no such word. And that's the effect that you are trying for. To be able to prove to people that you do know what you're talking about even if it does sound like a bag of wind.

In addition, you should try to maneuver people into talking about themselves. Always try to get the subject away from you and onto them. It is hard to do and it just takes repetition but you will get to be known as **"Mr. Personality."** Always ask them questions about themselves like,

"How's your family doing?"

Or

"How long have you worked for the company?"

Or anything. However, make sure that your questions are inquiring about themselves and that you don't give any impression that you're skeptical, hostile, derisive or challenging.

So always keep coming back to compliments in a pinch. For instance, tell a female co-worker or secretary,

"You know, you're too good for this place. I mean, NOBODY here has ever had the skills that you do!"

Then go back and identify with the persons belief,

"I believe the same as you do, that.......

I think that they all should!"

If you can ask a question that's likely to bring a yes, and ask questions that will lead to other statements. Actually questions are preferable to statements. The question can be simple enough,

"Tell me, would you do it again?"

Or

"Then what happened?"

You should appear sympathetic, encouraging, thoughtful and listening. Always think first, **"Can I make it more pleasant?"**

Again, be a people pleaser. Anyone who can **"shoot the shit"** is always well received anywhere. But the ones who can do it well, consistently and purposely are the ones who get ahead in this world. **In fact, you have to spend more time glad-handing and smooth talking than working!** And do this all of the time. Look around you and find the glad-hander or smoothtalker where you work. They are excellent at it! You'd be good at it too if that's all you did all day. **So take a hint from them and do exactly that, bullshit and glad-hand, whenever you can.**

CHAPTER 6

GRANDSTANDING – SHOW THEM WHAT YOU'VE GOT

You have to stand out or you're going to be overlooked. Anybody who wants to get to the top has to show and tell how great he or she is- everyday, every minute to everybody!!! The notion of teamwork is just so much hype. Most people advance in business or politics by playing lip service to the idea of teamwork whenever it is called for. So you have to be a bull headed individualist and keep reminding people of all your accomplishments even if there aren't any.

ESPECIALLY IF THERE AREN'T ANY!!

But grandstanding is more than whistle tooting, more than blowing your own horn, in fact it's more than an ego trip. Whether it's the mailperson or a secretary or the neighbor's kid. It doesn't matter – just impress them. First start to make **"teamwork"** speeches for the **"good"** of the company. About, let's all pull together for the good of the business.

RAH! RAH! RAH!

i.e.

"What do we want – productivity! When do we want it - NOW!!"

Keep on doing this and you **WILL** get noticed.

Then the next thing to do is make everything, even the most ordinary things, be dramatic. Such as the following:

a. **Taking off and cleaning your glasses. Spend at least five minutes at it. Make a grand show of blowing on the glasses and scroupuously cleaning them.**

b. **Making a phone call. Press each number very slowly. Talk like you own the phone and the person on the other end.**

c. **Straightening your desk. Move stuff around in slow motion. Like a guy doing 3 card Monte but very slowly.**

d. **Washing your hands. Act like a doctor scrubbing for surgery. Get a scrub brush and get under those nails.**

e. **Making an entrance. Be late so that all eyes are on you and you alone.**

Remember, be aware of every act that you do, because somebody is **ALWAYS** watching you. You've got to be continuously **"looking good"** to others all of the time. Because that's who you are trying to impress-

EVERYBODY!!

Be careful though – neighbors, co-workers, friends, they'll look at the way you talk, the clothes that you wear, how you fix your house up, the car that you drive – it all matters to them. And they'll talk about you. Everybody loves to gossip. It's a big job to be a good bullshit artist. Sometimes it seems that you've got to dress and talk like a swindler, like those fast talking guys on the street who are always trying to sell you a,

"solid gold watch 235 jewel movement – you can even count them little jewels ,see them –one, two, three, ...oh there's four and five. My lord, there's a lot of them"

But where they are trying to rip you off, you're not. Are you?

OF COURSE NOT!!!

You're just trying to be like those friendly gum chewing guys who are out for fun and adventure. But, that's just for show. Putting up a front like that is the ticket.

What you have to do is what senior officers in the Army do. Be willing to throw subordinates under a bus in a heartbeat to protect or advance their career. Use them and abuse them! Your focus should be on short-impact fixes that make you look good and get you your next promotion. Such as – fixing the copy machine so that it **NEVER** breaks down **(or keep blaming the mail room- this is especially good!)**

Or even having the boss's parking spot have bollards **(protective cones)** around it. Or make up a sign,

"Reserved for the top guy"

Anything quick that makes you look good.

So let's say that you've followed everything that I've told you so far, and your boss thinks that you're doing a super job, and now has given you responsibility for running a job or a project. Always use the words,

"My job"

or

"My money"

Frequently when talking about it to anyone who's on the job or not. It makes you look like only **YOU** are worrying about the company's money like it was your very own. And always give a dollar figure. It's impressive to anyone who doesn't know what you're talking about. Even though you know that it's didly.

"I'm in charge of 40 million dollars worth of projects."

or

"500 million dollars worth of accounts pass thru MY department."

or

"I have (or had) total running control of 9 different projects at the same time and completed them on time and under budget without even having the proper manpower."

WOW! WHAT A MAN!!!

Some other words to use to impress people on your job are,

"I'm wearing a different hat (or another hat)"

If you take on extra work that's not in your job description. Use this phrase when you're talking to higher ups about taking on additional or extra work.

"We put it to bed."

Or better,

"I put it to bed.

Again, higher ups love to use this expression when talking about a completed project.

Now, when things are really screwed up, avoid it or blame it on someone else. The higher ups will cover for you if you butter them up,

"Well, he's really not that bad."

To a report critical of you

or

"You don't seem to understand the problem."

To a mistake that you made

Then, when things start to look good, jump back in. They will remember that **YOU** were in charge, when it turned out good.

More important things to remember when talking to higher ups. If you see them, don't just say hello or good morning. Always add something of importance to them or the company,

"Hi, Mr. Smith. I'm working on YOUR job."

or

"Good morning Mr. Smith. I've been in since 5AM to get YOUR work out."

Now, if they keep on walking, that's fine, but if they stop, then that's your opportunity to mesmerize them about your job. About how fantastic you're doing it and the rub of it all, that you're doing it all by yourself and you don't have enough manpower. Sometimes, they may ask you how many people would you need to properly get the work out. **Tell them five hundred thousand, or six or seven million,** but make it many more times the figure that you need. I mean, how do they expect you to get the work out if they don't give you the right amount of people. This is the way that it should always come out.

If the boss should go on vacation or goes away on business, and joy or joys, leave you in charge, what do you do if anyone from another department comes in and jokes with some of the people in **YOUR** department?

Tell him that you are now responsible for the people in **YOUR** department, and that the boss left you in charge of **YOUR** department and that he shouldn't come in again doing it. Make up something, say,

"C'MON, you're holding MY MAN up!"

And then cry and whine that you have too much to do.

"I've got three projects near completion, two that I'm trying to get under way, and four projects that are brand new. I don't even know how I'm doing this. It's really unbelievable. I'm really short handed and need much more people."

And as always, no matter how much work you have to do, **DON'T DO ANY OF IT!** And then tell him that he's distracting **YOUR** man from doing his work. Also emphasize that **YOU** are responsible to the boss for the productivity in this department and don't come in again doing it! Just in case the higher ups are watching.

"C'mon, you're holding up production – don't you have anything to do back in your office?"

Afterwards, go over to your boss's supervisor, sit down perturbed and say,

"Those people in (fill-in) department. They think that this department is a joke."

Always say that you can get the job done faster than anybody else, whether you can or not, whether it's right or not. Bosses and higher ups think that you can just crank up the old printing press and get any job out, just like that. You have to agree with them and not laugh or disagree. It doesn't seem to matter if the field is medicine or publishing or engineering or banking or whatever. They always want it out yesterday. Or they'll ask you when are you going to finish it.

"When are you going to be done with this?"

Even if you tell them how much work that you've got to do, or how many intricate details that you must perform, or even if it's an art form like painting or photography, they don't care; **it's how fast can you get it done.** And nobody cares if a job turns out right, only if it's turned out fast. That's all production cares about or engineering or accounting or management. Who can get the job out the fastest. Higher ups and bosses will tell the President or CEO or Vice-President,

"Oh, it's a piece of cake. The "boys" can get it done like that."

As they snap their fingers.

And that's why budgets and estimates are usually way off. The bosses and higher ups don't know how long something will take to be done. So always say or imply,

"I can get this job out by Friday."

Meaning, that **YOU ARE** knowledgeable about how long it should take. And always, **ALWAYS,** say that you can get it out by Friday. It just sounds good.

So how fast can you get this job out?

Say,

"I can get this job done in 40 hours."

And you?

"I can get this job done in 20 hours!"

Or you?

"I can get this job done in 10 hours!"

How about you?

"I can get this job done, with both hands tied behind me, in one hour!!!"

Sound familiar? Like "Name that Tune", the old time game show on TV?

Well if you can get the job done in one hour, then do it. Get that job done!

And that's what everybody in management wants to hear. Your boss, his boss, the general manager, the Vice-President, the President, the CEO. That you can do a 40 hour job in 1 hour, or a year's job in one day!!!

And that's why so many bridges and buildings FALL DOWN!!

Then always talk to yourself. Or at least let others think that you are. This shows that you are so busy and loaded with work, that you're talking to yourself. And if anybody comments on you talking to yourself, and **they will**, say,

"I'm so loaded with work, I don't know if I'm coming or going. Would you believe that I'm talking to myself?"

Or

"I'm so busy here and I don't know how I'm going to get it out, that they've got me talking to myself."

So, when you talk to somebody and you want to emphacize what you're saying, talk as you write it down in front of them,

"So let's see if I got this right.

Job number is 1268

The client is Mr. Schmuck

Item number 1 is ....

Item number 2 is ....

Item number 3 is ...."

And so on and so on. People will think that you don't know which end is up. But if somebody else does it to you say,

"C'MON! C'MON! CUT THE BULLSHIT!!!"

CHAPTER 7

HOW TO WIN FAVOR WITH YOUR SUPERIOR

Do you remember that old saying –**"Handsome is as handsome does"**. **Well it's true!** The same goes for being **REALLY AMBITIOUS.** Or to put it bluntly – kissing ass. **There I said it!** You have to brown nose. You have to suck up to someone to really get ahead – your boss, his boss, anyone! There is no other way to put it. Kissing ass **IS** effective. Look around you- **IT WORKS!** Show me that it doesn't! Even if it sticks in your throat – **DO IT ANYWAY!!** Ass kissing, or brown nosing, is a time honored custom that everyone, has at one time or another, done. **But not well enough, because you're still where you are!** Instead of where you want to be. So how do you start? For openers, try flattering your boss or the person that you want to butter up. Be shameless in it, but never admit to putting him on, even if you've got to force yourself to keep from laughing.

"You know, you REALLY do have a tremendous amount of knowledge in this field."

or

"Even the bosses here KNOW that you are the best in the business!"

Always say that what you're saying is really sincere and the way that you really feel about something, even if you're just making it up. You wouldn't lie to him now would you? **OF COURSE NOT!!** This is the way that it should always sound when it comes across. That you are his best buddy and are looking out for him. But to become successful at kissing ass you must stay really close to the person, so always suck up to him. Take him out to lunch, say,

"This is on me."

Or buy him a drink, say,

"I saw that you had a very rough day today. The drinks are on me."

Or buy him a bottle of his favorite brand of liquor, or get him a woman, or do him favors that he knows only you can do for him. If he is a sports buff, get to be well versed on sports, know all of the scores of the teams. Play golf or tennis with him and let him win. But don't **EVER** let him win by a little, don't **EVER** let it be close- let him trounce you. This way you can say over and over again to everybody,

"He IS the best! He beat me something fierce."

Then the next thing is to treat him to dinner and a show, say,

"I just won two free tickets to a show (LIE!!!) How about celebrating with me?"

Or invite him over to your house for a barbeque, say,

"Sunday, I'm having a cookout, how about coming over. I told my wife about you and she's dying to meet you."

Get him to tell you about his family, his hobbies or interests. For instance, if he has a picture of himself on a sailboat, learn everything there is to know about sailing, so that he thinks that you are a kindred soul and can let his hair down with you. Make him feel that you are a friend, and not just an employee, are empathetic to him and show him that he has nothing to fear from you. Act like the chief of staff to a Senator or Congressman, know and do everything before your boss does it.

Even go so far as to always laugh at his jokes, but don't make it perfunctory, really mean it.

"Ha-ha- that's a classic."

Embelish it, and then tell others just within earshot,

"Listen to this –Mr. Jones just told me the greatest joke."

Afterwards, tell him,

"Mr. Jones, that really was a great joke. Seriously, did you ever think about becoming a comedian?"

Now, let's stop for a minutes.

WHOA! FULL STOP!!

Do you really think that after you do all of this that he's gonna feel that you're snowing him? **NEVER!!! Never in a hundred years. NEVER!!! Never in a thousand years!** He wants to believe it and everything else that you're doing for him. Everyone readily accepts agreement and praise and gifts blindly. This is true in politics, at the office, in organizations, anywhere. Keep on doing these methods and you will get advanced very quickly. So what are you waiting for?

Mow his lawn. That's right – **MOW HIS LAWN!!!**

"My doctor said that I need the exercise, can I mow your lawn too after I finish mine?"

Or take him to a ballgame, say,

"Hey, I just came into some incredible luck. Two seats for tonight's game, great seats. How about going?"

or even wash his car. There is nothing sacred, **NOTHING!! NOTHING!!**

"I'm trying out a new, very expensive car wash. I used it on mine and it's terrific. Can it stand the test on yours?"

But just doing this isn't enough, you have to go much, much further. If your boss has kids offer to take them to a ballgame or to an amusement park. Or ask your boss if you can take them fishing, boating, or hunting. Maybe even start a boy scout troop solely for your boss's kid, and you become the scoutmaster. Use them to your advantage; get them on your side. Then tell his kids to call you **"uncle"**. Tell them to tell their father that even **THEY** can see that most of the **"meaningful** "work in his department is done by you.

Isn't this fun?

Kissing ass can be just like a game, if you do it right. But keep it up, don't stop now. If your boss likes expensive cigars, buy them for him. I know of one guy who bought a case of Cuban cigars from overseas and had them shipped here. He then doled them out to his boss and those higher up to the point that they became dependant on him for furnishing them. Almost like a drug dealer or supplier. The outcome of this was that he got promoted very quickly.

Do the same with little French candies if no one smokes. Have a candy jar or small finger bowl that your boss or other people who pass by your desk can stop and take some. Or have little open jars of candy on your desk – maybe spearmint leaves one day, then orange slices the next or mixed nuts. Your boss and other people will stop by to talk and take a candy. It's a very small price to pay for getting the brownie points in. Because that's what you want – to have people who take a candy to talk to you. If someone passes your desk **(even if it's within 100 feet!)** that you want to talk to, like your boss or a higher up, say, **"Ya want some nuts?"** or use the type – pecans, walnuts, macadamians, almonds, filberts.

or

"How about a candy?" and raise the bowl towards them.

Although this sounds like a lot of work, and that I'm going into a tremendous amount of details, I assure you that it's worth it. If everybody is on a diet, have dietetic candies, say,

"Go ahead, take one, they're low calorie."

Or maybe have some assortment of dried fruits, like apricots or pears. Or bring in rolls or donuts or bagels in the morning. You will get to be known throughout the organization **FAST!!** Also, buy a newspaper each day, but don't read it. Keep it out so that as people pass by they can stop to look at it. I suggest keeping at least 3 or 4 newspapers out. Because knowing how people are, they will comment about something in it, and then you can start talking to them. If it's available **THEY WILL COME!!** Or even better, how about stopping them and saying,

"Hey, Jim, did you see this…."

And show them the headline or sports page. Keep after them. Always try to get the points in – the **BROWNIE POINTS!!** In with any higher up. Always say,

"Hi, how are you doing?"

or

"Good morning."

Or something, but never let a boss or higher up pass you by without talking to them. And even if you see them more than once in a day. Smile broadly in acknowledgement, nod your head yes as you pass by or something to say that you are there and notice me! But in most companies, you will probably see the same person 10 to 20 times a day. **Still, always say something!!!**

"What's up?"

or

"Did you hear….."

But always acknowledge them. Wave if they are too far away or they can see you but are in another part of the office than normally, or say their name emphatically,

"Big John!!!"

or ask them a non-threatening b.s. question,

"Any plans for the weekend?"

Most times, when bosses or higher ups do stop to talk they will start talking about somebody else. No matter what they say, **NEVER, NEVER** say anything bad about somebody else, especially, higher ups. Always give the persons good points. Because if you talk about someone else, the person will think that you'll talk about him also. And you want him to trust you. So, if a higher up says that another person is hyper or just plain crazy, just say that the person is,

"A vibrant, exciting individual."

But you must keep from laughing or cracking up no matter how phony it sounds.

Now, none of what I am describing should be difficult to accomplish. You should be able to start right now, wherever you are. The methods that brownnosers use are the same everywhere and while it does take some getting used to at first, it can be learned fairly easily.

For example, here's a very easy one. Demonstrate loyalty. Get yourself in your boss's favor, get him to love you. Make your boss feel that he is your hero; that you admire him for his successful position. Always boost your boss to others, even co-workers. As soon as your boss says something, even if it's the most stupid thing that you ever heard in your entire life, immediately turn to any co-worker nearby and say,

"Isn't that a TERRIFIC idea that Mr. Jones has?"

If he doesn't say so, it will immediately put him in disfavor with the boss. Also, always find the good points to any hair brained scheme or idea that your boss has. Never tell him the bad points – others will. Keep telling him what a **GREAT IDEA** it is and why. Again, you want to be a yes man, someone who your boss can bounce ideas and thoughts on without hearing negativity.

Another thing, circulate inter-office memos to those higher up saying that what your boss did, his pet project, was really a brilliant idea and that more supervisors should act like him in looking out for the companies benefit. If you can get your boss praise from **HIS** supervisor, chances are he'll remember you for the next raise or promotion or even a choice assignment. So solidify yourself with your boss and he'll make sure that you get the best too.

Next, justify **YOUR** job. Generate a lot of paperwork on nonsense. Become an impressive memo writer, such as writing intra-office and company wide memos on the importance of your job to the company,

"What is an accountant?"

The importance of **YOUR GROUP** to the operation and continued success to the company,

"How the Accounts Receivable Department Works"

Any stupidity,

"The Controller and his duties"

It doesn't matter, stupidity pays off. Also, if you should talk to any person in another department about the most idiotic thing,

"What is a Warehouse?"

Write a summary of the **"meeting"** and circulate it, and note if you gave them any documents,

"the outcome of the company softball game"

I repeat, stupidity pays off. As long as **YOU** don't give yourself away and tell them the truth or the real reasons. So always talk in generalities, beat around the bush, talk around and around the subject but **NEVER** give specifics. Become an impressive talker. Use 50 words instead of 10. Talk about the **"total picture"** of the job to anyone who come near, and if no one comes near, start yelling at the top of your lungs,

"C'MERE! C'MERE!!"

to anyone in view.

Call them by name and wave them over to you, put your arm around them, and then start telling them about your job and how difficult it is and how great you are handling it and that the rub of it all, that nobody recognizes what fantastic job that you're doing for the company. Even if it's the janitor or the delivery boy, it makes no difference; if you just keep talking about your job in this way, it'll get back to the top bosses soon enough.

You should also make up organization charts, draw meaningless diagrams about like how the work flows through the different departments, or oversimplify work objectives and circulate it to management. And by the way, **ALWAYS, ALWAYS** circulate everything to management, **ESPECIALLY** if it's nonsense. Bosses love to read nonsense. As long as it has their name on it and is presented in a professional way, they will read it.

So here's the truth. All management wants to see is how fast can you get something done, since it is the only thing that they can understand. If you tell them that you can create the earth in not 7 days but in 1 day, they'll love you for it. That is, until, the entire world falls apart, because you really needed 7 days to get it done. I'd really love to see one management type try to create the world in less than 7 days. **They can't!** That's why they are always asking **YOU** to do it faster.

So, when you talk or write, use terms or words that are meaningless, like:

"High-concept idea" –"This is a very HIGH- CONCEPT IDEA don't you think?"

or

"significant" –"This is a very SIGNIFICANT letter."

or

"important" – "I am doing a very IMPORTANT job."

or

"very true" – "Yes, VERY TRUE."

or

"critical" –"That is a CRITICAL factor"

or

"interfaced" –"This item has to be INTERFACED."

or

"overkilled"–"This job has been OVERKILLED."

Exaggerate words. Don't use just OK or Good, use,

"Terrific!!"

or

"Very Good."

or

"Brilliant!"

or

"Fantastic!"

or

"Super!"

or

"Superb!"

or

"WOW!!"

or

"Cool"

But use these words when talking to your boss or those higher up. You can use it to co-workers, but it won't be as effective.

Now, get to be known in your office, but not too well known. Start by saying good morning to everybody. It doesn't cost you anything and it makes you look reachable and human. But just make it look that way, don't actually be it.

Stay aloof, try to be visible, camouflage yourself- become a part of the woodwork. Don't be vocal or be so loud that everybody notices you. Remember that there is security in obscurity. That means, don't **YOU** be the one to upset the applecart and make waves in the office. Let someone else do it first and then see what type of reaction it gets. Observe, if it's a bad reaction, avoid it and the person like the plague. Say,

"I knew that it would never work."

in a smug attitude.

However, if it provokes a good reaction, then try to take over the idea. Become a credit grabber. Say,

"You know…I actually thought of this a long time ago, way before anyone else did."

No one can prove that you didn't. Then champion the idea. Go all out and tell **EVERY PERSON** that you see about it.

"C'MERE!! C'MERE!!!"

Soon, everybody will think that **YOU** came up with the idea and will associate it with you. Then at every moment you can proudly say,

"I came up with the fornicating idea!! Yup, it was me!!"

You should purposely strive to take credit for everything that turns out good in the office, so that every time your name is mentioned, getting things accomplished the best way, the correct way, will be associated with you.

Also, try to get a following of young people in the office. They are very guilable and naïve and can be easily awed and impressed. And of course they are easily led. Pick out the youngest people in your office and go after them. Be relentless and conquer them with your personal magnetism.

Young people are the corps of your army, or any army. So always get close to them and become their leader in the office or in any place of business. Lead them onward – become their mentor or guru and make them follow you blindly. They will anyway! Most brownnosers have a throng of young people to do their bidding. Young people are also good to use if you have any errands that you want done and you can also use them for any odd jobs that you don't want to do. I don't know why young people follow brownnosers, but I think that it has something to do with the Pied Piper. **What a line of b.s. he must have had!**

Now, there are also certain phrases which you should use on co-workers to show that if it wasn't for you, or your intervention on their behalf to the boss or higher-ups, that they wouldn't be there. Make it look like you are looking out for them and them only. Take them aside, and put your arm around them and speak in a hushed voice,

"Ya know, if it wasn't for me, you wouldn't be working on this special project. I recommended you to the boss for it."

or

"I covered for you yesterday."

or

"It was me. I gotta admit it. I recommended you for the raise." (promotion, job, etc.)

Petty, but effective.

In addition, you should always carry something with you whenever you leave your work area. This way, if you want to go visit somebody, or go into another area, no one can say that you're just stopping to b.s. Carry some papers, (**no blank ones showing!**) or folders (**several are a lot better!**), or charts or books. It looks like you're actually there on company business.

Or how about this. Let's say that you want to go into an area that you've never been in before or to check one area out or even to go into one that you have no business being in. Here's what to do. Carry a clipboard with a diagram on it, make up some boxes and scribble some lines on it. Or take some rolled up blueprints (**these are great!!**) and then you just stick your head into the office, gaze around an say while you nod to nobody in particular,

Slowly,

"uh-huh, uh-huh......"

And then quickly,

"very good, very good."

As you look at the papers or blueprints. And then continue to check out everything. If anybody asks what you're doing there (**they won't**) or if they say,

"Can I help you?"

You just say,

"I'm just checking out the seating arrangements."

Or

"I'm doing a survey for the new relocation."

It leaves just a hint that you're working for one of the big bosses on a possible re-shuffle of offices. It can quickly get rumors started of a re-organization.

If you can, try to become a specialist in one small area of your field. Let's say that if your department handles office supplies, you only do paper clips. So if somebody wants you to handle something big, like pencils, you say, well, **I only do paper clips**. See Bill, he handles pencils. And then you can use this as a reason for giving co-workers the rest of your work. Say that since you handle all of the "**paper clip**" jobs for the entire company, how do they expect you to do anything else. You will get to be known as a specialist, only working on paper clips, or some other small aspect of your field.

And then mesmerize them about what a great job you do and how much work you produce,

"What a job I am doing?"

or

"I am fantastic!!"

or

"I am the greatest!!"

or

"I am the best paper clipper in the company!"

or

"The entire industry knows that I am the best in the paper clipping field!!!"

But say it **LOUDLY**, over and over again. Always make like you're indespensible to the company and again say it very **LOUDLY, EVERY 2 MINUTES**,

"Do you believe how many times a day that they call on me for this!"

But say this phrase **OVER AND OVER AGAIN!!!**And then if you are given any "help", never let the "help", know the whole job, only a small part of it and only as it pertains to them. And don't tell them anything. Tell them,

"You work it out."

This way only you know the job and no one can take your place. You will become indespensible and they will always have to wait on you.

"I'm sorry, but the whole world has to stop – Mr. Smith is on vacation."

Also, say aloud, when you finish something, like nobody else has ever finished any projects before,

"WHEW!!! I finished it!!!!!"

or

"I just finished……..!"

or

"And here's another one that I finished!!!"

or

"FANTASTIC!!! I just finished…..!!"

It doesn't matter whom you say this to. Say it aloud to the whole office. Even if this is the most minute thing involved in your job, proclaim it loudly. A statement of everyday fact,

"WOW!!! I JUST FINISHED TAKING A PISS!!!"

Now if any co-worker says that you're not pulling your load or implies that you're goldbricking, say definitely not! That you are so doing it and in fact that you are doing more for the company than he is. And how dare he say that since he knows damn well that you handle all of the paper clip jobs for the company and that you've gotten awards for being the best paper clip specialist!! **So there!!**

But don't worry about direct confrontation; most co-workers are too conscientious to do it. They'll just grumble to themselves and say,

"Eventually it'll catch up with him."

or

"I can't believe that they allow him to get away with it."

Or they might even start a rumor on the grapevine.

Do you remember that song,

"I heard it on the grapevine"

Now this is the worst thing a brownnoser has to fear – the grapevine. But you can also use it to your advantage. More on this when we get to backstabbing.

Meanwhile, you go directly over to the boss and in as loud a voice as you can muster, tell him that this co-worker is not pulling his load and try to get him transferred or if that doesn't work, try to get him fired. (**it's you or him!!**)

In addition, whenever you talk to your boss, talk low so that it sounds like you're talking about something that you're trying to get- time off, a raise, permission to go to the bathroom, anything. Practice doing this so that others can't hear you.

Talking low just takes practice. Watch soap operas for a month straight and see how the men talk. You can get good at it quickly, since it's so easy, and then you can talk on the phone all day long and nobody will know it's about private or personal things.

Also, ask your boss if you can work through lunch and leave earlier. Or come in later and work the time thru lunch or stay later and make up the time. And then never work it. Or disappear for a few hours in the afternoon. This makes you look like a special or privileged person and this sets up other things, like how to get out of doing work and getting paid for it.

So don't start work promptly. Wait five or ten minutes – do personal stuff or just read the paper. Most bosses will allow this and again it shows everyone that you don't rush even for work and you'll start whenever you're damn good and ready. **Damn straight!!**

But to really get ahead fast, even a meteoric rise to the top, always say that what **YOU** are doing is a priority. That what someone else is doing definitely is **NOT!!** Make sure that the boss says that this is true. In fact really try to get others to leave you alone because you are working on a priority.

"It's a PRIORITY……I gotta get it out!!!"

Or shout aloud,

"PRIORITY!!! I GOT A NUMBER ONE VERY HIGH PRIORITY HERE!!

Then say,

"Everybody better leave me alone. I'VE GOT AN URGENT PRIORITY!!!"

The more you say that you're work is a priority, the more that everyone will believe you. Or at least the bosses will. So always keep talking about the urgent work that you have,

"PRIORITY!!!! I'VE GOT AN URGENT PRIORITY HERE!!!"

Also, try to delay doing your job or project so that other work will back up and you will look overworked and swamped with work. Say,

"I've got SOOO much work to do, I can't believe it!!!"

or

"Can you believe this?" Say this to no one in particular and point to the work. "Look at how much work that I have to do."

But when you do this, pad the amount of work that you actually have to do by filling the pile with blank sheets **(again none showing!)** ,charts of meaningless block diagrams, and assorted nonsense. You want to give the impression that the volume of work that you are holding is immense**. (and it better be!!!)** So take several reams of paper **(500 sheets**) and stick it inside your **"pile"** of work. It makes for an impressive show and tell. **(Do you remember show and tell from kindergarten?")**

I would also recommend keeping a listing of all of the jobs that you have to do and display it prominently.

"Look at these jobs – two million five hundred thousand…."

or

"Can you see that I have seven hundred and fifty-two jobs going out TONIGHT!!!"

And always tell the boss that you have **SOOOOO** much work to do, that you're really loaded, in fact that you're swamped with it, and that you don't know how in tarnation that you're going to get it out on time. Every time that you see your boss or anybody else for that matter, always bend their ear off about all of the work that you've got to do and tell them step by step and detail what you've got to do.

"Well, first I've got to do…and then I gotta….

And then I need to activate….and if that's not all, then I got……"

This way if a co-worker asks the boss for your help or new work comes in, you won't get it since the boss will say,

"He has too much to do."

So even if you have nothing to do, make something up – filing, copying, organizing, etc. or else the boss will ask you,

"Well, what have you got to do?"

And you don't ever, **EVER, EVER,** want that to happen.

Also, and this is very important, try to shove **YOUR** work onto your co-workers. This is what you should do. Go over to the boss and say that since you have **SOOOO** much work to do, can Bill or Johnny take a part of it.

And it's really only a small part, since you have to be free to work on the specialized part of it. Most bosses will agree to this, since bosses do not usually get involved in the details of the job. Once you get the boss to transfer this overload to others –give them the **WHOLE THING!!!** This way you're free to talk on the phone, take a walk, go visit others, etc. But if the boss doesn't do it (some bosses do work), you can get around it.

Here's what you do. If you haven't learned by now, you can buffalo co-workers. They are all conscientious slobs and they'll do the extra work. So be persuasive – talk them to death. Transfer your assignment over to them, say,

"Bill, I'm really backed up doing the Smith job. Could you help me out by doing ….."

If he won't, then ask for help from a higher up. Say that,

"Bill isn't helping me and Mr. Jones just doesn't realize how important my work is."

If you ham it up, most higher ups will usually call your boss in and tell him to immediately give you more help.

Also, and this is very important, get to know what words impress people in your field. Then say one or two of them each day, like you know what you're talking about.

"Valve in Vertical"

or

"Truss Beam"

or

"Linear Diffuser"

or

"15KVA Catenary"

You've got to always give the impression that you know what you're talking about even if you have absolutely no idea of what your field is about. **Again, that's why so many buildings and bridges fall down!!! Cover up your shortcomings!!! Use impressive words around higher ups whenever you see them.**

"Hey, Mr. Jones did you see the latest on the new Reduced Pressure Zone Backflow Preventer rules? It changes everything that we've done for the past hundred years. And now the DEP wants us to retrofit every building in the city. That's gonna cost 20 BILLION DOLLARS!!!"

That should get their attention and fast!

Again, try to impress them that you are very knowledgeable about your field even if you know nothing about it. Especially if you know nothing about it!!! (More on this when we get to "How to get a job when you know absolutely zip")

So here's what to do. In your office maintain a file of books that are impressive to people in your field. It makes you look like an expert in just having them. Display them prominently, since it really doesn't matter if you have ever read the book or even know what's in it – just show that you've got it. And offer to loan it to **ANYBODY**!! Possession is 9/10ths of knowledge – at least it **is to everybody else.** So by this reasoning to them, if you have it, you must know it.

Also, join any society that you can get a credential from that you belong to it. i.e. The Association of Brown Nosers, The Nuclear Society of Backstabbers, The Bullshit Artists League. Whatever, the society or association is in your field **– JOIN IT!!!**

Usually these societies won't ask you for proof of experience or degrees or what it is that you actually do. **All they want is your money!** So join at least 30 of them; cover the wall in your office or cubicle with as many of them as you can. Plaster your office with awards that you can also print up on your computer. The town gave you an award for helping the garbage men lift up and toss the garbage. **(they don't like to work hard)**

"Township of Brooklyn, New Jersey

Is pleased to present this award to

Leonard Love Matlick

For taking out the garbage 2000 times

Thru rain and snow and heat of day

AND helping our hard working garbage men

Lift the VERY heavy garbage bags up onto the truck"

Another thing is, that if you don't know what you're talking about, talk very **LOUD!!**

A lot of times you can bluster a person into believing that you know a lot. Most management or foremen types have very big mouths and talk very loudly; do the same. People will look at you like you're crazy, but they'll think that you're authoritative in the field.

And if you don't know how to do something, do not ever worry. Always ask a co-worker how he would do something.

"Bill, how would you do this?"

or

"Jim, you look like somebody who knows these type of things."

Most times, co-workers will tell you the answer. However, some may catch onto the game that you're trying to do and bluntly say,

"Hey! I have no time to spend with you, I've

got my own work to do."

Or the blunter person may say,

"Up yours! I ain't telling you a thing!"

But do not worry. Sometimes, you may find people like this. Just snow them, but not a dusting, make it a blizzard,

"Bill, I KNOW that you're a very knowledgeable person. I KNOW how to do this, but I was just trying to see how you would handle it. After all, each company has different rules."

And then do an about face and walk away. Go over to the boss and say,

"Bill is very intransient. I asked him a very simple question and he blew up at me. I guess that he doesn't know that much."

It seems that you always have to keep 'em guessing. So try to be like a politician. That means be foxy, be greasy, be very hard to pin down, fend off questions, deny everything, even when confronted. Watch politicians on the news and see how they handle questions that they don't want to answer. They talk like they are actors, like what they're saying is a bunch of fluff and not substance. So do the same. Take an acting course. Parade up and down in front of a mirror and practice. Practice, practice, **PRACTICE!!!** Delivery, timing, facial expressions – everything. To be a successful ass kisser, you must master it.

CHAPTER 8

STEALING A PERSON'S THUNDER

BACKSTABBING AS YOUR 2ND LANGUAGE

You should try at least once every minute to discredit those co-workers who are a challenge to you. Especially try it on those who possess some knowledge. Since you can't attack them on what they know, attack them on how they dress, how they talk, what their faults are, or any of their bad habits that you can pick up on. Constantly go after them and try to demean or discredit them. Act like a politician does or like a shark does on a defenseless prey. That's how ultimately **YOU** can get to be their boss!!! Whatever they say, you simply respond,

"Oh well."

In a tone that says that they don't know what they're talking about, as if they're talking through their hat.

Everyday, try to put down one or more of them. If one of your co-workers says what a great idea he has, **say it's not that great. Interrupt him constantly** so that he is prevented from making his point clear. **Insult him and his intelligence openly,**

"That's really a childish idea."

or

"We thought of that in kindergarten and you're first thinking of it NOW!!"

BUT SAY IT LOUD!! VERY, VERY, LOUD!!!

Make him look like a fool in front of everybody. Keep up the air of you are important – he definitely is not.

It gets better! Here's something that you should do right now to give you some idea of how far to go. Protest loudly whenever someone else gets a good thing, like a raise, gift, or promotion. Say,

"Hey, why not me?"

or

"What about me?"

or

"I deserve that too!"

And then say that this person didn't deserve it and how he got it; who did **HE** suck up to or brownnose. Then start a rumor on the grapevine that this person doesn't deserve what he got because he has bad breath, he drives an old car, he doesn't zip his fly.

ANYTHING!!!

Next purposely hide things. Don't give out information freely. Be guarded about what and to whom you give it out to. This will help you in the long run. For instance, let's say that you have some information that a co-worker desperately needs to perform his work.

DON'T GIVE IT TO THEM!!!

If the boss should ask them,

"Why didn't you finish it?"

And they say,

"I didn't have the information."

YOU calmly and matter-of-factly say,

"Of course you did, didn't you see this?"

And then you quickly pull out this vital information. This should give you the upper hand.

AAY, you gotta do what you gotta do!!

And in the same vein, purposely give out wrong or misleading information to a co-worker. Make them search in every direction but the correct one and waste their time.

Question: "Where is the Statue of Liberty located? I have to go to a meeting there."

Answer: **"The Statue of Liberty is located in Pennsylvania. You take the train to Pittsburgh and it's right there. (It's in New York City on an island!!) There's a train leaving in 5 minutes; if you rush you can make it."**

Don't give out any information either that you know the answer to and they don't.

Question: **"How much is 5+5?"**

Answer: **"5+5=25"**

DON'T BE A NINNY AND HELP THEM OUT!!!

They surely won't do it for you. Give them the wrong answer purposely. And if they use this information (5+5=25) and they say that you gave it to them **(which I'm sure they will),** you can always say,

"I thought he was asking what 5 times 5 is, and that is 25."

And one more important thing; don't sign your name to anything either. This way you can always blame it on someone else.

"I didn't do that; I would've signed it if I had. It must be George's responsibility."

Then, if you don't like a person in your department or in another department, write letters to the President or Vice-President that so and so is stopping the company from getting further ahead and make up a foolish reason why. Start a rumor,

"Harry is an alcoholic." (dope pusher, coke addict or even an adulterer)

or

"I can't work with George. He's unstable and unwilling to compromise. I think he's mentally ill and needs the help of a psychiatrist."

Or if that doesn't work, then you can always tattle to the boss or those higher up,

"Is somebody higher up protecting George? He's an idiot! Why would any company keep an imbecile like him?"

Also, if a higher up comes in to talk to a co-worker, immediately upstage him. **YOU** get center stage; **YOU deserve it!!!** Do this. Before the co-worker gets a chance to even say anything say this:

"Hey, Mr. Big Shot, here's something really interesting….."

or

"Hey Mr. Big Shot, before you see George……"

Or something else, but don't ever let that co-worker get to him first. Get that higher up to see **YOU first.** Establish your right to be much more important than the co-worker. Say something and then laugh,

"Hey, Mr. Very Big Shot, I bet that you came to see me right? ha, ha, ha"

And then when you talk to a higher up or anyone for that matter, always start bending their ear about how your boss doesn't seem to understand. That this other co-worker is pulling the wool over his eyes.

"Mr. Smith just isn't aware of it. He's TOO nice a guy."

And then start telling them again about how much work that you have, that you have even much more work that this co-worker does, and that it's not fair, and that this co-worker is **NOT** pulling his load like you are.

"I've got a 100 jobs to his 2. That's not equal – it should be, don't you think? He should be taking more of this work."

Know this. You are in a fight for your life, so always try to knock down this co-worker or make him look stupid; if he says,

"Of course."

You say,

"Never!"

If he says,

"Night."

You say,

"Day."

Whatever he says, you say the exact opposite and say it loud; purposely, obviously, emphatically, **VERY, VERY, LOUD!!!**

Then, if you should ever ask him for something that he has and you want it and that he's not using, badger him or threaten him into giving it to you.

"Well, if you don't give it to me, I'm gonna tell Mr. Jones!"

ALWAYS, ALWAYS go after any co-worker who's a threat to you. And that means **ANYBODY!!!!** And here's another always, **ALWAYS, ALWAYS,** buy coffee for your boss.

"You want coffee? I'm going for it anyway."

But if another co-worker does it, say out **LOUD,**

"YA BROWN NOSING THE BOSS, YA FUCK!!!!"

Don't be shy in defending your right to brownnose the boss. He's your meal ticket.

Remember that song, the one that goes, **"They smile in your face, the backstabbers."**

Well, it's true. You should also strive to smile in their face even though you don't like someone and just got finished putting the knife in their backs. Some may call it backstabbing or some other choice words, but so what. Always deny that you are doing it to them.

"ME? Bill, I would NEVER do that!"

or

"George, I love you. You wouldn't think that I'd do that? Never, I'd NEVER do that!"

Keep on denying it as you walk away,

"NEVER!!

and shake your head no.

And then rush over to your boss and say,

"George is a COMPLETE idiot!!!"

or how about,

"Bill REALLY is a horse's ASS!!!"

However, don't say anything while this co-worker is around, and never to the person's face. It's just not nice. **(Really, please try to keep from laughing)** Only do it behind the person's back. Or, when he turns sideways, but to his face, always try to smile and boost him up.

"My, but you're doing a fantastic job."

or

"That's really perseptive, Bill. Right on!!"

Anytime that this person does a good job, tell him, or even better, reward him.

"You did such a great job Bill, lunch is on me."

But behind his back, tell the boss that **YOU** did it, and take credit for it, using **"I"** or

"My" frequently. Forget this latest psychology of saying "We". It means nothing. It is **ALWAYS, I!!.**

"Although George did the job, I gotta admit it, I thought of it first. He did it under my direct supervision and I was primarily responsible for getting it out on time and under budget!!"

Never admit that a co-worker or underling does anything at all, that is of course, unless there is a mistake and then blame him for it of course,

"BILL REALLY BOTHCHED UP THAT JOB ROYALLY!!!"

Then, you should try to arrange to have your desk or office or spot located as close to the boss as possible. Tell him that there's a draft on your back from where you are now, or that the lighting is bad and you'll ruin your eyes, or make up some stupid excuse or anything!! But get located near him. This is **IMPORTANT!!** Again, this is **VERY** important and a key ingredient on becoming good at backstabbing or even brownnosing.

If you have to, badger or cajole a co-worker who's close to the boss now to switch places with you,

"Would you mind switching places (or desks) George, I've got this problem and I need to be close to the men's room."

And if he doesn't switch, complain to higher authority, your boss, personnel, the President, but you **MUST** get your way in this. Make up something,

BUT YOU'VE GOT TO BE NEAR YOUR BOSS!!!

That way you can exchange little ditties, friendlies, and words with your boss. You can cheer him up if he looks down in the dumps and you can also be his defender. For instance, if others in your department criticize something your boss says, just out of earshot of him show **YOUR** loyalty, **YOUR** allegiance to him. If they say,

"Why is he always changing things?"

Defend him so that your boss can hear it, but say it very loudly,

"HE HAS A GOOD REASON FOR IT!!!"

Then turn and smile broadly at your boss so that he knows that it was **YOU** who were defending him. **(Isn't this fun?)** Later, when you're able, go over to the boss and proceed to crawl all **OVER** the ass of the co-worker who had criticized him. Berate the co-worker and ask the boss why is he keeping him, and give him ample ammunition to get rid of him.

Here's another thing to do. Show your eagerness to help alleviate his burdens.

"Those timesheets are a real chore. You want me to do them?"
or
**"You don't have to initial all five hundred thousand copies.
I can do them for you."**

Not only show him that you're interested. **TELL HIM** that **"his problems are yours",** and what can you do to help. Take work home? Stay later?

ANYTHING!!!

Be shameless in it. The more sickening sounding the better.

"Why don't I pick you up in the morning. After all, we live in the same state."

or

"Five hundred miles is not that far. I'll pick you up."

Next , see what your boss likes and dislikes; if your boss says, "I hate everybody who wears a pink shirt!!!"

Never, ever, NEVER, EVER, wear a pink shirt!

Go in naked, but for God's sake, don't ever wear a color that he hates. Let him know that you are the same type and show the same reactions to things that he does. Let him identify you as being the same person he is.

Say,

"Yeah, I hate those who wear a pink shirt too.! They're ruining the country!!!"

If your boss likes people who are punctual,

NEVER, NEVER, come in late.

Always be on time or early. And don't ever be too anxious to leave at lunchtime or quitting time either – linger. Leave when your boss does, come in when he does; make yourself indespensible to him. Never leave your boss alone for a second. Anticipate his every thought. You must convince him that only **YOU** can do the job and that it's only **YOU** whom he can trust to do it **RIGHT**, the exact way that he himself would do it.

And another thing, don't ever say no to your boss either. Very few bosses like to hear,

"NO!"

from an underling. Never argue with your boss even if you know that you are right. Nobody ever achieved success who was constantly disagreeing with his immediate superior. So become a yes man. Always agree and ally yourself with him every time. Not to the point of always yessing him to death with,

"Yes,sir, YES SIR!!"

But yes him in other ways,

"You're absolutely right."

or

"Exactly."

or

"I agree."

or

"Yes, that's the way to do it."

or even

"Now I know why you're such an asset to the company. You're the best!"

Snow him, but not just a light dusting; make it sound like a blizzard.

If he throws something over to you say,

"Nice throw, what an arm you'd have for football."

If he throws a crumbled piece of paper into a wastebasket say,

"Three points!! You shoulda been a basketball player!"

Or really make the snowflakes fly, say,

"Do the Yankees (or name any pro team) know that you're here?"

Or even

"Say, did you play professional ball?"

Next always try to cheer up your boss if he looks down in the dumps. Say,

"Smile….it's becoming on you."

or

"I'm gonna come back there and cheer you up."

or

"I've got some good news….listen to this…."

or

"Job getting you down? It'll get better. It's not your fault. It's the way those higher ups have handled it."

But you've got to watch out when you do this. Don't be afraid of any comments from your boss – **he loves this stuff**! It's others that you have to beware of. If somebody jokes that you're sitting next to the boss, say sarcastically,

"Why, because you want to?"

Always retort to a challenge. If a co-worker says or implies,

"Well, there's gotta be somebody here who's responsible."

(meaning that you're not)

Immediately pounce on him,

"WHAT!!!!!! MEANING I'M NOT!!!!! Well let me tell you that I am much more responsible than you are!!! MUCH MORE!!!!"

Immediately say this to show him that you know the tricks that he's trying to do. Always open your mouth if a co-worker or anybody says a misconception about you or what you did and says it to a higher up. Even if you have to make a scene or start a fight, don't acquiece, don't keep your mouth shut.

FIGHT!!! IT'S YOUR LIFE AT STAKE HERE!!!

Let's say that you've been working on a special project for your boss for 2 months and the reason that it took so long was because a co-worker didn't give you the information that you needed. And you say to the boss, after he asks you what's taking so long,

"Well, I've had this for 2 months now, and …."

Just then, the co-worker hears this and realizes that he'll get into trouble for not giving you the information and he interrupts you from talking and says,

"Hey, hey…wait a minute, no I didn't!"

or

"That's not true!"

Or tries to cover himself because he knows that he is at fault,

SCREAM AT THE TOP OF YOUR LUNGS SO THAT THEY'LL HEAR YOU ON SATURN.

"YES, I DID!!!!!!!"

or

"NO, YOU DIDN'T!!!!

or

"YES, IT IS TRUE!!!!"

And then stab him to his face again and again at machine gun speed to your boss, while you still continue to yell,

"THE REASON THAT I COULDN'T GET FINISHED ON TIME WAS BECAUSE OF GEORGE!!!! HE DIDN'T GIVE ME THE INFORMATION!!!! IT IS HIS FAULT THAT I COULDN'T GET FINISHED!!!! HIS FAULT AND HIS FAULT ALONE!!!!!"

Then turn and face him,

"I CAME TO YOU EVERY DAY ASKING IF YOU HAD THE INFORMATION AND YOU SAID THAT YOU DIDN'T HAVE IT YET" (whether he did or not)

Don't let any person get away with anything. **TALK!!** That's why you were given a mouth. Forget about that the mouth is for eating. **IT'S NOT!!!** It's to defend yourself. **TALK BACK!!!**

You should always backstab and always deny as you stab them in the back again and again and this time twist the knife in there. As soon as they leave the area, rush over to your boss and say,

"I think that George has a REAL problem!!!"

or

"I think that Bill is unreasonable!"

Or some better ones to use,

"George is a lazy, backstabbing oaf!!!"

Or even,

"Why don't you get rid of him. He's an idiot!"

In addition, if you want to get a co-worker in disfavor, make several long distance calls on his phone to Greenland, or Mars, or find out what the largest amount anywhere in the world is to call and then call it fifty times a day. (**call during lunch or after hours**) And then get a copy of this phone bill and circulate it to the higher ups with a terse note that not everyone in your department is pulling for the company, and then sign your name to it. If this co-worker doesn't get called into the big shots, write another letter saying, what is wrong with the officers of this company, that they don't care about controlling costs? Say, that phone bills are important, and the employees who save the company money should be rewarded and those who don't should be warned and sign the **PRESIDENT'S** name to it and circulate it along with your phone bill and the co-workers.

If your company is worried about too many personal calls and you want to look good, use someone else's phone whenever you can. This way when they check the phone bills, it appears that you are saving the company money. And I would suggest bragging about it to **EVERYONE!!** Get a copy of the bill and again circulate it along with a letter to all of the big shots saying that more employees should look out for the companies benefit. And then sign your boss's name to it!!!

Aay, you want to get ahead, don't you?

Now, should anybody ask you a question or ask about something that's time consuming or difficult, you say **LOUDLY,**

"THAT'S SO SIMPLE!!! YOU FIGURE IT OUT!!!"

or

"THAT'S NO BIG DEAL!!"

or

"THAT'S NOTHING!!"

Always , ALWAYS, give simplistic answers to difficult situations. "We do that all of the time –it's easy." (defying gravity)

Again fluff off any hint that a problem is difficult to solve.

"I don't see that it's so hard!" (parting the seas) BUT HERE'S THE SECRET TO GETTING AHEAD!!

Never, repeat, **NEVER ,** give the answer to any question or problem. Let them figure it out. You must keep yourself above things like details and how a thing could possible work. (**time travel**) If you want to become a boss or a manager or CEO or whatever, this is a prime requisite. Then do this,

Make a statement out of thin air,

"Yes, it is!" or simply say,

"That's just it!" and walk away. Don't expand on it or feel that you have to. Or make up some stupid nonsensical remark. And if you can't thing up a good reason for somebody's question – **LIE!!!**

or

If somebody puts you on the spot –**LIE!!!**

or

Make up a logical sounding answer

or

"LIE!!!"

or

"DOUBLE TALK!!!"

or

"BAFFLE THEM!!!"

or

"LIE!!!"

And then cry and whine that you have too much to do.

"I've got three projects near completion, two that I'm trying to get under way, and four projects that are brand new. I don't even know how I'm doing this. It's really unbelievable. I'm really short handed and need more people."

And as always, no matter how much work you have to do, don't do any of it. Just concentrate on picking up minor inconsequential points and blowing them all out of proportion.

"This margin is off by one ten thousandth of an inch!!

Incredible!!! I can't do my work until somebody fixes this messed up form!!!"

And, joy of joys, if you are given help, (**YES!!**) give him everything so that you will be left alone. This way you can do whatever you want – play cards, call your bookie, try to put a hit on the closest female, work on personal projects – anything! But if anything goes wrong you can pin the blame on him. And then apologize to your boss for giving the job to such an idiot. But…if he should do a bang up job, and it turns out right…

YOU CAN TAKE THE CREDIT FOR IT!!! (how's that?)

You gotta have a patsy if you want to get far.

So, you should start thinking like a boss. Always ask a co-worker what he is working on, even if you have no business in asking him that. Tell him the boss told you to ask him. This way, you can tell the boss,

"Bill is working on……"

It starts to get the co-worker, and the boss too, feeling that you are responsible for the job and the person. But always deny that **YOU** are looking for position and power. **DENY! DENY! DENY!!!**

"Me? Nah. I'm just a little fish in the bowl."

Keep repeating this until you're a boss.

Now let's say that by now your boss thinks that you're doing a super job, and now has given you responsibility for running a small project. (**keeping track of ALL office supplies**!) Always use the words,

"My job."

or

"My money."

Frequently when talking about it to anyone who's on the job or not. It makes you look like only **YOU** are worrying about the company's money, like it was your very own. So always give a dollar figure. **Even if you KNOW that it's a bunch of didly!!**

"I'm in charge of 40 million dollars worth of projects!"

or

"500 million dollars worth of accounts pass thru MY department!"

or

"I have (or had) total running control of 9 different projects at the same time and completed all 9 of them on time and under budget without having the proper manpower!!!!" Wow! What a man!!!

Some other words to use to impress people on your job are,

"I'm wearing a different hat." (or another hat)

If you take on extra work that's not in your job description. Use this phrase when you're talking to higher ups only about taking on additional work.

"We put it to bed!"

or even better,

"I put it to bed!"

Again, higher ups love to use this expression when talking about a completed project.

Now, when things are really screwed up, avoid it or blame it on someone else.

"Well, you know…Joe Blow authorized it and he had all of the stuff."

If you butter up the higher ups, they will cover for you.

"Well, he's not that bad." (to a report critical of you)

or

"You don't seem to understand the problem." (to a mistake that you made)

Then, when things start to look good, jump back in. They will remember that **YOU** were in charge, when it turned out good.

"It was a difficult job, but I turned the project around!"

Some more important things to remember when talking to higher ups. If you see them, don't just say hello or good morning. Always add something of importance to them or to the company,

"Hi Mr. Schmuck. I'm working on YOUR job."

or

"Good Morning Mr. Idiot. I've been in since 5 AM to get YOUR work out."

If they keep walking that's fine, but if they stop, then that's your opportunity to mesmerize them about your job. **About how fantastic you're doing it and the rub of it all, that you're doing it all by yourself and you don't have enough manpower.**

Sometimes they may ask you how many people would you need to properly get the work out. **Tell them five hundred thousand, or six or seven million, but make it many more times the figure that you need. Say, "Two zillion, four hundred million would be sufficient to get a job out in one day the size of this project!"**

I mean, how do they expect you to get it out if they don't give you the right amount of people?

This is the way that it should always come out.

If by chance, the boss should go on vacation, and joy of joys, leaves you in charge (**stranger things have happened**), what do you do if anyone from another department comes in and jokes with some of the people in **YOUR** department?

Tell them that **YOU** are now responsible for the people in **YOUR** department and the boss left you in charge of **YOUR** department and that he shouldn't come in again doing it.

Make up something,say,

"C'mon! C'mon! You're holding MY MAN up!!!"

And then tell him that he's distracting **YOUR** man from doing his work. Also emphacize that you're responsible to the boss for the productivity in this department and don't come in again doing it. Just in case the higher ups are watching.

"C'MON! C'MON!! You're holding up production. Don't you have anything to do back in your office?"

Afterwards, go over to your boss's supervisor, sit down perturbed and say,

"Those people in the pencil department. They don't care about anybody's department but their own. They think that MY department, paper clips, are a joke."

Don't let nobody get away with nothing!!!

All throughout history, you will find that it was the backstabber who got ahead by plotting, by planning, actually setting up people to his own advantage. You may not be able to use their methods today, but it gives you some idea as to the extent that you have to go in backstabbing in order to really get far, far ahead.

Read about great backstabbers in history like Washington, Jefferson, Napoleon, and Macarthur, who were excellent at backstabbing.

Here's something that you can do right now. At night, after everyone leaves, go through their wastebaskets for any interesting notes or information that could be useful to you. Especially your boss or those higher up. It would also be nice if you could plant a bugging device near your boss's desk, so that you could listen in on those juicy conversations that you just **KNOW** or can guess are about you or your co-workers. It's nice to know what plans the boss has about you or others, so that you can plot and make plans.

Always be shameless in your b.s.ing and brownnosing and ruthless in your backstabbing. To what extent?

<u>**THERE IS NO EXTENT!!!!!!!!!!!!!!!!!!**</u>

If you want to succeed, there is no extent to what you should do. Just kneel and kiss their feet or snow them or stab them in the back until you get what you want. But always keep smiling. Never admit to putting someone on. You wouldn't lie to them, now would you? **OF COURSE NOT!!!** This is how it should always sound. You are sincere aren't you? (**YES!!!**)

CHAPTER 9

HOW TO FEND OFF EMBARASSING DIRECT QUESTIONS

You should be wary when people ask you questions. Believe me, it's not as you may think, that it is harmless and it is just to learn information about you. . They may be suckering you into something; they may be setting you up.

This is the challenge then, not only to being a smooth talker, but also in everyday life, in responding diplomatically to questions that you regard as inappropriate and downright rude. You have to learn the subtle art of the sidestep – fending off questions.

I can't impress this upon you strongly enough. It is the basis for all politicians and business and art strategy. Even if you overhear something from someone, and you want to set the record straight or respond with the correct answer to somebody's idiotic statement –

DON'T! DON'T DO IT!!!

See a big red sign first, **FEND OFF QUESTIONS!!!**

Start by being careful in your answers. If somebody asks you a direct question or a personal question that you don't want to answer, give a cagey response. If they say what time is it?

Lie!

Say,

"I don't know." (even if you do)

Give the wrong answer purposely;

"The time is 4PM." (when it's 3PM)

pause,

"uh"

answer the question with a question ,

"What was the question again?"

repeat the question,

"Oh yes. What was the correct time?"

Give yourself time to make up a lie.

"I don't have a watch on" (even if you do)

or

If they notice that you do have a watch on, say,

"Oh darn, my watch must have stopped."

Again, in a bind, always ask,

"What was the question?"

When somebody asks you a direct question. Then say,

"Oh."

Make it seem like you're out of it, not an airhead or mindless, but like the absent minded professor, in his own world of thought. And then say,

"Oh yes, I remember now."

And then nod your head in agreement. Wait several minutes or a really long time to answer.

"It's just that I'm so busy with 30 million jobs that I can't even remember if I'm coming or going."

And then walk away without answering. Don't even think that you have to. If they call after you, and press the question, turn and wave, and say,

"I'm too busy right now. Catch me later."

And make sure that they never do.

A good way to fend off a question is simply by saying,

"I'll answer that in a minute. Can I first ask you though….."

And then make up some stupid response or nonsense.

"Did you shower this morning?"

or

"Do you use a mouthwash?"

Use any stupidity to break the ice and then forget the question. Or if somebody asks you a question, never give a straight answer.

"Well, it definitely is possible…..but then again it may not be."

Hem and haw. Hedge.

"The sun will shine tomorrow, but there is a chance of rain….so it could be cloudy if it rains."

Always leave a line of retreat open, in case it's not right. Also, if somebody should interrupt you to ask a question or something,

DON'T STOP!!!

Finish the thing that you are doing. Look at them as if perturbed at the interruption. Say,

"One second, let me just finish this."

And then continue to do whatever you were doing for another couple of minutes.

IGNORE THEM!!!

And then say,

"Oh, I'm so sorry, it's just that this is so important."

This does two things. First it says that you're a very busy person and cannot be disturbed. Second, it says that you are more important than the person asking the question.

Sometime ago, there was a commercial for hair shampoo on television. In it a matronly woman abruptly stops this beautiful girl from walking towards her desk.

"Dear, how do you manage to keep your hair looking so great?" she asked.

Answer:

"I, uh………………….manage!" and then the girl walked on.

Beautiful response!

She fended off the question, paused, used the question in her answer and she kept the old bitty guessing by not revealing anything but leaving a trace of using secretive methods to keep her hair looking great. And she kept her cool.

If someone presses you for an answer or for some information, don't tell them too much. Leave them guessing. Say,

"I don't know."

Whether you do or don't.

So just don't react. Don't just answer by rote. We are trained since childhood to give an immediate response when asked a question. Pause and then think to yourself,

"What should I say?"

And don't do anything at all until you first pause and think.

If somebody asks you why the job didn't get out on time, say,

"I could have gotten it out on time, but I didn't have the proper information."

or

Blame it on other departments or people.

"It's all accountings fault. They promised me a job number and since I couldn't charge to the job, I wasn't able to do the work."

Always blame somebody else for your shortcomings. It doesn't matter if you could have done the work (**you were busy playing cards**), or that you even knew what to do (**you didn't know zip**) it's just all these other people can be used to your advantage.

Then write persuasive memos covering your ass.

"It's not only accountings fault, it's George's and Bill's fault too, for not getting me the job number. I would've finished it in plenty of time, plenty of time, if it wasn't for all of these time consuming factors."

Always repeat to everyone why you couldn't do it.

"Yes. I would have finished it in plenty of time. But that's the reason."

And then get them away from why you didn't do the job.

"It's just that I have 30 million other distractions."

And then blame others too.

"It's really Bill's fault. He didn't give me the job number. And that's the real reason the bridge fell down."

And as always,

DENY! DENY! DENY!!

"It's not my fault."

You should also make up some standard replies to nosy or embarrassing questions that keep coming up. You know the ones:

Question: "How old are you?"

Answer: **"I'm over 21."**

or

Question: "How much do you make?"

Answer: **"Not nearly enough for this job description."**

or

Question: "What do you pay for rent? (or your mortgage)"

Answer: **"I got a bargain. Two dollars a month."**

or

Question: "How much did your new car cost?"

Answer: **"They gave it to me almost for free."**

And then you can stiff them with curt answers:

"I don't want to talk about it."

or

"It's really none of your business."

I know of one older couple who got tired of hearing the standard question,

"How many grandchildren do you have?"

or

"You're a grandpa right?"

So instead of having to say something, they simply stated,

"Twenty – Ten sets of twins!"

That shuts them up.

Here is another thing that is very important in any job to fending off questions. Never sit back and relax or daydream. Somebody may sneak up behind you. Somebody is always waiting to get you in trouble. So always look busy even if you're not. Try to make comebackers to anything that anybody says. Like the following that a co-worker will just love to do to you:

"I hope that you're not sleeping (or relaxing) on company time."

Respond thusly,

"No, I'm in deep thought trying to come up with a solution for this. The boss has me working day and night seeing if I have a new method for inventing the solar system. And I do!!!"

Then zing it to them,

"Why are you interrupting me? I'm very busy. I'm going to tell the boss that you're preventing me from having the Universe not fall apart!!"

Here is another very important item. And this one is as important, maybe even more important than all the rest. Don't trust someone who can talk without stopping to take a breath. It means that there is something wrong with them, and that they are hiding something or don't know what they are talking about. Especially if someone can talk machine gun speed, then you especially have to watch out for this type of person.

It has been my experience that these type of people are also very sneaky, even more so then what I've talked about before, so you have to watch your back every minute with them. Now it may seem that I'm making a big deal out of a few type of people whom you may never meet. (**but you will!**) But I **KNOW** what I'm talking about and I just hope that you never meet up with these type of people. But if by chance you do then this is what you must do to save yourself. Put up a barricade. Say,

"STOP!!!"

and put you hand up like a stop sign.

Then say,

"Would you PLEASE slow down!!!"

Interrupt them, that's the only way to stop these type of people. Interrupt them and attack them at every opportunity, never let them get the upper hand. Constantly disrupt them from making their point clear. Always make it seem that anybody who can talk that fast has to have an ulterior motive **(and they do!),** one that he's hiding. And in most cases they do.

First and foremost in fending off questions, don't let anyone get away with any misconception about you, no matter how minor. Always jump down their throats as if they said a curse word. If you allow people, they will walk all over you and say that you enjoyed it.

TALK!!

That's what you were given a mouth for. Not to eat, but to defend yourself. Immediately cut them off or cut them down with a remark, should they say something about you that's not true. Most times, if you don't jump down their throats they will think it's true anyway.

For instance, if somebody makes a comment about your incessant gum chewing **(and you don't chew gum**!) immediately interrupt them. Yell as loud as you can that you should feel embarrassed,

"THAT'S NOT TRUE!!! I DON'T CHEW GUM!!!"

And then start on the fact that **THEY** are sloppy eaters. That **THEY** drop candy wrappers all around and on the floor. Or if they smoke, say that **THEY** pollute your air. Or anything to make them feel humiliated. **THEY** started it and **YOU** have to finish it. But always keep going after them and never let up. Don't just say that one remark and stop. Keep after them non-stop.

"THIS ISN'T THE ZOO. STOP FEEDING THE ANIMALS!! MICE AND COCKROACHES LOVE YOU!!"

Just remember to always interrupt them and never let them finish any misconception about you. Whether it's because you didn't finish something on time and now they're ultimately blaming you, or they're just trying to win brownie points with the boss, it doesn't matter. You just have to protect yourself in the clinches at all times.

You can attempt to avoid this happening if you don't do anything without first checking around to judge the outcome and how it will affect you. Now, I know that this is hard to do and a lot of times you can't, but you can set up certain things to plan on. An easy example. Your boss is counting the number of times that you go to the bathroom because you announce it to him every time.

"I'm gonna go take a piss."

If you know that he's purposely watching you go to the john, for heaven's sake,

DON'T TELL HIM!!!

Or if a guy is aggravated with his wife and he knows that he's gonna get aggravated when he talks to her, but he continually calls her during lunch. The simple thing to do is

DON'T CALL HER!!!

Certain things like this you can see what the outcome will be and although these are simplistic, they show what I mean.

Also, don't volunteer information to anybody. Even if you know the answer,

KEEP YOUR MOUTH SHUT AND DON'T TELL ANYONE!!!

Let them find out for themselves. Has anybody in your recent history volunteered information to you when you needed it or asked for help? **OF COURSE NOT!!**

So why should you. Don't be a ninny and help someone out, since you are not helping yourself or your career. The simple rule here is,

IT'S ME FIRST. FUCK EVERYBODY ELSE!!!

And while on the same subject, don't loan anything to anybody either. Remember Ben Franklin's statement,

"Neither a lender or borrower be"

It's true! But don't loan because you'll never get it back. For instance, if somebody asks you or makes a general statement aloud,

"Anybody here have a screwdriver?"

SAY NO!!!

Don't volunteer it if you have it. Lie outright if they ask you. And even if they remember that you have one, say that you don't,

"I left it in China."

Be selfish for your own sanity and the safety of your possessions. Invariably the people who are forever borrowing tools, money, information, never return them. They are counting on your being Mr. Nice Guy again and again.

ENOUGH!! SAY NO!!!

If anybody, anywhere, asks you a question, always say,

"I'll have to get back to you."

And it doesn't matter what they ask you or even if they ask you if it's sunny out or cold or raining, always say,

"I'll have to get back to you."

This way, it starts to set up a feeling inside you of never having to respond to a question.

You can always add, as if in an afterthought,

"I don't have my papers with me."

Or

"I haven't been outside"

Or

The good old,

"I've been in the bathroom all morning long."

CHAPTER 10

HOW TO GET A JOB

(ESPECIALLY IF YOU KNOW ZIP)

One of the things that I've learned from working all over this country, is that there is always a job available. **No really there is!** To all those who say in a down economy- **NUTS!** Hear me out. It just boils down to 2 things: How far are you willing to travel to get a job and how much money are you willing to lower your expectations in order to accept. Once you can settle these two important things, everything else will work itself out.

I've known people who refuse to move out of a small town in the Mid-West or South to find something, even in **THEIR** own field. To get a job (any job) you cannot be that inflexible; smooth talkers have to be flexible. You have to give a lot to get a little.

Contrary to public belief, getting a job is easy, especially if you know nothing at all. You first have to decide what you want to do – become an accountant, engineer, lawyer, stock trader, nuclear physicist, astronaut, brain surgeon, etc. However, some jobs like brain surgery do require some prior knowledge, even if you did stay at a Holiday Inn Express.

But if you should choose a profession like brain surgery, there are so many books being written today on how to operate, that this shouldn't pose too much of a problem, if that's what you want to do. So once you decide on what type of job you want to do, this is what you do first.

Rent a Post Office Box or those rental boxes that say "Suite 179" (**like Mail Boxes**) and make up an ad to put in the newspaper or on-line classifieds.

"MANY JOBS! HIGH SALARY!
HIRING FOR IMMEDIATE OPENINGS
RUSH YOUR RESUME!! NOW!! RIGHT NOW!!!
to: Suite 179
P.O.Box
Anywhere,USA"

Once you get some resumes in, this is what you do. Rent a hotel room in a very nice hotel, to give the impression that you are on the up and up, and contact as many as you want in order to get some idea of the field that you want to go into. The people that you interview will gladly give you all of their back-up material as well as their references. Such as their medical boards (**if you choose brain surgery**), where they went to school, and many other things that they want you to know about them.

So, interview these people intently, asking questions that sound like you know what you are talking about, such as:

"How would you do a brainal rectolomy? (to a brain surgeon) or something like that. Look in a medical book and find some really good questions to ask. I would also tape record the interviews so that you can pick up on their actions and reactions to questions. (this is exactly how an actor rehearses for a role in a movie)

Take concopuous notes and always appear sympathetic, and waiting on their every response. How you do this will reflect on how **YOUR** interview for a job goes.

And once you do a bunch of interviews, then all you do is pick the best one and copy it. That's it. Then it's yours and you've got a foot in the door.

Armed with an impressive sounding resume to get in with, leaves only the interview to pass. And this can be a piece of cake too. All it does is take guts, to do the rest, but you will find yourself in another field or job quite easily.

You just go from interview to interview, carrying a pocket tape recorder, which will get you to find out what questions **THEY** ask. Even highly technical questions.

Such as,

"How would you do a brainal rectolotomy?" (for brain surgery)

With the ammunition you got from interviewing a real brain surgeon, this should now be a piece of cake. Trust me.

Next, see if there are any books published in the field.

Brain surgery has a lot of books published, so does engineering and law. **I can personally attest to that!**

Now sending out the best resume may not work sometimes, so you have to send out a lot. Send 10,000 resumes out, if that doesn't work, send 20,000, 30,000, 100,000!! It doesn't matter – make your job getting a job.

If you have to, go out of town to get a job. If you've got a house, wife, kids, leave them there and you go out of town – **rent a room!**

Don't apply to the same company for several positions. For instance, if you're applying to a hospital for a brain surgery position, don't also apply for a janitor's position. Somehow, it doesn't work – they will find out. You don't want to look desperate and not discriminating.

A word about resumes; don't go over 2 pages, or use colored paper. Don't use bad grammar, such as

"I could never spell engineer before, and now I are one."

Use bold face to make important things stand out and organize it logically. Ask yourself, what would a brain surgeon or an engineer say? But don't use stuff that the interviewer never heard of, such as abbreviations or specific jargon.

Be tenacious, but don't keep calling them more than once a day. Call every week or every two weeks, and alternate between calling and e-mails.

Forget references. 75% of today's job-seekers do not have their references checked by prospective employers. The reason is that companies are afraid of lawsuits. The pace of lawsuits filed by prospective employees and those of employees have tripled in the past few years. Also, most companies will not talk about a previous employee because they may get sued. So what are you waiting for? Push thru them.

Now eventually, using these methods will get you a job. Once you get on the job you may get fired after a few minutes, because you know absolutely nothing about it. But most bosses are usually afraid to admit that they hired an imbecile, so they might assign somebody to show you the ropes. If not, go back to the previous stage and the next company, at least you will have some experience, even if it's 3 minutes worth.

Eventually, going from company to company and being fired for inexperience and then jumping right back in, you will quickly gain experience and gain some insight into what the field is about. This is how all b.s. artists start.

Try to answer questions in an interview with a one word response. For example, if they ask technical questions, such as,

"How would you put in a seismic restraint?"

Answer: **"Strongly."**

or

"What is the maximum dimension for supporting a 6 inch plastic pipe?"

Answer: **"Hanging."**

Take their questions and pick up on one word in the question. Of course you need to have some smarts in responding to technical questions, but you don't have any idea of what it's about. Just listen to what they are saying and pick up on minor words.

So, in the first question, you would pick up on the word – **restraint**, and then you would strongly restrain it. In the second question, you would pick up on the word – **support**, and then you would hang it. It's a play on words, an interview.

They ask questions to trip you up so that they don't have to pay you top dollar. It's not about what you know. So play the game the way they do. Here's some other things to do in order to control the interview. (and **YOU** control the interview, not the person interviewing **YOU**.)

Keep the interview climate open and relaxed. Ask the interviewer open ended questions starting with words like what, when and how.

"What sort of specific area of engineering work do you do here?" (for an engineering position)

or

"When you operate, do you have enough staff to assist me? (for a brain surgeon position)

or

"How many members of the bar do you have on staff?" (for a lawyer position)

Use why sparingly. It often places the interviewer on the defensive.

"Why don't you have a liquor cabinet here for prospective employees?" (of course if you're an accomplished alcoholic, it might not be the right question to ask)

Try to parrot back all the supposedly right answers – get the interviewer to provide as much information before the interview. Probe the interviewer and ask how he did an accomplishment. Pretend that the interviewer works for **YOU** and ask him how **HE** solved the problems.

"You turned a loss into a profit in one year? Wow! That's some accomplishment.

How did you do it?"

In going thru an interview, you've got to listen not only to what people say, but also to what they mean. You have to appear very personable (**the most important quality**), presentable (**come dressed to the nines),** and technically knowledgeable (**you really don't have to if you can do the other two)**

Generally, first impressions **DO** make a difference. Be conservative in your clothes. Dress in clothes that you think your boss would wear. Don't wear black leather to an interview. Don't wear frayed shirts, ties or old clothes.

Don't wear blazers with school emblems. Don't scrimp on shoes. The more expensive looking the better. If you're a man avoid jewelry that's not functional, like a watch. If you're a woman, keep it simple. Also don't overwhelm the interviewer with a heavy odor of cologne or perfume. And if you're a woman, **try to flirt, but don't ask him if he wants to get laid**.

These are the basics, but you should consult a book on grooming. More jobs were lost by people who didn't shower (**BO**) then those who did, and not on what they knew.

Also, try to prepare stereotyped answers for questions that you think the interviewer will ask, such as,

"Tell me about yourself."

Answer:

"I'm a self-starter, goals oriented person who gets in early and gets the work done even before it's asked of me."

or

"I'm really a wonderful person, as you will soon find out. I take out the garbage, I'm friendly to old ladies and little kids and dogs. In fact, I've been given the "Nice Guy" award three years in a row!"

Or something to that effect. You want to give the impression that you are wonderful, pleasant and also a good worker. You are, aren't you?

OF COURSE YOU ARE!!!

And that's what you have to show them**. Not hard! Not hard at all!! Now go out and get that job!!**

CHAPTER 11

CHARISMA – HOW TO DEVELOP IT

Charisma is that inner glow that radiates from you. It is a form of psychic energy that people can feel and even swear that they see. I remember myself seeing the former Mayor of New York City, Abe Beame, radiate with charisma as he was going down the street, shaking hands with all would be followers of his mayoral campaign. He literally had a presence that was inspiring. But it is an attitude and a manner that others think that they are seeing. Those who possess it usually have an air of energy and vitality. They are also very observant, noticing and mentally recording things, not just gazing into the distance.

Charismatic people smile easily, effortlessly. They are a very comfortable person to be with. You like to be with them since they are very likeable. But charisma is not born, it is developed. Although it is most often seen in politicians, charisma IS easy to develop. You don't have to be a politician or a leader, but they all have it. It's also known as "star quality" in performers.

Just imagine a spotlight on you wherever you walk. Visualize this as an aura extending from yourself and igniting every person that you meet or who steps within this area as being enthralled with you. I know that this sounds like a bunch of b.s., but give it a chance – **it does work!**

Whether male or female, project an image that tells others what your position is. This image is more of an attitude and a manner. You have to look as if you know what you're doing.. Move and act purposefully, even when you're going on the elevator. Most charismatic people tend to possess certain items in extraordinary amounts, such as a high-energy level, vitality, courage, composure under stress, a clear direction, a strong sense of movement towards ones goals and above all, the determination to succeed.Learning how to be charismatic is a skill that is learned as any other skill, by studying, practicing, and absorbing it until it is mastered.

So how do you do it? First, smile frequently. Make reassuring gestures with your eyes, face and hands. Have a warmth and playfullness in your manner that your presence shows emotional support, understanding and strength. Speak in a low tone that will sooth and reassure. Exude natural charm. People will tend to seek you out if they perceive you as a charismatic individual because they want to improve their own self.

Next, get a tape recorder and listen to your voice. Dissect your voice until you sound confident and magnetic. Hire a speech coach to improve your speaking voice. Changing your voice to one that is magnetic may take time, and is not an overnight thing. It has taken you years to come up with your present voice, so don't think it will happen immediately. I wish it would.

But, if you have the determination to succeed, **it will happen.**

Again, practice speaking in front of a mirror or visualize yourself speaking to people at work or on TV with a voice that you think is charismatic, and you'll be surprised at how soon your voice will change. **For the better!**

Most charismatic people also use a lot of hand gestures, so do the same. Giving a thumb's up to someone, saying what great job they did is a great one. Or giving the "**finger**" to someone is also effective, but in a negative way. However, if you take that same finger and point it downward, you can use it to make a point, almost like an expletive, but the other way.

You can also do what Nixon did, and raise up both arms in victory, or what Churchill did with two fingers in a V. Or you can use your hands like a garbage man directing a truck **to "c'mon back, c'mon back**." You can also use this to tell someone to come closer or join me.

Again, hand gestures are great to add emphasis to what you are saying or doing. Most charismatic people are also touchy-feely types. Most men cannot do this, but women can; hugging, kissing, etc. goes a long way. But since men cannot touch or hug other men or can't come closer to women without being considered a pervert, flattery can go a long way. A lot of people, expect charismatic people or charming people to be flatterers. And they are! **So what are you waiting for – do the same!!!**

Charismatic people have an image that sets them apart from others. Not because of their accomplishments, but because of their image. They are expected to do well and when they do achieve something, everybody notices it and they are recognized for it. Charismatic people continue to act in ways that will get them approval or kudos by others. Again, image is everything.

Image is more of an attitude than how you look. But, make no mistake about it, looks **DO** matter. Most charismatic people are not overweight. How they dress does not call attention to themselves. But you won't see wrinkles on their clothes or clothes that are ill-fitting.

Again, image is important. You need to show an image of "**you can depend on me**". You have to act and talk like a charismatic person. So how do you do it?

First, when you sit in a chair,

SIT UP STRAIGHT! DON'T SLOUCH!

Don't cross your legs. When you walk, walk like you're going to a meeting that you're late for.

WALK FAST!!

But don't appear harried. When you stand up,

STAND UP STRAIGHT! DON'T HUNCH OVER!

Look like you know where you are going and in the right direction. Look everyone in the eyes. Look at them in one eye, right or left does not matter, but look straight at them. And don't avert other people's eyes. They will think that you are hiding something or have a poor self-image.

Have a nice personality. Be positive, not negative. Be persuasive.

You also have to give the impression that you are competent. You don't have to be competant, you can be an idiot, but you just have to give the impression that you know what you are doing. So try to organize your thoughts **BEFORE** you start speaking.

Remember that old saying, "**Put brain into motion before opening mouth.**" **It's true!** Just don't give a running dialogue of everything and everybody. Say nothing or yes answers. (**never no**) Be brief, be spontaneous, be direct. A few simple thoughts, nothing more.

Again, you can't appear rushed or harried. Try not to let anyone or anything affect you. Always try to stay calm or at least give the impression that you are calm. Imagine that you are the captain of a ship and are trying to steer a course during a storm while everybody else is trying to abandon ship. Just give the impression that you are in control and calm. No matter what happens.

Another thing – listen to people,

DON'T TALK SO MUCH!

Ask them, **"and then what?"** or **"you don't mean that you actually**...."

KEEP QUESTIONING THEM!

Make them feel that you are waiting on their every word, that they are spilling out gems of wisdom or experience. **(try to keep from laughing-please)**

Make even the most simplistic thing that they did be of such importance to you that you hang on their every word.

"You copied 500 pages! WOW! That's fantastic! Tell me more, and don't spare the details – How did you do it? Was it hard – it must have been."

Even on stupid things, don't accept general statements.

"Please be more specific – don't say the sun rose, how did it rise, did it shine on you? Did you actually see the sunrise?"

BE DECISIVE! !

Always state the problem and then give the answer.

"We're going to do this! And then we're going to do that!"

But always give a solution to a problem – don't just keep repeating,

"Oh boy, do we have a problem here!"

People want solutions, they don't want others to keep repeating the problem. They are looking for someone (**YOU!**) for help. **Give it to them!** Don't waste a person's time with nonsense. **Talk straight.**

And when you talk, talk about the challenge, not just all of the obstacles.

"Wouldn't it be great to walk on water – can't you just see it!"

Each charismatic attribute that I've mentioned so far can be acquired fairly easily. But you must work at it by conciously making it happen.

Also, don't be jugemental or critical,

"Boy, that was stupid!" or "You're a horse's ass for doing that!"

Just make a simple imperative statement.

Suggest. Show. Clarify.

Then when you walk into a room, people need to notice you. You have to make a striking presence. You have to look about the room and be ready to accept contact with **ANY PERSON.** People can sense this in your eyes. So you have to have a comfortable look when you look into their eyes. Have a twinkle in your eyes, a playful look, that says, I'm not a threat.

You also have to hear people out, and never rush in or interject to make a point, and **NEVER** steal a person's thunder. (**not yet anyway**)

Your whole face has to light up when you smile (**eyes wide open, grinning from ear to ear**) and when you laugh make people want to laugh with you too. Make your laughter contageous. And this is not just confidence, this is

CHARISMA!!

While the other person is talking, look at them intently, and again mentally wait your turn until the other person finishes.

Also say,

"Uh-huh, uh-huh" from time to time and nod your head in agreement. And then emphacize with what the other person is saying. For instance, if it's a calamity, say,

"My goodness! That's HORRIBLE!"

Charasmatic people are also very courteous. From the biggest to the littlest employer, charismatic people always are courteous in small things, but they do matter.

i.e. **Treat any employee with respect. If a janitor has just finished mopping up a floor, ask them if you can walk across it. Ask a visitor if they would like to use the phone. Open the door when walking with a person of the opposite sex. Remember names; charismatic people develop a knack for remembering a person's name.**

Also, promptly return telephone calls and respond quickly to e-mails and letters. You may be busy, but if you don't respond in a prompt manner, they will always remember that too. One day is acceptable to some people, because of schedule conflicts, but I try to cut it to ½ day if possible. Or if I can't respond, I call them and say that I'm working on **THEIR** job but I just had a previous engagement, and will reply as soon as I get back to the office.

This most people will accept. Nobody likes to be kept waiting. And speaking of waiting, never keep a visitor waiting more than 5 minutes. Stick your head out of your office, and acknowledge them.

"I'll be with you in a minute. How's everything? Ok? Just a minute more."

To be charismatic, you have to have incredible empathic skills, be a great communicator in talking at a level with which people can understand

and also have a jolly disposition and make people feel alive. Not hard !**NOT HARD!**

Just look at former President's, they've done it. It's not so hard if you break it down and put it into a routine. For instance, write it down and then rehearse it.

Not only that, but you also have to praise people in public, like in a group setting.

"Roger here found a way to screw two women at once and that was brilliant. Absolutely BRILLIANT!!"

You have to be so confident that the sheer brazenness of it will seem remarkable.

You should try to refer to or quote another person, especially those that have some importance in your job or career. Referring to what another person has said is flattering whether or not your statement is accurate. Most people will object to a complete misrepresentation of their comments, but forgive a slight inaccuracy.

For instance, the previous comment about screwing two women at once, Roger will be slightly flattered that you chose him to boost his ego, and he won't say anything about it. However, if you said that Roger couldn't even screw **ONE** woman at all, then he would get upset. He will crawl all over you if you said that, like,

"What do you mean that I can't screw any woman at all!!!"

So always try to boost someone's ego. Referring to and quoting another person, has two very important items when it comes to charisma.

First, the people that you refer to and quote will be drawn to you, thus increasing your base of those who regard you as charismatic. Secondly, since charisma is based to a large amount of what other people think of you, the larger the number means the more charismatic that you are in reality.

Another thing about being charismatic. Try to share credit. It gives the impression that you are confident to recognize that other people helped you. Again, to share what Roger above did, give credit to him.

"I couldn't have done it without Roger showing me the way to do it. And he is a master at it!!"

Always acknowledge the contributions of others. It projects charisma and magnetism.

To be charismatic, you have to make others feel good. One way to do this is to use what's called a confirmation behavior on your part; it seems to have a therapeutic effect on other people. It adds to the feelings of self-worth on the person that you are giving praise by your words or actions. Praise may be considered flattery, but using praise makes another person feel important and needed. It's another way of giving a person a compliment. But you have to concentrate on a specific behavior. Such as, saying to a secretary,

"My you stapled those pages perfectly!"

Most people glow when you point to a specific task that they did.

"Stan, you folded those napkins the best that I've ever seen! Have you ever tried doing it with paper towels?"

It doesn't matter what it is! Keep praising co-workers, even supervisors on what they've done.

"Mr. Smith, nobody in this State, no, even this country, has the skills you have in making pottery!"

Any form of flattery to others gives them a positive feedback about what they did. The ability to do this makes people be drawn closer to those who give it.

Also, you have to show a touch of warmth in your personality. This also makes you appear charismatic. Such as handwriting a short note to say thank them for what they did for you, and signing it less formally, with your nickname or shortened first name.

Remember names of people that you don't see frequently; it makes them feel important.

Charismatic people have a knack to remember names and can in a millisecond see somebody that they haven't seen for awhile and remember everything about them. All people who are in a leadership position have learned this and it's really not hard.

First, carefully listen to the person's name and repeat it several times. Ask the person if you are pronouncing it right. Ask for the person's business card, and concentrate when you hear the name.

With self-discipline and practice, you can take on many of the traits, characteristics, and actions of a charismatic person. Charisma is a type of charm combined with special qualities that inspire others. Developing charisma can have a big impact on your career and personal life.

Diplomacy is a big asset and one that many charismatic people possess. If you are in an adverse situation with someone, never immediately pounce on them or go to a rebuttal of what they said or stated. Always, always, try to break the ice first,

"Hey, Al. Have you got a minute? I wanted to go over a couple of things."

And then **EASE** into it by asking,

"Wow! Some weather, huh? I hope it stops snowing soon."

Or

"Hey, how's your family doing? I hear that your daughter just graduated from college. I bet that you are proud."

And after awhile, **EASE into what you really want to talk about.**

"I know that you are concerned about shit happening, but the project is going really well, with just some minor speed bumps and I know that was what you were concerned about."

Politics means being polite, and that's what you have to be, even if it is sticking in your craw.

Diplomacy will get you far, charisma, will get you further!

CHAPTER 12

BLUFFING

BECOME CONFIDENT IN LANGUAGE AND DEMEANOR

Bluffing means to pull a fast one, to outsmart someone, like, in a poker game. You bluff with only a pair of cards (sometimes **NOTHING!**) to outsmart someone with a full house to give in.

But bluffing is also hoodwinking someone with your banter to beguile or bamboozle them. Your demeanor is such that you challenge them constantly as you talk the walk, and that basically is what b.s.ing is all about- you know or have knowledge as you try to tell everyone that you know

EVERYTHING!

And once you've learned the basics – it's quite easy. You do not have to study anything to succeed. You really are disguising your lack of knowledge to all observers.

Most b.s.ers are bold and confident. And it's true. You hoodwink someone by assuming a fictitious front. Again, bluffing means someone who relies on an assumed appearance and speech. You must hold your own against a social, or business opponent. You do not want to be outwitted by somebody who knows more than you do. You must talk in a normal way to sound like it's the truth **(like a politician does!).** Learn how to steal the conversation away from a persons' specialty to any of the fifteen million other subjects that they don't know anything about such as,

"Say, did you hear about the latest hydrogeology change to the Infrastructure that Congress want to put through?"

Or

"Was there any truth to the report that Neoproerozoic Ned Mountain formation are not in the Early Orovician time period."

But to become successful at bluffing the main thing is to get right the manner or style that you want to take on. Such as, you have to put most of your remarks in the form of a question, especially when someone puts you on the defensive or tries to put you down,

"Don't you think that you would have learned that in kindergarten? I DID!!"

This way you don't concede. **TO ANYONE!!**

Always use words like professional workspeak, such as:

"Programmatic"

or

"Process"

or

"Infrastructure"

Then never commit yourself. Always use a saying that you can always retract at a later date,

"You know, there is something to be said for barbecuing on the fly."

If you can't think of the right words to say, then try a cynical or disbelieving look. A feint like this can be a major force in bluffing. Also, never try to give an answer; try to play for more time. You can always say,

"I will have to think that over…" (about taking a hike or jumping off of the Brooklyn Bridge)

But you should always try to interrupt them. **Interject blatantly!**

ABOUT ANYTHING!!

It could be from a surprised,

"Oh!"

to a quiet,

"Hmm"

Or you can always interject **a contemptuous snort or even a sardonic laugh** into their rambling commentary. And by far the best way to interrupt them is by saying,

"Really?"

in a questioning and even doubting tone.

The whole meaning of doing first class bluffing is to make the other people uncertain as to exactly what you mean.

So what do you really mean?

This is the way that it should always come out. This can be achieved several ways. Just make sure that you always leave it open as to whether you still do or don't.

You get what I mean?

It doesn't matter what it is. But to be successful at this, it has to be carried out with complete conviction.

Now if you encounter it in someone else, always use the same enthusiasm that they do. For instance, if someone is bluffing you that the New York Yankees actually started out as a professional football team (**and you know that it is b.s.**)just counter with,

"Actually, they started out as a professional cricket team. (which is like baseball anyway)" The other person is now trapped in their own b.s.

But the real art form when it comes to bluffing, is to say one thing and do a gesture about something else. Like gestulating like an umpire,

"SAFE!"

While you say,

"OUT!"

Or giving a thumbs up and saying,

"NO WAY!"

This can throw off even the best b.s.er. As most soldier's or spies know, disguise or camouflage can throw people off balance, and this is essentially what you want to do in bluffing.

It's not only speech that bluffing comes into play, but also in appearance. So if your bluff is that you are a **"smithy by trade"**, you have an apron that is soiled or a large hammer hanging around. (**a forge going is great too**!), and you talk about the horse that you shod that won the Preakness.

As you can see, props also come into play with camouflage. And one of the best that I've used is the drink (**whether it's alcoholic or not**). Always offer to refill a person's glass as the way to interrupt them from asking you pertinent questions.

"My, you've almost finished your drink – I'll get you another."

(never ask them if you can get them another, you just say that **I WILL** get you another) And then you disappear to find someone else that is not interested in blowing your bluff.

But overall, the way that your delivery comes out is how good a bluff that you can pull off. Try to adopt a slow, measured and considered tone of voice, as if you know what you are saying. (**you do, don't you**?)

It gives the impression that you carefully thought this out. This does give the effect of being self-assured. And again, the reason that you do this is to make sure that nobody will contradict you.

As in all forms of b.s.ing, rehearsal is tantamount to success.

PRACTICE! PRACTICE! PRACTICE!!

To a b.s.er, practicing and rehearsal is the same as

LOCATION! LOCATION! LOCATION!!

Is to the success of a retail store. Now, if you've tried and still can't develop your delivery (**TRY AGAIN!!**) there are still a number of equally helpful and time proven alternatives to try. Most of these have been performed by politicians, TV news anchors and others.

You must make sure that no one calls your bluff. For instance, say that you have spent a considerable amount of time in setting up something, like in organizing your own baseball team.

(EVEN THOUGH YOU DON'T PLAY BASEBALL!!)

And by organizing your own baseball team **(let's say a minor league team)** you will make 150 million dollars. Along comes some naysayer who says, "We don't need another baseball team; we already have six teams in the area."

So, they're calling your bluff. You should then say,

"Of course we need another team!" (look insulted.) "Have you forgotten about the blind, the disabled and the women that are the major players?"

Bluffing has to be developed into a fine art form. And state of the art bluffers prefer these following measures.

Be sincere. Make your voice sound so sincere that it reeks of sincerity.

Don't let your voice be demanding or pressured. Make it sound like the President. Be earnest or at least sincere.

Either one carries with it the conviction of tone. But don't be both. Either earnest or sincere. Too much of a good thing surely will fail. Of the two, I've always liked earnest. Like the play, the importance of being earnest.

Smiling is a necessary form of bluffing too. For some reason, people with a lot of teeth smile a lot. I don't know why, but adopt this as your strategy too. However, don't have a foolish smile that you turn on and off. It should come out naturally. Let it ooze out of you like melted butter. But don't smile when you are engaged in a negative conversation. Or vice versa.

You can also resort to taking on an offensive tone when you're bluffing. But you don't want to frighten somebody. It's a delicate twist; to try to scare somebody but not doing it. Just employ so many words at machine gun speed that your opponents are outplayed by this breathless farce. Again, employ so many words in this bluff so that it becomes inevitably successful.

Now, nobody ever dreams of questioning the character actor who played Darth Vader, because he has the right tone of voice – confident and controlled. You can make up on the spur of the moment a bluffing nature.

Mocking is also a good form of bluffing, but you have to be sure of this like Cary Grant used to do it. He was a master at it. Don't over emphacize the content of your bluffing.

Your delivery should also be nice. This generally works well because people don't want to hurt the feelings of those people who appear pleasant.

In this, you pretend to be good, honest, just like you or me. The supreme master of this type of bluff was President Bush, both Junior and Senior, who tried to get themselves reelected by this simple but wholly effective method.

The principal thing to remember in bluffing is that it is the superficial aspect of b.s.ing that is the art, and not the subject. You are always bound at some time to get into a combat with someone who is a conversationalist. So pick another conversation, it does not matter. The truth is that most times, bluffers have not persuaded you to do this.

You don't have to know or study anything – just make it seem like you did. Just collect or have an amazing amount of solid fact disguised as frivolous observation.

Most everything is one long bluff from start to finish, so that anything you say, provided you say it with enough authority, will carry you through. Most people are very susceptible to being persuaded that what they think they see is not what they actually do see.

There is also an important lesson here. Namely that the key to a lot of skills **(like being popular or getting into college)** is simply to fake them, and that the illusion of knowledge is often more important **(and certainly easier to acquire)** than the knowledge itself. If you really do believe that you can do something, chances are you can.

So what can't you bluff?

Not too many things. Today, all you really need to know is how to turn on your computer and you can learn anything. You don't need to know how to fix a car or do your taxes. We have mechanics and accountants for that.

So let's say that you want to fake a Mafia hit man. I don't know that you would, but if you do, then this is what you do.

You have to stare. You have to have a mean intent in your eyes. Keeping eye contact with people is a good one. If you can give them that stare and look them in the eye, sooner or later they're going to look away. Then you know that you've got them and they'll think that you're a Mafia hit man.

You do not resort to pulling out a gun or even talking like a gumbah. Just use the words from a movie like "Goodfellas" and talk like you're going to do a heist or a hit. Presto-

You are a Mafia hit man!!

CHAPTER 13

HOW TO MAKE A DATE WITH SUCCESS

First, announce your arrival. Like any first date with the opposite sex, making a date is never easy. It's that first impression that counts. To make a date with success requires cunning, skill and the knowledge that everybody else had had a date with it before. And if its reputation is a little tarnished, **SO WHAT!** Everybody had had their turn, so now it's yours.

Second, you have to make yourself available. Be in the right place at the right time. Go to specific places that will insure success. Dress as if you're going out on a date. Look sexy – let it radiate out from you. Talk to everybody, whether they can help you or not. And don't forget those of the opposite sex – they can help, even in a back handed way. **(the grapevine!)**

Look spiffy and confident,say,

"I LOOK GREAT!!"

Or

"I AM THE BEST DRESSED PERSON HERE!!"

Or

"I AM BRILLIANT!!"

Or anything! No b.s., but it helps get you in the right frame of mind to be available when success comes along. And every day, success **DOES** come along. Whether it stops by you is up to one person – **YOU!!**

Also, try to avoid negative people; they tend to discourage you and stand in your way. They delight in singling you out to tell you one of their most depressing stories or why **YOU** can't make it. They are mired in mud and they want to bring you down **with them** – avoid them like the plague – **CUT THEM OFF!!!!**

"Success" is a term that really is neither male nor female, not spirit nor corporal, but you have to think of them as such in order to gain admittance to their world. And their world is out there. You may find this hard to believe **(and I did at first)** but it is a state of mind, a feeling of confidence that comes over you that attracts success to all who will attempt and court them. But they are out there and you have to find them and go out on a date with them. There is one simple way to announce to the world that you want to be successful. It's like dating – you have to show that you are sexy and available. And like going out, it does take some courage – you have to go out alone and you have to do it with some confidence.

Take a good look at yourself in the mirror. Stand there and focus on your good points. Pick your three best qualities and say them out loud to yourself.

"I'M HANDSOME!!"

Or

"I'M THE BEST (ENGINEER, ACCOUNTANT,RECRUITER,ETC) THERE IS!!"

Or

"NOBODY IS BETTER THAN ME IN MY FIELD!!"

Whatever! Also, get rid of negative influences. Don't listen to people who put you down, or constantly point out your faults**. (such as friends or family members)**

Think of your worst date ever, and bear in mind that this date with success that you're on, can't be possibly be worse. I'll let you in on a little secret, **IT'S GOING TO BE BETTER!**

So see yourself as others see you. Be aware of what image that you are projecting to those around you. On a date with anyone (**especially on a date with success**)

PHYSICAL ATTRACTION IS CRUCIAL!

Once you become aware of what your image is to other people, then you can do something about it. When you do, it will make yourself desirable to success and it will get you more dates with success. Remember, you may have to change your day-to-day look in order to attract attention to success at first. Once success gets to know you, what you wear isn't going to matter as much as who you are.

I know that you are probably thinking that this is a lot of b.s., but sex appeal is all about confidence. It's not about how much you weigh, how long your hair is, or even if you have any. It's not as obvious as wearing a tight dress or driving a sports car.

IT'S ABOUT HOW YOU CARRY YOURSELF!

Start feeling and thinking sexy thoughts. The opposite sex (**success**) can pick up your feelings about your own sensuality. The way that you carry yourself and how you behave. These things tell the opposite sex (**success**) how you feel about yourself sexually.

Once you have made the connection, that's half the battle. But what do you do once you've got their ear? First, don't tell them you whole life story. When you start a conversation, reminisce about a pleasant experience that you had.

"I WAS THE FIRST ONE TO GO OVER NIAGRA FALLS IN A BEER KEG. NO REALLY IT'S TRUE!"

From three you can get into other topics, such as why you want to make this connection.

And don't just talk for 20 minutes and not getting to the point. Nothing drives a person crazier than waiting while they finish what they are talking about and not getting to the point of what they want.

After small talk, and things seem to be going well, ask the person for lunch, dinner, a meeting, etc. Find out what would be a good time, place, and day for the two of you to meet to discuss what you mutually want. Be clear with the plans so that nobody is confused about what to wear or where you are going. Again, this is not about sex, this is about getting ahead and making your mark on the world.

Now, conversations can reveal a lot about the type of person you are trying to get to know. No matter how successful or great-looking they appear, they become less attractive or more attractive, depending on what comes spewing out of their mouth. So there are conversation do's. Talk about things in the news. Be well-versed and well-read about the world. Specifically do not tell someone that you don't read the newspaper or watch the news. Headlines can give you a synopsis of what's going on in the world.

"Did you hear about the Emperor's new clothes –AU NATURAL!"

Talk about the weather, especially if there is some sort of unusual natural occurance that has taken place.

"Wow! What a storm! It was raining for 40 days and 40 nights. Don't you think that we ought to get an ARK?"

Talk about movies, music, books. Talk about the concert that you want to go to or your favorite movie stars.

"I just saw Gone with the Wind for the 200ᵗʰ time. I can never get enough of that movie."

Talk about sports.

"Say, how about those Jets, huh? About time, don't you think?"

But the best thing of all is to talk about the one thing that all of us humans do –EAT!!

"Say, do you eat food? Well so do I and you're not going to believe this but……"

If you go to an art gallery or museum or some cultural event, say,

"Culture is great, isn't it?" (and so is success!)

It doesn't matter what you say as long as you say something. Use any saying to start a conversation.

"Some election, huh?"

Next, in terms of time, make the time to make a date with success. Pick things to do. Invest time in this process; just like you would in finding a job or an apartment.

For example if you were going for a job interview, you would research the company, buy a new suit, and get your resume looking its best. The same is true with a date with success. Invest in yourself so that you'll give off the best impression. You should consider losing those five pounds if you need to, updating your hairstyle and doing anything that you might need or want to do, so that you make the best impression that you can possible make.

Furthermore, there is the money issue. In terms of money, you may have to spend some, so be prepared that this might occur. Buy some new things, new clothes or accessories. Invest in one really nice outfit that makes you feel confident and good about yourself. Make sure that you look good, whatever the cost. Success will realize this and act on you.

So how does success approach you? The first thing to do is look like you are enjoying yourself wherever you are. Even if you have to,

FAKE IT!

So this means that you walk around with a sparkly, a grin, or a wide smile. The bottom line here is to look like you want to be approached. You don't have to flaunt it to look approachable, just give off vibes when you are out in public that you want to be approached.

AND YOU WILL BE!!

So the ultimate question is where can I go to make a date with success? Opportunities are everywhere; at the office, at the mall, at the race track, supermarket, the airport. All you have to do is put yourself in places where you can find yourself in public places.

Get to know other people in other departments. For instance, if you work in Claims, talk to the people in accounting or marketing. Ask them to go to lunch or for coffee. What starts out about an outing between workplace friends can become an event with lots of potential. Again, this isn't about getting a love connection started, it's about getting yourself out there.

Find people with the same interests is your best starting agenda. Because it's like the old saying,

"birds of a feather, flock together."

And it's true! You can "**feel**" when others are like you. Just stay with them as much as possible.

Making a date with success calls for planning. Staying an hour later at the end of the day in order to get all of your work done is no longer the answer. Now it is also your responsibility to make certain that everyone else gets his work done too. Your first responsibility, then, is to learn what everyone else in your department does, and how to do it yourself in case the need arises.

You're working on 10 projects at once and **they are all due today!** If you drop one project, that's the one project higher management will pick up on, not that you worked on 10 projects at the same time.

So you're thinking ahead. Suppose that you're the last one left in the office and the boss asks you to revise a BIM model. If you don't know how, it will have to wait until morning, and the boss will be annoyed. **If you do, score another point for you**. He will remember that you're the person who helped him. So to repeat, learn what everyone else in your department does and how to do it yourself in case the need arises.

Once you know what everyone else's job entails, it is time to develop your own style. There is no one way to become an effective person that success wants to marry. Every successful person will give you one set of answers. This should not bother you. There is never only one way to do anything.

Learn the names of everyone that you see regularly. Learning and using people's names makes people feel better about your relationship with them.

Don't be embarrassed to ask them; what you should do is simply ask their name and start using it. **"Hi Len"**

Sit and talk with colleagues at lunch or at the coffee or water machine. You need to communicate with those whom we work with when they're not at their desks. Just take the time to get to know the person you work with on a much more personal level. And don't forget to ask them about their family, where they go to the gym, what problems that they are facing in their daily lives. This stuff definitely matters. Show that you take an interest in them.

To make a date with success you also have to dress the part and also acquire some items that will insure your success. Most people can recognize just by looking at a person's '**dress**' if they are successful or not. So it is not all that expensive to put on a good '**show**' to say that you are an up and coming star.

You don't have to buy a $5000 suit or dress, but wear blue, grey or beige suits or shades of those colors. The darker the suit the more confidence it reflects. And whenever you buy a suit, buy shirts and ties to wear with it.

Make your mark in the business world with elan and elegance. You need a symbol of your ongoing commitment to excellence. So get good expensive, well polished shoes. Get a decent watch **(it doesn't have to be a Rolex**), have a **REAL** leather briefcase that shows that it was used a lot – a **"serious briefcase"**. People usually believe what they see, and not what they hear. So make sure that your clothes and accessories are what a successful person wears.

And act like a successful person. Talk to everybody; say something as you pass a person in the corridor that you know,

"Uncle Len" and nod your head.

Or

"Big Len...how's it going?"

It doesn't matter what you say as long as you acknowledge the person. In the military you would salute an officer as they pass by, but since we don't have that in corporate life (**and we don't have medals and rank either**), you still have to say something as you walk the halls of life.

Also be well-versed and well-read about the world. It doesn't really matter what you say as long as you say something. Most cable or news channels will give you a synopsis of what's going on in the world or in the most recent innovation in technology.

Say,

"I hear that they're having a revolution in the world of toys. They are becoming more life-like. Yeah, Pinnocio is the latest story-book character to come to life." Then say,

"No, really, his nose grows when he tells a lie."

Again, it doesn't matter what you say, but say something. Talk about anything – the weather is always changing.

"It's really bad out there. It is heavy thunderstorms and lightning. I hope that you didn't park too far away."

Care about them and you will surprisingly find that they will care about you. When this happens on a regular basis, success **WILL COME YOUR WAY.**

CHAPTER 14

NITPICKING

You must train yourself to pick up on small inconsequential points and of course, blow them all out of proportion.

If a margin on a paper is off by one thousandth of an inch, you scream,

"HOW COULD YOU DO THIS!! This margin is off! I'm gonna have to tell Mr. Shithead (the boss) about this."

But don't ever stop. Continue to go off the wall as you rant and rave.

"Never in the history of this company or in my extensive experience has a margin been off! And now this!! No,No,No! This will never do. This work is slipshod and poor!!"

Continue to pick up on minor inconsequential points. Those without any knowledge (**higher ups**) will agree with you since they don't know either.

Keep this up and you will soon be known as a pain in the ass. But, in a strange way, that's what you want. Because if people (co-workers, underlings) start to fear you, then you're well on your way to the top. Just remember to jump and attack anything that is not correct or the "**proper**" way of doing something (**the sun didn't come up this morning)**

ANYTHING!

Harp on that one thing, even if it really is unimportant. (**you better tell that Sun to get in here early) ESPECIALLY** if it's unimportant.

Let's say that you're checking some figures and you find a mistake. Quell the urge to be hasty and run over to show your boss that you found an error. First make sure that it **IS** a mistake.

On the sheet that you're looking at, you see 5 and 5 and you know that the answer is 10 but the answer says 25. Don't rush over to the boss and say,

SEE, THE JERK WHO DID THIS CAN'T ADD!"

Your boss may say that it is really 5 times 5, which does equal 25 and you may wind up with egg all over your face for jumping the gun too soon. If however, it **IS** 5+5, which is 10 and the answer says 25, then quick like a bunny, run over to your boss and proclaim in a voice so loud that everyone across the country can hear,

"SEE, THE JERK WHO DID THIS CAN'T ADD!!"
CAUTION!!

Make sure that it wasn't the boss who did it and now you're calling him a jerk. If it was the boss's mistake, then as tactfully as you can, ask him to re-check these figures, that maybe an underling gave him the wrong information. And oh joy, if this is the case, then join him in crawling **ALL OVER** the ass of the underling, berating him for giving the boss the wrong information.

DOUBLE CAUTION!!!!

Make sure that it wasn't **YOU** who gave the boss the wrong information. If this is the case, then as quickly as you can, pass the buck and blame whomever left the company, saying that **HE** gave you this wrong information. No one can prove that he didn't.

Also, don't volunteer information to a co-worker; let him find out for himself. He wouldn't tell you, now would he? So why should you help him. Especially if a co-worker is getting more money than you are, don't be a ninny and show him how to do something; let him find out for himself. This

way he may goof up and look overpaid. And then you can say aloud so that everybody can hear,

"GEE, THE HIGH PRICED GUYS THAT THEY HAVE IN THIS DEPARTMENT. THEY DON'T EVEN KNOW THE BASICS!"

Then laugh as if you're teasing. (**but you're not!!**)

Another thing, don't volunteer to do anyone else's job either. Don't be helpful because no one is gonna show you how or help you.

Let's say that a co-worker says that he's swamped with work and could you do him a big favor and handle a part of it, and it's only such a small part since he's doing all of the really heavy and technical stuff.

DON'T! DON'T! DON'T! LET HIM DO IT!!!!

First – **He won't appreciate it.**

Second – If it isn't right he'll say that **YOU did a terrible job.**

Third (**most important**) – If anything goes wrong with any part of it, (**including his own part), he'll blame it on you to the boss and you'll wind up holding your schwanz and going "uuuuuhhhhhh."**

So don't help anyone else out. Just do your own stuff. However if **YOU'RE** swamped with work, try to get a co-worker to help you out and then you can do all of these wonderful things to him.

Here's another don't. Unless you know absolutely for sure, first hand knowledge, never, **NEVER** take information from someone else and count on it or use it as fact. **THEY LIE!!!**

Only what you can see with your own eyes or what you know to be true is the only thing that you should count on. Trust nobody, **NOBODY!** Only trust yourself. Whom do I trust? –**ME!** So unless you know for sure, don't spread it further. Don't take this information from others and tell your co-workers. Because if it isn't 150% right it'll come back to haunt you.

They'll say,

"But you said."

And you'll look like shit because you took the wrong information from somebody without checking it out and they'll pounce on you. Believe no one, not even relatives, unless you know absolutely, positively, 1000% for sure. (**and even then don't believe them!**)

Then, rather than accept when something goes wrong, yell your head off, so that the whole office can hear you. If you feel embarrassed and everybody stops and looks at you, then you know that you've screamed loud enough.

MAKE A SCENE!

Do this especially when you have finished your work and you are all prepared to do something and then somebody else isn't (**another person or another department**)

Say that you were all prepared to do it but the other person wasn't and demand a change in schedule. And say that you want it noted for the record and also do this:

GET EVERYTHING SIGNED IN INK! PENCIL CAN BE ERASED!

Then make a copy of everything and date it to make sure that nobody tried to change the original. And whenever somebody brings their copy over, you take out yours and compare the two very closely.

VERY CLOSELY!!

But a lot of times, "**they**" (**bosses, other departments, higher ups**) keep changing the rules. You've always got to be shifting and be flexible in the office. If you bring back to a person who set the ground rules.

"Well, you said….."

Or

"You told me to do it this way."

Guess what? They changed the rules again. They'll say,

"Well that was before….."

Or

They'll boldface, outright **LIE!!**

"I NEVER SAID IT!"

Or something else that is absolute bullshit. And you'll wind up like before, **holding your schwanz again and going,**

"Uuuuuuuuuhhhhhhhhhh"

Just be like a tree and bend. Offer no resistance if this happens. Say to yourself,

"You want to do your own thing fella, that's okay by me, but I'll get you next time."

Just keep a record – and get it signed in ink and then in six months from now when things go wrong **(and inevitably they will!)** you can pull out your copy and blame it on them.

NOW THAT'S OFFICE POLITICS!!!

Also, do you remember that old admonition,

"Red sky in the morning, sailor's warning."

Well, it wasn't just a maritime forewarning of a storm you know. Old time sayings bear true even today. For example, you're talking to 2 or 3 co-workers and one of them gets hit in the face with bird dung. Out of nowhere, he looks up and says,

"The sky is falling."

You look up and the sky is blue and in one piece and no other bird has deposited anything on anyone else. But the other guys around you agree with him.

THEY AGREE WITH HIM!!!

"Yup, the sky sure is falling."

You know for **SURE** that from what you've been seeing in the sky with your own two eyes that the sky is **NOT** falling. And that this idiot got hit in the face with bird shit.

Don't open your mouth to contradict., because when you're outnumbered 2 to 1 or 3 to 1, you'll look like a fool, even though you **KNOW** that you are right and they are definitely wrong.

You can't prove idiots like Chicken Little wrong when other idiots agree with them. Nor can you tell the Emperor that he's naked. They'll give you fifty reasons why they're right and you're wrong. Wait until the numbers are on your side.

Also this tells you that these co-workers are idiots, which you should note for future reference, so that now you can attack them whenever you see them again, since you now know that they are unsure of themselves. The best way to handle this situation is not to agree with or even acknowledge that they are wrong when they say,

"The sky is falling!"

But simply say,

"Well, I have to get back to work."

Or just walk away. But then go directly over to the boss and say,

"You're NOT going to believe this, but I was just talking to Jim and do you know what this guy said (laugh)…that the sky is falling." (laugh very hard)

Usually, a boss will say,

"Whaaaat?" or shake his head in disbelief and agree with you that this guy is an idiot and so are all the others. However, if the boss says,

"That's right, the sky IS falling, and I got hit with a piece of it too."

And again, if you know that the sky is **definitely NOT** falling – don't argue, back off. Be like a politician. Say,

"Uh….well, that's what I said. I agreed with him but Jose said that the sky is NOT falling. Can you believe that?" (pin the blame on someone else)

Then casually walk away. Note for future reference that the boss is an idiot too. But don't press a point with him – agree. You don't get ahead by proving the boss wrong.

But you can get ahead by pretending to be the fastest to do something even if you aren't.

Don't let supervisor's rush you into doing your job faster. They never remember that they ever rushed you – all they will remember is if they find one of your mistakes that only happened because they rushed you. So don't rush. Tell him, that you are just one person and how can he expect you to get this out so fast.

They don't want it wrong, now do they?

If someone presses you for an answer or for some information, don't tell them too much. Leave them guessing. Say,

"I don't know."

Whether you do or don't; so don't just react. Don't just answer; pause and then think to yourself,

"What should I say?"

And don't say anything at all until you first pause and think. Say that you could have gotten it out on time, but you didn't have the proper information or blame it on other departments or people. Write persuasive memos covering your ass. Because the bottom line here is to save your ass, no matter what. Tell them that Jay was away for two days and you were out in the field or that you were on 30 other jobs that he was pressing you for and that's why. But you tried, you really did, and you promise to make it better in the future.

A prime don't, is to remember that don't ever say anything bad about the company ,even in a joking way.

It will come back to haunt you!!

For instance, did you ever wonder what goes on when your boss and his boss are discussing your raise or promotion. Listen to this scenario:

Your boss: "Len is fantastic! He does a tremendous job. I don't know what I'd do without him."

His boss: "I don't give a damn how good he is. What does he do wrong? What's bad about him. What's the dirt?"

This is an actual tape from a bugged office. **(try it yourself)** So you can see that the higher ups don't care if you're any good. You just have to protect yourself that nothing bad can be said about you.

Again, never say anything bad about the company, your boss, his boss, anybody! Even if you're having problems with the job, never say anything bad about the companies policies or the problem.

Bad: **"This company sucks!!"**

Good: **"This is the greatest company in the world."**

Bad: **"Nobody does a f....kin' thing right here."**

Good: **"It's great to work in this type of atmosphere."**

Bad: **"The boss is an asshole!!"**

Good: **"Mr. Matlick is our greatest asset."**

So always be careful about what you say. And then, never refuse to go to a company sponsored dinner, picnic, or retirement dinner. Say,

"I wouldn't miss a free dinner." (then laugh)

Always make sure to go to all company functions. However, let's say that a function is planned for a certain day or time that isn't good for you. Tell them,

"It's in the best interests of the company that we change it to…"

And then make up some absurd reason. Like the Martian division won't be able to make it if left that way.

Now, if your work area is unusually quiet, or if co-workers in your area don't talk much, say something stupid aloud.

How many times where you work does someone say something moronic aloud and he keeps repeating it throughout the day and all of a sudden everybody picks up on it and then it's the **"in"** word or phrase to say. **Do it too!**

ANYTHING!!!

Stupid sounds break the ice; again it shows that you're uninhibited. Or use expletives in unexpected places and at unexpected times. In the office, at a meeting, in church, or even at your desk.

"S-H-I-T!" (spelled and then said loudly) or use **"Merd!!"**- (it means the same)

Or

"GAR-BAGE!!"

Or

"FUCK!!!"(said aloud)

Then never admit to anything ever going wrong or to ever having a problem. Everything that you have is perfect. Everything that you do is wonderful. Even if others tell you what goes wrong in their lives, you say nothing. Your home, your car, your children are perfect; they are the best and you do not have any problems. However, you must learn to temper this and not spread it around. Be careful of how much good news that you tell to people. This may sound crazy, but most people aren't interested in good news; they like only bad.

People are very jealous of good things happening to you. For example, suppose that you went around telling people,

"I just won $100,000,000 in the lottery!"

Or

"I've got the greatest house! They put it in Architectural Digest!!"

Or

"I just got a $5000 a week raise!"

Or

"I just……"

Whatever; see how long people would come near you. Spreading good news is like spreading a disease like AIDS, people will avoid you. And people really like bad news. It makes them feel good that it isn't them that these terrible things are happening to.

Most people go around saying what bad things happened, what bad things that they read in the newspaper and saw on TV and isn't it terrible and isn't it awful, and oh what a mess and guess who died, and who's sick and what went wrong. And to this,

EVERYBODY LISTENS!

Here are some more don't do's that I've discovered to be helpful in avoiding conflicts and in getting along with people.

First and foremost, don't let anyone get away with any misconception about you, no matter how minor.

Always jump down their throats as if they said a curse word. If you allow people they will walk all over you and say that you enjoyed it.

Talk!

That's why you were given a mouth for; not to eat, but to defend yourself. Immediately cut them off or cut them down with a remark, should they say something about you that's not true. Most times, if you don't jump down their throats, they will think that it's true anyway.

For instance, if somebody makes a comment about your incessant gum chewing (**and you don't even chew gum**) immediately interrupt them. That's the first step. Yell as loud as you can that you should feel embarrassed that everybody is watching you. Or if somebody yells,

"Sshhh!"

then you know that you're yelling correctly. And then just say,

"THAT'S NOT TRUE!!!"

"I DON'T CHEW GUM!!"

And then start on the fact that **THEY are sloppy eaters**.

That they drop candy wrappers all around and on the floor.

Or if they smoke, that they pollute

YOUR AIR!

Or anything to make them feel humiliated. They started it and you have to finish it. But keep going after them and never let up. Just remember to always interrupt them and never let them finish any misconception about you.

Whether it's because you didn't finish something on time and now that they're blaming you, or that they're just trying to win brownie points with the boss, it doesn't matter. You just have to protect yourself in the clinches, like a prizefighter does. Because, and don't forget, that this is a fight, and one that you have to win all of the time.

But why would people do anything to you? Because people will do things that benefit themselves rather than you if they believe that you will do things to them. You will have people who yell at you, demean your abilities, scream at you and call at you over something that you did or didn't do at work. You will find this type of person extremely frequently here- they are little Caesars, little dictators who have a serious rage problem.

You have to focus on the long range goal, and forget the garbage along the way. Just ask yourself, "Will this get me closer to where I want to be.?"

If you serve well, you eventually become the boss.

You don't get ahead by being Mr. Nice Guy. You get ahead by nitpicking on everything and everybody, no matter how big or how small. If you work at a regular job, there's a quitting time, but if you want to make it to the top, then you do not have one. You do not have a life outside of your job. Your career is your life. You work until you've done possibly everything. Then you go to sleep. That is your life.

There is the two most fundamental edicts that you will have to learn:

Tell them only what they want to hear

Show them only what they want to see.

There is a weakness among bosses and others for being taken in by what they want to hear and see; don't you be taken in by them.

Here is where careful listening can pay off for you. Keep a sharp focus on everything they say. Sooner or later they'll come out with something that you can twist into something that is like the solution you are looking for.

Then pounce on it!

Say something like,

"You've got it!"

They say what?

And you just say,

"That's it!"

Whatever IT is.

Whenever they ask again what you mean (and they will), you say,

"Whatever you said was a great idea."

And they will find that they are surprisingly receptive to listening to you now.

The common perception of success is to only think of yourself and to do what you want to do, without the slightest concern for how others may be affected by your actions.

AND ITS TRUE!!!

A safer, more effective way to get ahead is to observe your bosses, to figure out their likes and dislikes, and to give them what they want without sacrificing what you want. The biggest challenge involved in meeting someone's needs is to figure out what those needs are. Figuring out other people's needs is not easy.

Most people have a hidden agenda and they will beat around the bush before even coming close to saying what they want.

But if you learn how to identify and meet the needs of others – good for you!

Just meeting the needs marginally will probably not be enough. You have to meet them with overkill.

Make believe that reaching your bosses and others goals without you would be difficult if not impossible. These people must feel that they wouldn't want to risk angering you, because if they lose you, the company would fall apart.

This is the way it should always sound, like you are indispensable to the company, that they are not being reasonable and they definitely aren't being logical.

This is when you know that you can trip them up, and that they can't meet their needs without you.

Be ready to take action and be compelled to do something, anything. You have to take action, frequently engaging in an aggressive, hipshooting response. Because you don't have a lack of concern with learning, this action taking occurs unfettered by strategy, theory or analysis.

Don't be frustrated by confusion and whining. Have a compulsion to act, and be very unsympathetic to the pain and stress of others. Hey, it's you or them!

Another biggie on the don't list is don't believe anybody since they don't know. Only believe what you can see and what you can hear is what you should believe. Remember the "**I'm from Missouri statement.**" Even if "**they**" say,

"Everybody does…"

Don't you believe it, they lie!

People who just assume, just love to spout theories that are actually bullshit. They know nothing so they tend to cover up for their shortcomings and then they pick you as an easy target to let go with one of their fabulous stories. And this type of person can go on and on for hours about what you should do or shouldn't do. They'll bring every expert in the world to back them up, but again don't you believe it. It's just another case of b.s.

So don't count on anything or anybody. And don't count on a person to do something **UNTIL** he does it. If he says, yeah, I'll do it,

DON'T BELIEVE HIM!

Because you can't trust events or people ,i.e. don't count on expected money until you actually receive it. If you don't count on anything or anybody, then you'll never be hurt and you'll never wind up hold your schwanz because someone that you "**trusted**" said that they were going to do something that you were counting on.

This happens a lot if the people who didn't do what they were supposed to blame you for their inaction. Just say,

"**Hey, my job is done, that 's not part of the job. It's yours.**"

Or say,

"**How come that you're not on top of this?**"

Then also have an excuse if this happens to you. And even after you show them what they missed or what they said, they'll say,

"**I never said it.**"

Or some other bullshit, but at least you're defending your own ass from being pounced on. Because "**they**" always seem to produce a "**witness**" who will lie thru their teeth for them. If, however, emotions get strained and you get into a screaming match, **(and you will!)** always end with,

"I hope that we can still part friends."

The big don't in all of this, is I hope that in any case that you are not arguing with your boss. Because even if your are 100,000,000 per cent right, never argue with your boss. No boss, foreman, lead man or minor boss likes to hear that he's wrong from an underling (even if he's 150% wrong). It doesn't pay to argue about it even if you're right.

Another part of the same don't is don't butt into a conversation to correct a wrong statement that someone made. Even if you **KNOW** it's ridiculous, don't do it. Only comment if he tells you about it, and then the best thing to do is to put him on.

Suppose somebody asks you for a lift home. Either a stranger, acquaintance, co-worker, or relative and you don't really want to take them. **(You don't have to!!)** Say,

"Gee, I'd really like to, but I'm not going directly home. I'm going _____ (bowling, shopping,out of state, out of the country, out of this world)"

Or

"I'm not going in that direction. It's really out of my way."

Or

"I'm going to take a haircut, and I'm late for the appointment." (lie, make up someplace- an affair, my girlfriend's place, or dinner)

Or

"I can't. I'm going to _____" (another city, world, Mars)

Again, try to fend off;

Say no-

"NO!!"

or anything, but get out of it. You are not the appointed soft touch to take anybody home. This is also excellent training on other things that you don't want to do; you don't have to you know.

Another thing that is good advice, is if you get an itch, don't scratch it. If a fly lands on your face, don't push it away. Appear that it has every right to be there. Here's how you can learn this simple trick.

Don't fidget. Practice keeping your eye steady on one thing without excessive eye movement or blinking.

CONCENTRATE!!

Start holding it steady for a couple of seconds. Then try for 30 seconds. Then a minute. Then for a couple of minutes. Then for 20 minutes. And then for an hour. It builds patience and calmness. This is the same training that kings and queens, marines and astronauts get.

So if everybody else around you is falling apart you will appear strong in the firmament. Leaders, bosses, and foremen are selected from this type who can do this well. I can and

SO CAN YOU!!

Then, here's another simple don't. Don't be seen going to the bathroom. I know that it sounds crazy and maybe it is, but go during lunch or before and after working hours. Practice holding it in. Try not to drink too much water or coffee since that makes you go often. Try to appear super-human, that you can hold it in better than anybody.

But, actually sneak whenever you go. Carry a paper or folder or say that you're going to check on such and such a department while you're really going to relieve yourself. The only time that you can go to the bathroom is if a higher up says,

"I gotta go to the john."

It makes you appear weaker than others if you go to the bathroom too often. And that's what you don't want to do.

If you keep doing this faithfully, you will eventually get into a supervisory position. And when you get to be a boss, this should be your philosophy:

"I don't know how long that I'm gonna be in this position, but while I'm here , I'm going to take them for all they got."

To be a successful boss you must develop an attitude of staying cool and being indifferent to any emergency or unexpected situation. No matter what it is or what the emergency or calamity, or situation – stay calm and indifferent. This takes time and lots of practice, since, it very rarely comes naturally, but you must master it.

Let's say that an underling curses you out, using every foul word in the book. And if you're good at backstabbing or nitpicking, this will definitely occur. You don't say anything until he finishes because he won't let you. Then you calmly and unruffled, say,

"Calm down, calm down. I'm not mad at you, why should you be mad at me?"

or

"I take it that you have a problem. Can we talk about it?"

This will probably incense him and infuriate him more and he will start cursing you again. Don't crack under this strain. Don't lose your cool. No matter what he says, just say in a very unruffled voice,

"I see that you are being unreasonable. Why can't we discuss it further?"

Since this situation generally seems to happen right in front of higher ups, it will show them that you can handle people. **They'll remember it.**

Or, let's say that someone comes running up to you and says,

"The world is coming to an end!"

Mustering up all the courage that you can, and in a calm, unruffled and totally indifferent voice, say,

"Oh really, what time?"

Don't let anyone know that you're really shaking in your boots. Give the impression that you are bored with it all.

Now, if you are a boss, you will have to delegate the work. But what happens if you don't know anything at all about the job. (this again is also called the Schumck theory)

You just do this. Describe the work, but only in general terms and only as it was described to you. Don't pin yourself down and don't go into details.

Details are what can trip you up, especially if an underling knows more than you. So be very vague.

If the underling questions it say,

"You work it out."

Or if he explains it as,

"Is this what you mean?"

Say,

"That's the general idea."

But keep fending it off. If he asks you a question that you don't know the answer to, make up one and then walk away. And if it's wrong, say that you never said it. He's not going to call you a liar.

And once you are a boss there are so many things that you can do and get away with it. For example, say one big word and then disappear for the day. Tell them nothing.

"I hear that we're having a consolidation in this department."

Don't tell them what it is. Just walk away. Keep 'em guessing. If somebody asks when or what it is, say,

"I don't know."

Then forget to. Say,

"Well, it's 2 PM. Let's adjourn it."

And as you are getting up to leave, always say,

"My, that was a worthwhile meeting. I'm glad I called it."

Finally, don't rely on the traditional advice of successful people, they rarely know the reason for their success. If you asked them, they'll find pat answers to give like,

"Smiling big."

Or

"Maintaining a positive outlook."

Or

"Luck."

Don't believe any of it. Most of them won't admit it, but they made it to the top by simply, **"playing the game"**. And you have it in you to do the same. Trust me **(you do don't you?)**

Then there are little sublities that are not apparent but are very important nevertheless.

For instance, if your boss is short and you are tall, stoop down and make him feel big. Or if you're walking with your boss, always let him set the pace don't you.

Then, be the first to hold the door open for your boss and keep it open until he passes through. And if a lot of higher ups are walking out the door, drop everything and,

RUN!!.

And get to the door first, ahead of all the others and hold it open. I know that it sounds like this is just little petty thing, but pettiness makes you get ahead, and fast!

Also, if you can, try to be ahead of your boss every step of the way. If he says,

"Is it done?"

Say,

"It's on your desk already."

Or if he says,

"Tell purchasing to do…."

Say,

"I already did."

Again, you must make yourself indespensible to your boss. Not once, but every time . And of course, blatant brownnosing is still by far the way to do it. Because if you can get your boss on your side, to become your mentor, he will look out for you every time. He can be a marvelous advisor when you no longer work for him, he can help your career move along and he can act as your defender if something should go wrong and he needs to cover your ass.

Now just one mentor might not be enough. A mentor should always be an executive farther up in the ranks who is identified with success. And there is nothing wrong with making up a plan and working toward success as long as you make sure that you are not aboveboard. You should never tell people your goals; they may feel threatened. Like, if somebody says or implies that you're important, say,

"Me? Nah, I'm a nobody here."

Or

"No, I'm a nothing here."

And then imply that **HE is!** Get it off of your back and onto theirs. Move those feet with fancy steps!

Now if you want to learn how to do something, hire an expert in the field to show you. This goes for anything and all throughout history, great leaders have hired actors to instruct him in how to get ahead.

For instance, Napoleon, he hired an actor to instruct him how to walk and talk like an emperor. You can do the same. Not that you're going to be like he was, but to similar feats. Hire an actor to show you how to walk and talk and think like a boss. Your boss; his boss, it doesn't matter. All bosses talk the same and act the same. You just have to show the same mannerisms and presto! **You're a boss!**

But always grovel. **On your knees if you have to!**

Let me explain. Stand up when a senior executive enters the office. This is very similar to the Army when you have to stand up when an officer enters the room. It's the same here. Because if you remain seated its shows a lack of interest and most of all a lack of respect. Senior bosses **WANT** underlings to fawn all over them.

If you're in a car with your boss or higher ups, mention a little ditty that you've learned about your competition. And that also includes your co-workers. And if you have to, make fast subject switches, say from talking about the status of the banking industry to Yuppies invading supermarkets. **It doesn't matter, say anything.** Also try to make statements that are based on fluff or conjecture, not on knowledge or experience.

Again, try to show the person an attitude that is the same as his. Ally yourself with them each and every time. First try not to give any impression at all- be bland. Appear sure of something that he fears, so that he knows he can trust you. Try to become skillful at putting the other person at ease. Find out what he considers to be the worst impression and avoid making it. Try to agree with specific points the other person makes. Appear to be ignorant with co-workers and let them show you how smart they are. Then show them how impressed you are. The secret is not to let anything or anyone to throw you, to recover immediately and not to fall apart, just keep on going.

Whether it's too hot or too cold, never admit to it bothering you. Let everyone else complain and seem like an old woman.- you must be like a rock. Never let weather affect you. **(at least show this side of you to others like your boss and those higher up**)

If you don't know how to do something, ask a co-worker if you can have a copy of the work that they did. But don't use any of it. Read it to try to find out any mistakes that this person did. And then point out those mistakes to your boss. Always try to knock people down, belittle them and make them

look like fools. Because if you don't, then they are gonna do it to you

FIRST!!

This is what it is all about. So every chance, every opportunity, make a comment about your co-workers to them, about them, on them – to anybody you see. Again, **BEFORE** they do it to you.

Or else become adept at come-backers. Those little ranking outs and put downs that co-workers, neighbors, and relatives are very good at. But you can be too. Listen,

If anyone else get's in earlier than you say,

"What do you do – sleep here?"

However if somebody else does it to you say,

"I gotta get this work out."

And how many times does some co-worker say sarcastic remarks each day to put you down, like,

"I see that you're not working too hard."

You say,

"I'm taking after you."

Or if they say,

"Don't work too hard."

You say,

"Don't worry, I won't."

You have to have an act that you keep using about everything. Even when you're not feeling well, it seems that you have to put on an act. It comes down to this scene. If you're sick or have a cold, say it loudly and often about how sick you are and that you're still at work. **(and it doesn't matter if you are sick, just use this routine to get sympathy)**

"Oh, I got a runny nose, and a sore throat, and a sick stomache and the runs and this hurts me and that hurts me, and I'm taking tea with lemon and sucking candy and asperin, and oh, I do feel terrible, AND IF I DIDN'T HAVE SOOOO MUCH WORK TO GET DONE, I'D GO HOME!!"

Make everybody, especially the bosses, know that even though you're deathly sick, that you're still holding out and staying at work because you're needed there.

So just do this, whine and complain a lot, but only when you know that others are watching you and only to the highest authority.

Then in addition to whining, you must comment on anything that passes your desk. For instance, if anyone from another department says that from now on to get a pencil, you have to turn in your stub, write some nonsense such as the following:

"In reviewing the attached I am assuming that you have it under control and that you recognize the responsibilities involved with the constraints that are established on costs. I'm sure that all other individuals will give you their best assistance."

This is known as language-eez, or blatant nitpicking.

To do nitpicking to the highest degree means always try and see what others are doing or what they are working on. Even be so bold as to ask them,

"Say Bill, what are you doing?"

And joy of joys, if they are **NOT** working on anything, **TELL THE BOSS!**

Don't yell out loudly,

"Bill is goofing off!"

No, rat on them but do it in a nice way **(unless you don't like the person and then it's perfectly acceptable to yell out)**

"BILL IS GOOFING OFF!!"

Quickly go over to the boss and say,

"Well, since Bill is not working on anything really busy, and since I AM SOOO BUSY, CAN HE DO SOME WORK FOR ME." (like for the next 30 years)

And don't forget to use whatever you have around as a weapon.

If somebody says,

"Can you get an audience with the Pope?"

Always say yes and brag,

"He depends upon my advice constantly."

Do this as if you are privy to high level decisions. Then honestly try to get an audience or an appointment. **(in writing if possible, so that you have proof)**. You never know, sometimes the bigger a person, they are more lonely and he may want a non-threatening friendship. If he says no, just tell them,

"Well, he's too busy, but I tried, I really did. But, the next time I see him, I'll get you his autograph."

And then forget that you ever said anything.

CHAPTER 15

LEARNING HOW TO BECOME AN A #1 ASSHOLE

Learning how to become an A #1 asshole isn't hard. In fact, in today's world it's extremely easy. To become an asshole means never saying **"excuse me".** It means going out of your way to screw everybody else **FIRST,** before they can even get a chance to do it to you. In other words, you've got to be mean, rotten, selfish, and above all –**arrogant!!** Forget that you ever heard of common decency; you've got to be a heel and step on everybody.

Sound ruthless? Of course. It is an attack philosophy to prevent you from being attacked from all sides. It seems that wherever you go, people are constantly trying to intimidate you, cause you grief and aggravation, and to complicate your life. This, because you were taught by your parents, even by your teachers, **NOT** to do it first to anybody. Be like a sleeping giant, until you are awakened they said. Wait until they do it first to you and then defend yourself, you were told.

GARBAGE!!!!

Aren't you tired of getting it socked to you while everybody else does as he pleases?

You can change this very easily, yes you can. **Really**. Start off by not being Mr. Nice guy anymore. Let's say that you open a door and there is someone right behind you. Don't be a nice guy and hold it open-

SLAM IT SHUT!!

If you can, wait and then let it go right in the person's face. If they don't say anything, keep on going. However, if they say something like,

"Hey!"

or scarcastically,

"THANKS FOR HOLDING THE DOOR!!!"

Turn around quickly, but keep on walking and then smile broadly.

Don't turn around for at least 30 seconds and then wave and continue on your way.

But never, **NEVER, NEVER!!** Say,

"sorry" or **"excuse me"**

Don't ever acknowledge that the person exists or that you made a social mistake. Don't use,

"I didn't see you."

Take it out of your vocabulary. This way it wasn't **YOUR** fault. It is just a general statement.

So go ahead, kick them when they're down, gouge their eyes out –

"ATTACK!!!"

You can win these little victories time and time again if you just say to yourself,

"I'm the only one here that counts."

Just don't care, don't give a shit for anyone else, but you. Wherever you go remember that,

"I'm here and I'm the only one that matters."

Or

"You can leave now – the great one has arrived!"

An attack philosophy is the ultimate in assertiveness training. First, convince yourself that you are above all others. Not a snob attitude, but an attack attitude that says that you are just better than everybody else is.

AND YOU ARE!!!

Now the best way to learn this is to watch others do it. Just copy what someone else has done that was mean, nasty, rotten, arrogant, in other words – a son of a bitch.

If you go to work on a commuter bus or train, or even walking in the street, you have an opportunity to observe some pros at it. Look for the one on a bus who is blocking the aisle with his arms on his hips so that you can't pass by, or spread out in the seat like he owns the bus (**HE DOES!**), talking up a storm to a guy in the next seat.

Watch him closely; he has the manners of a pig, a child who never grew up or who had parents who never corrected his bad manners. He sneezes and doesn't try to cover it up with his hands. He slinks down in the seat as if he were at home (**HE IS!**), and not amongst strangers. He is in a world all by himself, as if he were the only person that is on that bus. He utters aloud any instantaneous response,

"SHIT! FUCK! WHATEVER!"

He belches loudly, farts constantly, etc. So learn from him; there isn't anybody in the world but him – so do as you please. Life is made for **YOUR enjoyment,** not everybody else's. Just don't care what other people think.

For instance, if you're in a supermarket, merely imagine that you are the only person there. Purposely block the aisle. Take your time. Don't care who has to go by. Don't care who's in a hurry, only **YOU** matter!! And that's the way it should be, isn't it? Nobody gives a damn about you – **NOW DO THEY?**

Simply do this now. Start by having a chip on your shoulder. Then dare everyone, to,

"Go ahead – knock it off!!!"

Years ago, nobody messed with a gunfighter or warrior or even today's man who has machismo. **But if you're a wimp they will!!** That's why I say that nobody will dare mess with you if you go out of your way to attack them. But I'm not talking about physical violence. **NO!** I'm saying that he aggression and the ferocity of the attacker **IS** the philosophy. (**the best defense is still a good offense**)

You should" **ATTACK**" everything equally whether it's talking on the phone (**DEMAND!**), driving a car (**NO DEFENSIVE DRIVING!!**), walking in the street (**STARE THEM DOWN!!**), **anything!**

So let this be your motto,

"Don't be nice – be nasty"

Once you can accept this, changing your personality to being nasty and selfish, then you can become one of us. **The Few. The Proud. The Assholes!** And if you get good enough at it, who knows, you may become king of our society. It's like a college fraternity (**We all behave the exact same way!**)

It's so easy to become indifferent to others or to do anything you want regardless of the consequences. This is also a prime pre-requisite for becoming a Mafia hit man or a politician.

Again, the best way to learn this is to watch others do it. And today, there is plenty of opportunity to do this. In this age, manners and ethics don't seem to mean anything anymore. Assholes abound today and it's very easy to follow their fine example. Watch everything that other bastards (**uh, I mean asshole**s) do. If something impresses you and looks good to you, then do the exact same thing in the exact same way.

For instance, if you don't like someone, write an anonymous letter to the IRS saying that this person bragged that he cheated on his income tax. Nobody can say that he didn't! And nobody can prove that it was you who put the feds on them. Or if a doctor charges you for something that was not done, write a letter to the governing body saying that the procedure was never done.

And isn't it nice to give somebody else aggravation for a change. **Instead of YOU!** Now this is what I mean by being nasty. Purposely going out of your way to be cruel. To kick them when they're down.

It is fun!

If you can do this, you are well on your way to becoming a great asshole.

Here's another good one. If you are in another's territory (**their office or desk**) and are surprised by them, act as if you own it and have every right to be there. This is excellent practice on how to become a con artist also. Keep thinking that they aren't there, that they don't even exist. Usually they won't say anything anyway. Remember that **YOU are Mr. Bigshot** and your rights are more important than the rights of others.

Let's say that you are at a check-out counter in a supermarket and there is somebody ahead of you. Purposely mix your stuff with theirs or put it as close to theirs as possible. If they give you a dirty look or say anything like,

"Hey, that's my stuff!"

Simply say,

"Stick it!! (emphacized with an index finger)

Or

"Do I look like a priest? Tell somebody else!!"

Remember, don't be nice – **BE NASTY!!**

If you do this faithfully, you'll soon be a master at it and you'll quickly know if you're succeeding. If they start calling you a bastard or other well chosen pieces of curse words, you will be already on your way to an A+ in the course.

But, it does take a certain amount of courage to do what I'm saying – personal courage. Call it –**GUTS, BALLS, COOLIONEES,** or whatever to put your head under the guillotine every time just for the sake of daring someone to chop it off.

GO AHEAD! MAKE MY DAY! I DARE YOU!!

And as with anything you can't get ahead without it.

Just be selfish and think of only **YOUR** desires, **YOUR** ambition, **YOUR** happiness – first, second, always and **EVERY** time.

NEVER BE CONSIDERATE! NEVER THINK OF ANYBODY'S FEELINGS!!

Act as ruthless as those teen-age goons who blast portable radios everywhere they go without any concern for anybody else. It's not too late. You can still make it to the top. Do what you want to do regardless of consequences. Do everything as if you were a little kid and the things that you liked then – caring only about your instant self-gratification.

So revitalize yourself, revitalize your life, your tastes, your wants, go back to what you were **BEFORE** others broke your will and forced you into **THEIR** mold. It's easy. Just do what everyone else does who gets it their way by attacking. The garbage man gets it his way because he wants you to arrange your garbage into neat little piles of plastic bags, the conductor wants all tickets ready, the mailman wants zip codes and return addresses, etc. So do the same things. **DEMAND!!!** You want? **YOU GET!!!**

These tradesmen get it their way because they have told you to do it this way or else! They won't do what **YOU** want.

Well, do the same!

These fights are everyday battles – on the bus or train to work, at the supermarket or gas station, at home and at work. Little insults and intimidations, these are what you are fighting. Because, if you can win these little victories time and time again, you've won the war.

And if you follow what other assholes do, then,

CONGRATULATIONS!! YOU HAVE WON THE WAR!!!

Now, you have to protect yourself at all times and at all costs especially against the "**average individual**". This is made up of people that you meet in the street, family, co-workers, civil service employees, or gas station attendants. You don't have to worry about other assholes or b.s. artists; they won't harm you. **But the "average individual" will!!**

They'll do it to you in verbal attacks of unloading on you a barrage of nonsense! Such as the following scenario.

Let's say that you pull into a gas station for $10 of gas and you give the attendant a $20 bill. Sarcastically, he says,

"What's with this! Everybody is giving me 20's!!"

ATTACK!! TALK BACK!!

Say,

"WELL HOW ABOUT A 50 THEN?"

Or

"WELL, I'M NOT EVERYBODY!"

Or

"GEE, I WISH THAT I COULD HAVE SUCH AN EASY JOB AND JUST BITCH ALL DAY!!"

Or say something else. But don't just take it.

ATTACK!!!

Don't let anybody get away with anything at your expense. You want to survive? Then you've got to attack them and respond every time.

I would strongly, **VERY STRONGLY INDEED,** suggest that you keep a card file on responses to average situations. If somebody throws you with a saying or a put down or something that you couldn't handle immediately; then **IMMEDIATELY WRITE DOWN A GOOD RESPONSE.** Average situations keep repeating themselves and the next time that something like this comes up you'll be ready for them. Next time, you'll **TEAR THEIR HEAD OFF!!**

Here's a good example. When you're talking on the phone to a large company, the bank, or the phone company, always, **ALWAYS GET THE NAME OF THE PERSON THAT YOU ARE TALKING TO AT THE BEGINNING AND BEFORE HANGING UP.** Interrupt them immediately when they say, "Debrah Jones…." Or any name and say," **Can you please repeat that ..slowly (or how do you spell that)"** This saves you loads of aggravation the next time that you call because they didn't do what you wanted them to do. And you **WILL CALL AGAIN!!** Most large places seem to have a penchant for screwing things up the first time. And for some reason these institutions ignore your first call as if it never happened. So when you call back it sounds stupid to say,

"I don't know who I spoke to, but I called last week…."

And then you have to go through the whole story again, and they'll probably tell you that you have the wrong department or the wrong person and it gives you a whole lot of grief. If you've got the person's name you just tell them,

"LOOK!! I CALLED YOU! LAST WEEK AND I SPOKE TO YOU! AND YOU! DIDN'T TAKE CARE OF IT. NOW WHY DIDN'T YOU!!!

This puts them on the defensive and not you. Also, when calling large places, let the phone ring a minimum of 10 or 20 times. Eventually it will get on the nerves of somebody there and they'll pick it up. Or try 30 or 40 rings if necessary. Letting it ring only 3 or 4 times does nothing to hardened employees from these places. They joke about it at your expense.

Another thing, don't continue to be Mr. Nice Guy and keep anything in. If somebody does something to you that you don't like,

YELL YOUR HEAD OFF!!

Also curtly cut off people who complain to you about everything, just for the sake of finding a soft touch to tell it to. Cab drivers, mechanics, and relatives fall into this category. Say,

"HEY!! Find another guy to complain to!!"

or

"Dump your problems in a garbage can – NOT HERE!!!"

or even better, have a sign that says,

NO DUMPING ALLOWED!

And point to it whenever anybody tries to give you grief. Only when you can **CONTINUALLY** give it back to people will they leave you alone and not try to step on you.

Now, since these situations keep happening again and again, always try to make up a response to different situations. If you're in a restaurant and you drop a fork or utensil, **ATTACK!!** Don't even give someone a chance to say,

"Butterfingers!"

Say,

"THERE'S GREASE ALL OVER THIS!!!"

or

"Actually, I was mad at myself and that's why I threw it down."

But get on top of the situation. Don't let anything pass without commenting on it, since someone else will. **They're doing it now to you aren't they?**

However, if somebody should do something to somebody else, and not you, then keep your mouth shut, **SHUT!!**

You are not the appointed defender of everybody else; let them worry about themselves. They don't come to your defense, now do they? **Do they? OF COURSE NOT!!!** So don't worry about others and don't even consider others. They simply don't exist. Never fight for others either. Only consider and only fight for yourself. You and nobody else. Look out for you; you're number one. All the rest is weakness. So always, **ALWAYS,** preface doing something for someone else by asking,

"Would they do it for me?"

If they would do it, fine, then I say do it for them. But c'mon, do you honestly think that they will do it for you?

OF COURSE NOT!!!

They are only interested in themselves and they wouldn't lift a finger to help you. So don't help them!

Why even common courtesy of the road doesn't even hold any water any more. You can't even practice defensive driving because if you do, some other asshole will be there ahead of you. But there are ways to handle it, and that is to go on the offensive.

If you're driving on a one lane in each direction road and someone's tailgating you. There's a double solid line, so he can't pass you. You're doing the speed limit but he wants to go 100MPH above that, and you are in **HIS WAY!** And he's tailgating you very, **VERY**, closely. I'd let him!

First, I'd wait until an S curve or a blind curve that comes up. Then I'd pull my car as close to the double line that I can. A lot of times, cars coming in the opposite direction, will cross the solid line into your lane. What I do next when I see this, is to swerve quickly out of the way. If the guy behind you is tailgating as close as I think he'll be – surprise, surprise, surprise. This usually solves the problem.

If however, **YOU** are the guy **DOING** the tailgating, then my hat's off to you. So if you survive this situation, what I'd do then is to cross the double solid line **(the wimp in front of you won't!)** and give him the **"finger"** as I honk my horn. This makes you the attacker and not the attackee.

A lot of people get mugged in a large city because they are not the attacker. The reason a mugger picks out a target, is he thinks that the person is a wimp, an easy mark. But this is what you have to do in that situation.

STARE THEM DOWN!!!

I have noticed that most people do not make eye contact with an attacker. If you want to survive you must!

STARE AT THEM!!! DIRECTLY!! IN THE EYES!!!

And don't divert your eyes away from them, let them submit to you. The first one who gives in is the weaker and **HE LOSES!!!** You have to attack your enemies at every opportunity. Here's an example.

A woman passenger is on the train or a bus and she's talking up 2 seats, one with her coat and luggage on them. **She is the asshole and is the attacker!** But don't **YOU** say excuse me, since when one asshole meets another **(even of the opposite sex)** just make eye contact with her. If she doesn't move her stuff away, **then just sit on it**! Believe me she'll move fast enough. And if she says anything, just stare her down. You have every right to a paying seat.

Now, this also goes for old people, who think that because of their advanced age that they get special privileges. **THEY DON'T!!**

And it definitely goes for those teenagers who usually sprawl out their radios on another seat and it definitely goes for any man or gang of hoodlums. Although with a gang of hoodlums, I would back off, since they have every right to an extra seat because **THEY** are the attacker. And it is the attacker who you leave alone.

But if you are a shark then you don't have to leave them alone. Because a shark is the ultimate attacker. Now a shark, once he decides on a prey, zooms in on it until he has it.

DO THE SAME!!

An asshole is actually a shark (**but in sheep's clothing**) and you should have the same traits. Let no one or nothing deter you. If you can't get it from attacking straight on, then go around. But keep coming on no matter how many times they push you away. Once you are ready to start your attack, make no waves, make no sounds; just have a sheer determination to win. Challenge anyone who violates your territory or possession, no matter how small the infringement. Assert your rights.

Like a shark, eat anything (**TAKE!!!**) that's thrown your way. But you are better than a shark. Man, not a shark is the **SUPREME** predator. **And that's called an asshole!!**

If you're an asshole, at least you are getting yours. So to all you emotional 98 pound weaklings – don't be taken constantly. **ATTACK!!!**Learn the assholes creed:

DON'T BE NICE – BE NASTY!!!!

CHAPTER 16

LEARNING CONFIDENCE THE "EASY WAY"

There is an easy way to learn confidence and a hard way. The easy way may not be palatable to you because it smacks of a term called **"confidence man"** or con man. I am not talking about milking an old woman out of her life savings. No, I'm talking about the confidence that this con artist has in going after anybody to get what he wants – and that is confidence **"the easy way"**.

You can see the **"easy way"** of gaining confidence by going into any car dealership and watch how the salesman acts. Or even better, watch how an **"infomercial"** on TV sells something. That's the **"easy way"** of learning confidence. So to learn the **"easy way"** the best thing to do is to start by cheating. No, no – I'm not talking here about cheating on your taxes (**which is illegal).** I'm talking about cheating as a way to learn confidence.

Now cheating, like lying, is a time honored trait that anyone can acquire fairly easily. And contrary to public belief, cheaters **ARE** held in high esteem **(at least by thieves).**

But there are certain ground rules even for cheating and the first is to make everybody know that honesty is and always will be **YOUR** policy. It doesn't really matter whether it is or it is not. Cheaters abound today and it seems that you can't believe anyone anymore. So even if honesty is **NOT** your policy, you should always say that it is and reinforce it aloud. Tell people,

"You can trust ME."

Keep a straight face when you say this and reek of friendliness and charm and honesty. Make them think that you are above all that petty stuff, like cheating. Get them to have confidence in you and believe that you are

straight and aboveboard in your dealings and that you would **NEVER** do anything as dastardly as being dishonest. Now would you?

OF COURSE NOT!!!

You're just a good ole boy, not some slick Yankee horsetrader.

You should strive everyday to give people the impression that you are looking out for their benefit, even ham it up to the point that it seems that you're giving them something for nothing. **You are aren't you?**

OF COURSE YOU ARE !!

Now I now that it's gonna seem hard to believe, and it took me awhile too, but as long as you **TELL** people that you're honest and aboveboard, they'll believe you. They really do. **And it works!**

So act like a car salesman. Tell them what a fantastic deal that you're giving them, so much so that you're sacrificing **EVERYTHING;** that you're taking a really **BIG, BIG, it's actually a HUMONGOUS!** loss. (**it also helps if you add a tinge of crying to your voice**)

But by golly,because they are such a terrific person, here's what a great deal you'll give them. That you'll break down and give it away. **TO THEM!!** Only to them. (**now look away to the side and back to them as if you only want them to hear**)and for this one time only **FOR NOTHING!!!**

Yes, you are giving it to them FOR NOTHING!!!

This is the way that it should always come across; true sincerity. It works wonders. **It really does!!** But if by chance they are skeptical and they don't believe you, then do this next.

CRY! WHINE! YELL!

Throw a temper tantrum!!

Swear that you have no money, swear that they are taking advantage of you and that you can't put another penny into the deal.

Then purposely stop and change this act and calm down. Put your arm around them and tell them in a hushed voice and that they are your bosom buddy., their best friend, and that you wouldn't ever cheat them and what kind of person do they think that you are?

BUT, since they **ARE** such a truly wonderful person, and that you don't do this for everyone....but only for them, that you'll not only give them that at such an unbelieveable low price of **NOTHING!!**, **BUT** you'll throw in......if they will only take it. **AND NOT ONLY THAT!!!**You'll give them....**AND MORE!! AND LOTS AND LOTS MORE!!!**

Isn't this fun? And a hell of a lot easier than taking candy away from a baby too (**just try**).

Now, you don't have to be a fast talking salesman to do this, you can do it also, even if you have no training or even an inkling to be one. Just by using your wits and taking advantage of every situation you can turn anything into going the way that you want it to.

It's like a guy who owns a stationary store and picks up some complimentary packs of cigarettes that are being given away. He pulls off the complimentary sticker and sells them. **Not hard!** In fact, it's quite easy to be a polite sleezeball. Ethics. Smethics. Who cares? This is the way you make money.

You never know at that moment if you can turn it into something good for you or something that you can use. Even something as ordinary as somebody giving you a business card.

TAKE IT!!

For instance, municipal employees, especially those in the higher grades, love to impress people by giving out business cards with their name and occupation on it. I collect these whenever I can or else I have them made up.

Let's say that tonight I'm going to a restaurant for dinner. I take a Health Inspector's card with me. Whether I like the food or not, I take a few bites and then I call the waitress over and say that the food is spoiled. Usually, she will bring it back to the chef, who will say in a huff, of course not, it **MUST** be my imagination, that his food is excellent and **PERFECT!** And the waitress will usually concour with him,

"We **NEVER** had any complaints before."

I then say that I should know, pulling out my Health Inspector's card, and say,

"If I was on duty, I would close this place down!!"

Or even if you are in another city, say in an adamant tone,

"I this place was in MY city, you wouldn't get away with this. I would close it down for good!"

What happens then, usually is a pronounced apology, and that of course that I should know if the food is spoiled, and the chef blames his suppliers, vowing that he'll never use them again, and you get a meal on the house of whatever you want.

You can use this routine in many different restaurants because of the following:

Ninety- five percent of restaurants use frozen shrimp even though their menu's advertise it as fresh. And how about that seventy percent of fruit salads in restaurants are labeled fresh fruit cup, use canned fruit or fruit with preservatives. Also, eighty percent call domestic blue cheese, Roquefort. Additionally, three quarters of restaurants serve baked ham that isn't baked. And they also get you when they give you Merlot, when you ask for Bordeaux. And all restaurants call ground beef, sirloin. Now who's the cheater, the restaurant or you?

Again, cheating is done by nearly everyone, but what you have to do is to make is sound palatable, like you're not doing it purposely. That cheating just happened, the way it would if you tripped over something in the street and all of a sudden

THERE IT WAS! OOPS!! I NEVER SAW IT!!!

For example, construction jobs are always behind schedule. Let's say that a company is constructing a building or a bridge and they can't wait for the time it takes to get new pipe delivered. They'll look for shortcuts and unethical arrangements to meet their schedule. Here's where you come into the picture.

You can buy rejected pipe from a pipe mill and the best part is that you can buy it for almost nothing. The mill sells it because it wants to get something for its mistakes. Now you can easily spot it because it comes with a yellow band around the ends. Then this is what you do. Pull the yellow band off.

THAT'S IT!!

Simple? **And then you sell it of course as new pipe!!!**

Go over to the job superintendent and say that you just **HAPPEN** to have a whole job lot of new pipe and that you can deliver it immediately. Of course, forget to tell them that this rejected pipe is not new pipe, **(well, nobody actually USED IT!!)** and sell it to them at full price.

Now you know why so many pipes break and bridges fall down!!

Always try to get away with something, even if you know that you can't –**TRY!** You just may. How about a mundane thing like parking at an airport.

Usually the daily parking lot is a lot cheaper than the hourly lot, but you have to walk a lot farther to the terminal. Now, most airports have mechanical devices to issue parking tickets, so here's an easy thing that you can do and get away with. Go get a ticket from the daily lot, but don't pull in. Pull directly **BACK!** Next, go over to the hourly parking lot, take a ticket and go park wherever there is a spot. Destroy the hourly parking ticket. When you are ready to leave, just give the attendant the daily ticket. You've just saved yourself about 50% and a lot of convenience. **CAUTION!!** Some of the larger airports have gotten wind to this scheme and have installed devices that if you pull back you will ruin your tires. So, always check if this is there; but smaller airports you can still get away with this.

Remember this. You've got to be a conniver to become good at cheating. So when somebody says that you positively, absolutely, definitely and most certainly cannot do something; always, always, try to finagle another way to do it. This is what is called,

"Cheating."

And here's another. How about if you're in a bar or a cocktail lounge. It's crowded and it's dimly lit. Put down a ten or twenty dollar bill on the bar when you order, and then just before the bartender brings your drink, switch it to a dollar bill. A lot of times, the bar is so noisy and crowded and poorly lit that the bartender will still think that it is the ten or twenty that he first saw and sometimes he will give you back all of the change.

Or how many times does a cashier or a person give you a $5 or $10 dollar bill in mistake as change for a dollar bill. Don't be honest Abe and say,

"You gave me too much."

KEEP IT!!!

Or if he says something and realizes his mistake, say,

"Oh, I didn't notice." And then laugh.

Pettiness is what makes you wealthy.

Next, buy things on sale and then return them for full price when they go off sale. Say that you lost your receipt. I usually buy it the day before it goes off sale. You'll get anywhere from $5 to $50 or more each time that you do it. And you can do this a lot with stuff from stores like Sear, Macy's or Penny's which do not question merchandise under their own store brand. Start out slow with one store and going from department to department and then expand it to hitting all stores in an area in one day. You can easily clean $1000 or more a day.

Try cheating for what you've always wanted. If you'd like an expensive in the ground swimming pool, but in no way could you ever afford it, just cheating will get it for you. Become a distributor and for almost nothing can you get one. First write to the swimming pool manufacturer and say that you'll become a distributor for their pools, but that you'll need to have a sample of their very best pool. All you have to do is to pay for the installation and you'll get one. And the best part of this deal is that you don't have to sell any afterwards. You just agree to show their pool on your property for several weekends for one summer. Neat, huh?

And you can pull this distributorship angle with just about anything: landscaping, fireplaces, even rental cars.

As a qualifier for something to cheat on, I would say that

THERE ISN'T ANY!!!

Cheat on everything, especially those that you can get for nothing.

For instance, aren't you tired of paying exhorbatant utility bills? Who isn't. Then take a course offered by most meter companies on the operation of meters – water, gas, electric, etc. The course costs anywhere from $60 to $100 and it's given in adult education curriculums. You will learn, how, by using a simple screwdriver, you can fiddle with your water meter or electric meter or any fuel meter to register the minimum bill while you use as much as you want.

Most cheaters are wealthy and this is how they get that way. And here's another way they get wealthy – they pay minimum postage! How? Again, here's a method that the Post Office doesn't want people to know about.

You can't get mail delivered without postage, it's true. But the mail scanners, the postmen and the routers, don't look to see if there isn't enough postage on it, only is there postage at all. Cheaters don't use full stamps of whatever a stamp costs. If it cost 50 cents or more they use 1 cent stamps. They put 4 or 5 one cent stamps on it so it looks good and they mail it. Now occasionally the post office will catch one or two and send it back for improper postage. But more times than not, they will deliver it or ask the addressee for the postage due and not you.

Here's another one that you can get for nothing. Book clubs are usually good for this. They offer tremendous values of paying only 10 cents or a dollar to join and you get 3 or 4 books worth maybe $100. What I do is to send away for it and they they will usually say that if I'm not satisfied in 10 days that I can keep the books and cancel membership. That's exactly what I do.

I tell them that I'm not satisfied and I keep the books and I cancel membership. And then I send away again, using the name of a different family member (brother, sister, wife, husband, mother, etc) I get the same thing and do the exact method I've described – keep the books and cancel membership.

Then after I go through all the family (and I include cousins and uncles twice removed), the book club will send to the first name that I sent in, have I reconsidered and they'll make another offer of more books at less money to join. So I agree. I join, get the books and cancel membership again. And I go through all of the family again. This way, you can build up a whole library. And you can do this with record clubs, DVD, tape clubs, even some stamp and coin clubs will offer tremendous deals.

And then a lot of times, the book clubs will offer whole volumes of author's books, which I collect and when I get a pile of them together, I sell them to a book dealer. So now I've gotten money for nothing. If there is a way to cheat, you have to find it.

You've got to be a cheater if you want to get ahead. Each day make up one or more unethical, illegal or immoral schemes. If you can't think of one, steal an idea that somebody else did. A cheater is **NOT** gonna call **YOU** a thief!! **He's gonna call you his idol!!**

CHAPTER 17

HOW TO PULL A FAST ONE

Pulling a fast one (**over somebody's eyes**) like a grifter, is a mixture of theatrics, pressure, and hype that combine to play on people's emotions and sometimes abuse them. It's also a well-oiled sales pitch which appeals to he person's greed or fantasy. Pulling a fast one then, creates a deep need in a person or strikes a chord in which people are willing to pay a high price for something that they have absolutely no use for. (**like in buying the Brooklyn Bridge**)

So, when trying to pull a fast one, just make a fuss over them, personalize it, and flash a winning smile (**hide your shark teeth!**). Say with a cocky sincerity,

"You have my word on it."

But don't emulate the fast talking huckster who's always trying to sell you something sleezy or underhanded. Always try for the "**Burt Reynolds effect**". Like the character he played in "**Smokey and the Bandit**"; a gum chewing, friendly old saw that you would give your last nickel to.

This is the way it should always sound. You have to make it sound sincere for them to believe you when you say,

"Trust me".

Now, if you're not the outgoing type, I know that it's gonna seem hard at first, but you can still become successful at pulling a fast one. Here's an example of something that you can try right now and which is not illegal and can become very profitable.

Since every person wants some form of recognition by his peers or to be thought famous, start a **"Who's Who"** of a particular field. Since very few people get to be included in the real, "Who's Who", you can get literally thousands of people to pay top dollar to be listed there. And what's so good about it, it's completely, absolutely and 100%....legal.

This is how it works. Get a mailing list of say accountants or teachers or computer programmers and then make up a form letter, offering them to be listed in a "Who's Who in America" of accountants or teachers or computer programmers. Say something like,

"It is my pleasure to inform you that because of your outstanding accomplishments in the field of *"bullshitting"*, you have been identified as a candidate for the forthcoming Who's Who in U.S. Accountants" (or bullshit artists) This is indeed a great honor to be so termed by your peers. I commend you for the achievement that has brought your name to the attention of our staff. We believe that you deserve to have your accomplishments recorded in a directory that will attest to your credentials for the whole world to see. I look forward to receiving your completed application form and check for $5000.00"

ISN'T THIS GREAT?

You can charge anywhere from $100 to $1000 or $5000 for the privilege of having their name published in a book.

And that's the best part of pulling a fast one. If you make it sound impressive enough you can sell them on anything, even snobbery.

Here's another variation that you can capitalize on. First start an **"association"** in a particular field or of a general nature, i.e. "Association of Energy Users" or how about the "American Society of Consumers". Or even better, "The Association of Computer Operators." Or "The DVD society of America." **ANYTHING!!** Maybe even have a blu-ray chapter.

This is what you do. Make up an application form and charge a membership fee for anywhere from $10 to $100. You can also get money by charging for an affiliate member if they're not interested now. (**so you can promote the cause for whatever that you're doing**) Then, if you can get a whole bunch of people to join, you can hold an annual "**congress**" of members and charge anywhere from $250 to $1000 for the privilege of attending. And again, if they can't attend, you ask them for money to promote the cause of the members that do.

Always try to look for things that you can make money at. But only do those that not only can you get away with, but don't hurt anybody. Like a rip-off that makes people cheer for its success, i.e. "**Pet Rock**". It's not a rip-off, it's not a rock, it's a book. There is a fine distinction between unethical and illegal and as long as you don't violate that line you can get away with things that are not illegal but just sound that way.

For instance, here's a very simple fast one that you can try right now, that 's not illegal and just seems to be a little shady. **Trust me, you can do it!**

Rent a meeting room in a hotel and advertise something that is **"in"** – UFO's, astrology, jogging, nuclear, or energy, any health related or aerobics item,

WHATEVER!

Then write an hour to an hour and a half speech on the subject. If you can, rent a video tape about the subject or slides are always good to bring along. Next, print up an advertisement and distribute it to local stores. For example, let's say that your fast one is UFO's, write it up as;

UFO'S

A discussion featuring that well known expert

Dr. Leonard Love Matlick on the topic,

"Is someone out there?"

All-right Hotel Friday

Grand Ballroom 8:30PM

And then all you have to do is talk about it. If you can, get a friend to also do this, and you've got your **"expert"** in the field to speak on the subject. Also, it goes over better if there is more than one person talking about it.

And you can simply be the **"moderator"** of this discussion group. You can get anywhere from 100 to 500 people at $10 or $20 or even $50 to just listen to you. That's how guilable people are; **they want to be ripped off!**

So always try to get in on **"in"** fads, whatever the latest craze of fad is, that is what you should cater to. Most successful grifters do and if not there are still three basic rules to try to follow:

One – Pull a fast one on an unsuspecting boob

Two – Never give a sucker an even break

Three – A sucker is born every minute (also called a fool and his money are soon parted)

Armed with these three basic and simple rules you shouldn't have any problems. In fact, adhering to them will make you get wealthy very fast. In this particular age or any age for that matter, people are very guilable and you can sell them on anything. The Emperor's new clothes for instance. Simply cash in on something that is nothing, general knowledge that everybody knows about. The most successful grifters cater their racket to what is nonsense, fluff, worthless crap. Just do the same and you'll do very well. Here's a good one.

Place a classified ad,

"ESTABLISH SUCCESSFUL CONSULTING BUSINESS SEND $20 FOR DETAILS TO…….."

And then when you get some answers, go to the Library and under business opportunities, copy several pages of them and send them back. There is plenty of general information there to satisfy any person looking to start a successful consulting business. You're just gathering it and selling it, which is exactly what any business is. You're simply providing a service. Or copy what somebody else did. Buy one copy of something that you see advertised and sell it in the exact same way. Put it in the same magazine or direct mail piece, in the same print, even use the same words!

Everybody does it, why not you?

Or how about this. Write a pamphlet on something called,

"HOW TO BE A BETTER PERSON"

Now you don't have to be a writer either, so don't worry. All you do is then write the ten commandments, or something similar on ten separate pages. Such as,

"SMILE!"

On one page, and then,

"TALK ABOUT HAPPY THINGS ONLY!"

On the next page, and then,

"BE CONSIDERATE!"

And so on with the rest of the pages. Underline each word and sell it by mail for $10 or $20. **It works!!**

If you would respond to any mail advertisement that's exactly what you would get. And that's how you avoid legal hassles. As long as you give them a product or service and don't mail them a bunch of bricks, the law and the postal inspector's will leave you alone. It's always those sleazy con men that give pulling a fast one a bad name.

There is also an enormous amount of free material that the government publishes that you can copy. You don't even have to change the name. Just re-publish it under your name. How about those tax guides that you see in the bookstores, on-line and in the magazines on how to fill out your income tax return, **are an exact copy of the federal tax guide word for word!!**

And like I said before, always copy what somebody else is doing or has done. It saves you time and money and if it's a scam already going on, no other con artist will say that you're stealing his ideas. **There IS honesty amongst conmen as well as thieves you know!**

So when you copy something, do it in the exact same way and in the exact same publication or mailing. If something is **"in" like gold coins**, tell them to send for a special **"report"** for only $20 and then copy what others are already saying about it. You can get it free from other con artists that advertise. And they are **ALL** con artists. Here's what others have done in the rare coin scam.

"500% PROFIT!!!"

"To find out how gold coins could work for you send just $20 for the exclusive report."

Use the same method that they are using as far as print style and form. You can use classified advertising, or display advertising or even direct mail. It doesn't really matter. Just get one and copy it exactly. And again, look for what ongoing cons or scams are doing right now. How about this one that is being advertised due to the popularity of lotteries.

"MAN WINS $500 MILLION LOTTERY USING SPECIAL REPORT"

This report explains how to win any state lottery no matter where you live.

Rush $20 plus $4 handling for special disclosure report."

Or if you don't want to use the mails, try this con that has been going on for years. Most church's use it and also places like the VFW or American Legion to get a lot of money quickly. Buy an expensive car like a Cadillac or Porsche and raffle it off. But don't even wait for the car. **Rent the car for a month!** Then make up raffles that say,

"RAFFLING OFF A 2014 PORSCH 914"

"$100 PER RAFFLE TICKET

LIMIT OF 500 TO BE SOLD

RAFFLE WILL BE HELD AT......

CALL FOR TICKETS .... "

And then sell 1000 of them! This way you can buy the car for cash and you also have a nice profit for yourself. And you can do this with anything, but it works well with expensive cars that people think that they have a good chance of winning it. (**BUT THEY DON'T!!**)

Or here's yet another way to pull a fast one. Let's say that you don't want to do any of the things that I've mentioned, but just want to get a better paying job in another field. (also see How to get a Job (**especially if you know zip**) But the catch is that you don't know anything at all about the field. Here's what to do. Rent a Post Office Box and then advertise in the newspaper, or on-line,

**"MANY JOBS – HI RATES, LOADS OF OVERTIME
RUSH RESUME TO P.O.BOX ...."**

And give the box number. Then pick out the best resume and copy it. This is also good if you want to switch fields. At least with someone else's resume, it'll get you past the front door. And that's what you want. If you can at least get a foot in, then you can bullshit your way up the ladder.

Everybody does it, why not you?

There are certain requirements that to pull a fast one that you must possess. Renting a Post Office Box is definitely one of them. There are so many things that you can do with a P.O.Box that it is a necessity. In addition, most con men (**professionally speaking**) have an alias and so should you. But change your first name or middle name. That way you don't need a court order and it's legal. You can always say that it is your nickname.

Sometimes a name just happens to **"hit" or strikes your fancy;** that's the one to use. Another requirement if you want to sell something is to hire out of work actors as salesmen. They can sell it easier, since they have the training in putting on an act.

If none of what I told you interests you, don't go away. I've been saving this next one for those that are hard to convince. Offer advice. Simple? **It is!** Start a one page newsletter for business or any other subject like astrology, UFO's, health, aerobics, food, etc. Again it doesn't matter if you know anything at all about the subject; only if you can lie but with an unabashed face about it.

You can buy a mailing list from a direct mail place of whatever group of people or interest you want. And also of a general nature too, and send an offering to them to subscribe to your newsletter. Everyone wants advice that's **"in the know"**.

Or start a service on how to pull a fast one that isn't illegal, and that you can make money off of. Call it something like,

"Rent a fast one" or something to that effect.

And in it you just tell them how to pull it off. Read the local paper or on-line and collect them. Everyday one con artist or another is always getting arrested for some con or another that didn't work. Simply repeat it, but don't tell the con artist that it didn't work. Con artists are just as stupid as everyone else, maybe even more. They have to have somebody to trust, so it **might as well be you.**

CHAPTER 18

HOW TO BECOME A LADIES MAN

Any man has what it takes to become a **ladies man**– even you. You don't have to be handsome or sexy or tall or even a **"hunk"**. All that you need to possess is a good line. And, after what you've learned so far, it's not that hard to acquire; in fact, I'll let you in on a little secret – it's really child's play.

Women fall so easily for a guy with a decent line of bullshit that it's downright sickening. They're really just suckers who can't seem to resist any smooth talker with an ability to snow them. And you can also learn to become this sly fox type very easily too. Simply do this now.

First, try to spend a lot of time around women. Any woman. Become their confident, their friend; b.s. them blatantly and brownnose them. Because if you're constantly around women you'll have a better chance of making it with them. And you never know with whom you'll be able to hit upon. However, at first, don't have any favorites. Just keep on doing it with every woman that you see, whether you care for them or not. And if you do this all of the time, you will quickly get to be known as a **"ladies man"**.

Now a ladies man is actually a b.s. artist, and they all have one common trait; they can make women feel at ease by smooth talking them. They set them up and then make their move; and you have it in you to do the same. **And they are such easy pickings!!**

For instance, tell them anything but keep a straight face,

"Your birthday's TODAY?"

(fake a surprised look) and then the set up,

"Do you know that statistically, and this is no bull, that the most intelligent and the best looking people are born in May."

You can also change the month to whatever they say. But don't just make up one statement and stop. Talk non-stop. Let it ooze out of you like oil. **Go ahead – shmalze it up.** Impress them with what you do or downright lie or just say something outrageous if they ask what you do.

"I design toilet seats."

And then continue with,

"No, seriously I do, and you can't believe how important the contour is. If the angle is not just right…Well, it's like a boomerang – it comes right back to you."

No matter what they say, b.s. them. Just keep this act up and keep on b.s.ing them, that's the ticket. That's what they want to hear. And that's how to make it with a woman. **Any woman!!**

However, you need to be a little too deliberate in your act – slower and more pensive like soap opera actors do. Study them. Also study how beauty contest winners get the attention of judges – stop, look them right in the eye and smile your brains out.

And since you are being judged, flash those baby blues at anything in a skirt. It doesn't matter if they're married, or young, or old, or beautiful or plain or whatever.

It doesn't matter!!

Just start going out with a lot of different women. If you become a ladies man, you can get a lot of women to have an affair with you or a simple one-nighter, and that what you want isn't it?

OF COURSE IT IS!!

Any man wants that, and it's really not that hard to do once you know what to look for.

Picking up and successfully seducing today's woman requires skill, intelligence, wit, judgment, discretion, cunning and savvy. But if you want to make it with a lot of women (**and who doesn't!**) then you have to learn where the girls are, how you can attract their attention, and hopefully induce them to perform sexually for you.

Your best chances for scores among women are in the service sector. Those that you see daily. And this is where you have to do battle to win a woman. Not on a once a week date, but daily. Women working the service industry of the economy – cocktail waitresses, airline stewardesses, car rental girls, secretaries, nurses, etc. are a lot more susceptible to a casual pickup and carnal interlude.

For instance, if you know that you're gonna be at a certain place that one of these women are going to be, make up flash cards of something to say and make it sound witty. A lot of times a witty or chance remark at a bar, a wisecrack or a suave gesture on a plane, will get you a date. And once you have that, it's ¾ of the way to getting whatever you want from her. Let's say that you cash your check at the same bank branch each week or make a deposit there or whatever – **hit on the girl teller!** Every time that you see her make a comment about something, even if it's stupidity or nonsense. Again, each time that you see her, make up something, even if it's stupidity or nonsense. But open your mouth (**SAY AAHH**) and talk to her.

TALK TO HER!!!

It doesn't matter if it's sexual innuendo or humor, you can just talk about fact or anything that comes to mind like,

"My, what a dreary looking day, don't you think? (said in winter)

Make up general statements, but keep on going, don't stop even if there is a **"lull"** in-between. Always fall back on flattery to make small talk.

"My, but you have such a winning smile!"

You can do better than this. Just make up flash cards and rehearse it and keep the act up.

If you are in a bar, talk about the merits of ice or no ice in a drink, any nonsense – salted or unsalted margaritas,

ANYTHING!!

But make the moment count. Don't be inhibited. If you're in an elevator with a woman say,

"We've GOT to stop meeting like this."

or

"Don't tell them what we did last night."

Again, make it better than this. A woman hears this type of stuff all of the time from men, so start with something fresh. Or use it to your advantage. Say,

"I'll bet that you hear this all of the time from guys."

Be spontaneous. If a woman smiles at you on the street, or even if she doesn't,

YOU DO IT!!

Say something to her- say hello, ask for directions, make up something smart to say – but start talking.

Another thing –stay loose. Try to be relaxed (**re-laxed**). Don't act like a loser; act like a winner (**at least show them that!**) If they look at you, pretend that this happens to you all of the time. That you are a handsome hunk that women drool over.

AND YOU ARE!!

Go to unobtrusive places to meet women – museums, your job; ski clubs are good, even if you don't know how to ski. Aerobics classes are even better, since you get to see a lot of women in the skimpiest of outfits (**and you'll probably be the token male there!**).

Supermarkets are great as well as malls. And don't forget department stores, but pick the stores carefully.

You will have a better chance if you meet a woman at places where you spend leisure time. If the female shares your tastes and views you will at least be able to converse with her on an intelligent level and not in the more prevalent of a parent to child. Some suggestions here are political rallies or organizations, art exhibitions, car and boat shows and music recitals.

Even hotels are a great place to meet women. I wait by the front desk until a woman comes to check in. I purposely listen attentively until the desk clerk says to the bellboy,

"Take Miss Wonderful up to room 7345."

Then I wait a few minutes until she has a chance to relax and then I go and knock on her door. Most women alone in a strange town **WANT** company and some of them may be succeptible because they are lonely. A lot of these will consider a simple one nighter if you just make them feel welcome. Say,

"Hi, I'm the guy in the next room."

Now, some hotels even cater to the woman traveler. They set up little get togethers on a concierge floor. A lot of women are intimidated by a bar. It's your job to make them feel at ease. At least until you can get them alone.

(hide that lecherous smile)

Another great place to meet women is those bars that feature male dancers catering to women only. Here's my plan; it's very simple. I wait until the show is over and then I make my move. Usually I am the only male there. The women are usually too horny from the show to resist.

If all else fails, you can try singles bars. Here, there are scores of imbibing women who desperately want to meet you. They line up against the bar like a chorus line, swinging their crossed legs to tempt you. And all you do is go from one to another down the line saying,

"Isn't this a wild place?"

Or some other bit of sexual innuendo. But don't let the price of an alcoholic beverage cost you and cost you. Make sure that you see the woman when you don't have any alcohol in your system. It changes the whole picture and the female knows it. The woman that looked beautiful to you drunk, looks terrible sober. So if you're gonna go on the make, drink soda or ask for a drink straight with a water chaser, and then when nobody is looking spill the drink into a plant or just hold it.

Take your time and choose carefully. Do not choose a woman who is too young as she has not had time to develop her talents properly. Do not choose one too old as she may not have been able to secure a husband and is doing this as a final measure.

A lot of times it seems like an auction because you can interest them by nodding your head or signaling with your hand. However, there is no auctioneer and you must ask her several pertinent questions. i.e. Does she go to these places often? Where does she live? What kind of work does she do? How old is she? etc. All of these types of questions should lead to an invitation to dance, or a date, or a late night snack or to hers or yours home address.

This is similar to getting merchandise on approval. However, there is no catalog to select from and you must make a cursory examination in the few hours that you have with her. You should use this time to find out if she meets certain basic requirements that you may have such as body type, personality, etc. and of course, how well she performs sexually.

Don't be surprised if the woman fails to permit you all of the usual amenities of sex on the first "**date**". They think that if they expose their bodies and let the male see what he is getting it will damage the merchandise. Be smart and persist though, since your future sex life with this woman depends upon it. Usually, the woman will give in after hearing you say the words,

"I love you."

Like some magic potion, it works fairly well and you are allowed to make physical contact. Future sex with this female is determined by how well she performs. And if you should find one that does not suit you, return her immediately with a terse note sent back to her mother. If more mothers would be held responsible for their daughters bedroom activities, fewer women would be returned or divorced for lack of sex.

The physical exam should be rated AAA for excellent, AA for very good, F for fair, P for Poor and NFG for **no F....g good**! Only those with an AA rating or above should be selected. Return all others and stamp them with your mark as a warning to all other males. Get rid of others by saying,

"See ya around." (probably in the next century."

Now it is a worthwhile idea to maintain a stable of eligible women. This is true womanizing. Get **"engaged"** to several women at one time. Females will not like it but you will. This way it permits you all of the usual marital dividends without getting married. And you can always postpone marriage indefinetly. Don't settle on the first female to come along even if she does pay the most fantastic dividend you ever had. Better to take your time and sample as many females as possible rather than take the very first one.

I've always admired men who can get more than one woman to perform sex with them. Like pimps. I can never understand the social stigma associated with being one. Imagine the balls, the sheer charisma involved to get 3 or 4 women to perform for you. Personally, I think that we should give them medals for their machismo. I know that their women do. In general, women have always put the ladies man on a higher pedestal, and that's only natural; **men are more accustomed to a pedestal – all gods are!!**

So how do you know what to look for? Most men treat the subject of women rather haphazardly. They pay more attention to the selection of their cars than they do their women. In addition to sexual attraction there are other factors, much more subtle, in determining the right woman for you. The first rule is of course to look for those that possess a good figure, for if its not good to start with, it will quickly go from bad to worse. Forget those who brag that they've lost a lot of weight, they will put it back immediately after they've got you. Stay away from fat ones too or you'll be sorry. They are very selfish creatures, only concerned with stuffing themselves and they are very, **VERY**, lazy. Also, they are not at all jolly and can at times be very surly.

Women are also devious, so discard at once, those that wear enormous amounts of strings and pulls to keep their figures in one place. Men don't wear spanx, but women do! Even though we have outlawed cruel and unusual traps for animals as being barbaric and uncivilized, women have not and will use every trick in the book to give the impression of a good figure.

REMEMBER!

Real backsides **DO NOT** have seams. So be ever on your guard. That bulky sweater maybe **ALL OF HER INSTEAD OF A SWEATER!!**

Above all, test the vocal chords of the woman you choose since you don't want one with a shrill tone. Make sure that her voice is soft, pleasant, and sultry even when she's bad tempered, or else you most certainly will regret that you didn't check this out every time that she opens her

BIG-FAT-MOUTH!!

And since we're talking about her mouth, let's talk about the language that she uses. Most women are **NOT, repeat not,** the dainty little creatures that you think they are.

NO! NO! THEY ARE NOT!!!

They maintain an arsenal of foul words that your drill sergeant didn't use and some of them use it as formidable weapons. When they're with other women they use words like"**f… this**" **and "f…that"** all of the time and they're always talking about **"what a hunk" some guy is. Disgusting!!**

In fact, the opinion that most men have of women is just the opposite of what they really are. Women are ruthless, exacting, suspicious, calculating, jealous, and cold-blooded. They are all hard- hearted Hannah's!!

ALL OF THEM!!

It seems that to be on top you gotta act like a bastard with women. They respect only those who treat them like shit. Oh, they'll say no, that they will only love a man who treats her gently. But that's a lot of bunk. They will constantly talk about the son-of-a-bitch who treated her rough with admiration. They just love to be hurt. Women are truly sadists!

So when you talk to a woman, treat her like you would, your best hunting dog- firm with a tone of command in your voice, and like you're talking to an infant or an idiot. I don't know which one a woman is, but they need constant re-assuring, much like any dog or baby would.

Also, and this is very important, you want a woman who is sexy. Forget the comedians, those with a good sense of humor; go after the sexpots. All women have the same basic equipment it's true, but some know how to use it better than others.

Look for a woman who will give you the maximum in sexual pleasure. Forget those who you have to expend too much energy or time coaxing her or showing her new pleasures. You'll wind up forsaking your own. In this you must be extremely selfish. Go after a woman who is very aggressive in bed. Those women will always keep you content in bed at least until you can find another, sexier woman to take her place!

There are also several more things that you should look for in a woman. My research has born out that booming voices among other things, shatter glasses and ear drums, so you don't want a woman with an usually large mouth either. Forget oral sex, these are very bad if you are ambitious.

They are always saying the wrong things at the wrong time, especially when you are all prepared to impress someone important, like your boss. Many promising careers have been smashed because of women that possess big mouths.

And while you're looking at her mouth, find out how her teeth are. Women are sneaky and she may want several thousand dollars worth of caps and has been waiting for you to arrive on the scene before she gets the work done.

You don't have to be gross to find this out, after all, she's not a horse! But make her laugh. Her guard will be down and if she laughs heartily enough you can quickly gaze into her mouth. One more pointer on laughter though, make her laugh hard. Women love a man with a sense of humor and it will give you some impression of the way that she laughs. The lilt of female laughter however, should **NOT** resemble the cackle of a hen, because if it does, you will late berate yourself as a dumb cluck for selecting her.

If you have hopes of climbing the social ladder, you'll need a woman who's the perfect hostess. Look for one that not only can prepare unusual hor d'ors, but knows when and how far to open her mouth. A lot of women can be very obnoxious, always at the wrong times. Look for the ones that went to a finishing school, or those that are from the social elite. You will have a better chance at making it.

Seek out a woman then who will help you out in your career, not just reap the benefits of your hard work. For instance, let's say that you are a writer. Get a woman who'll prod you, who'll feed your ego, who'll type your manuscripts, who'll call your agent or publisher and set up appointments, etc. A woman who'll work for your benefit, not hers, that's the one to choose.

This type of woman must also be a gourmet cook, an excellent seamstress, a whiz at cleaning furniture and keeping the house sparkling, be able to have and rear 10 or 15 children, and of course still have time to work, attend every social function with an area of 3000 square miles, and also do charitable or humanitarian work or contribute their "all" to a cause of questionable merit.

So if you think that you can't find a woman like the one I've just described, you're wrong –

DEAD WRONG!! They **ARE OUT THERE!!**

You can't settle for less. Don't compromise at all. If you use this as a guide you'll find her. Look at any successful man and you'll find that his woman fits **EVERY** one of these traits. He didn't compromise and neither should you. That is of course unless you don't want success and if that's the case, then the woman that you're seeing right now will do nicely!

Ok, so now you know what to look for. But what are you up against? What does a woman look for?

Most women are always looking for **"Mr. Right"**. You know that guy, that famous knight in shining armor. But who is he? Who is Mr. Right to a woman? He is one of the following although not necessarily in this order:

- A male model that has just signed a contract for a starring role in a movie.
- Any billionaire
- The President of the United States (or about to be)
- A 4 star General or ship of the line Captain
- A professional athlete with a Super Bowl or World Series Ring
- Someone who has climbed Mt. Everest or at least Pikes Peak (NOT by car)
- A TV soap opera actor
- The present winner of the Mr. Universe contest
- Anyone (**even you**) who can take out the garbage

Now also for a price, you can phony up some id's and say that you're so and so in order to impress a woman. It's really easy. Pick out a person that's famous, but not too famous.

i.e. a race car driver who has won the Indy 500

a character actor who's name is famous, but whose face is not

you can even pick up on who is the latest most read writer and say it's **YOU!!**

It doesn't matter who you impersonate. Usually, you can impersonate him for one or two or even three nights. You just have to get enough time so that the woman can impress her girlfriends with you. I know that this seems dumb to you and to me also, but women are very succeptible to impression.

"See whom I'm going out with!" she'll say to her friends so that they're dying with envy.

"You're SO lucky." They'll say.

And at that time you can do almost anything you want with her; she's yours. Again, make up an act and impress them. Say, that you're a soldier of fortune. **(that's always a good one)**

"Remember that spy plane that was shot down by the _____ (fill in any country). Well, don't believe that. It was ME! I did it. I shoot them down on a free-lance basis. Really."

Keep this act up even if they scoff at who you are trying to impersonate. A woman will believe almost any type of horse-shit. They are truly simple creatures.

BEWARE THOUGH!!!

They are **NOT** stupid! Although you are looking at her with just sex in mind, a woman isn't going to be that foolhardy. She'll look at you coldly; you're just a number on her list of many eligible suitors. She may think of you in terms of romance, true enough, but also what you do for a living and is it a glamorous job (**in her girlfriends eyes**), how much money you make (**and does it approach the national debt),** what properties you own (**which she can take in a settlement),** and as always, how will she look in her girlfriends eyes if she picks you (**are you up to their standards as a hunk**). She will even check the mortality rates for your height and weight. After all, you're going to be her future supporter.

Sound ruthless?

OF COURSE!! AND VERY EXPENSIVE FOR YOU!!

Just to live with a woman is the largest single investment that you will ever make in your life. In fact, just to maintain her you will have to figure on at least the following a year:

- Winter, spring, summer and fall outfits
- Complete jewelry collection
- New or late model car
- Vacation every year, preferable at the most expensive and far away places
- Doctor and Dental bills
- Money to go shopping with each day
- A night out with her girlfriends, so that when **YOU** come home from a hard days work**, SHE** can relax (**whatever does she do?)**

- Every new electrical appliance or fad that comes out
- Rooms of furniture changed every few years to what is "in"
- And of course, a home, preferably one that in **NO** way can you afford

In addition to these known costs there are other costs that are not so apparent, but must also be taken into account in determining supporting a woman.

After these maintenance costs that I've mentioned, it will also mean a minimum of one quart of liquor a day **FOR YOU!!** It might also mean care in a hospital for a duodenal ulcer caused by stress, or the more usual care from a competent psychiatrist. To give you some idea of what you are up again, from birth onward, women must practice for hours a day, the words,

"I WANT!! I WANT!! I WANT!!!"

It is best to have a constant source of money or else a good pair of earplugs (**Earco model 14 is the best. It has given me many hours of golden silence**)

So if women are so ruthless in their search for a desirable mate and to guard against possibly picking out the wrong woman for you, I suggest that you make her fill out a standard form (**like they do for computerized dating**). This form should contain past medical information (**has she ever had measles, mumps, chicken pox**), present medical information (**herpes, AIDS, VD**) ,does she have any condition that requires constant medical attention (allergies, acne), is she on a special diet? Does she need a diet? (**you can testify to that**) Does she have a craving for expensive and unusual foods (**oysters in champagne at 4AM?**)

This form should contain about 1000 or so questions. If she gets more than one wrong,

CHOOSE ANOTHER!!

It is just as easy to choose the right girl than be stuck with the wrong one for the rest of your natural life. Should you be foolish to pick any with more than one thing wrong – woe to you. Which by the way, is what the dictionary defines as a woman – a bringer of woe.

The woman selected should also be tested to make sure that she knows all of the homemaking skills such as cooking, mending, nursing, child rearing, washing floors, cleaning furniture, chauffeuring, and valet services among others.

If the woman you select does not know how to do these things or if they blatantly refuse to do these minimal tasks, (**"I wasn't raised to do them! These princesses will say**) then you will have to bear the additional expense of providing these services.

The old adage of a good cook makes a good woman still hold true.

A woman's mother's duties entailed training her in these useful functions so you should be able to get the most of what you are selecting. It is just as easy to find a female that is brilliantly trained in these skills as it is to find those who are not.

CAUTION!!

Females are very tricky. They may even have their mother's prepare a meal and then say that they cooked it. Or another devious ploy is to have a quality restaurant deliver a complete dinner and say that **THEY** are a gourmet cook.

NONSENSE!!

Females aren't gourmets, they are gourmands!!

To prove this, did you ever see the way a female eats in a restaurant? A horde of starving vultures can't consume as much. Therefore, to make sure that the female has the necessary skills of homemaking, watch while she does them.

So now that you're up against, what is your strategy? Simply, to find and make as many women as you can –**THAT** is essentially what being a ladies man is. Actually, there is no being a bad ladies man either, since if you out with more than one woman that's good – **kudos to you!!!**

CHAPTER 19

BECOMING EXTRA ORDINARY (NOT HARD!)

Geronimo, the famous American Indian chief, was once asked should underlings suck up to their boss (**meaning him**!) He said,

"Of course not, but the Authorities decided it that way, and they are the ones that rule."

So back then, and even before his time, sucking up to the boss was standard practice, and everyone did it. Bosses, CEO's, CFO's, COO's, etc. are the Authorities having jurisdiction and they still dictate that brownnosing, b.s.ing and backstabbing (**the 3 b's remember?**) are what makes a person get ahead. (**and fast!**) You may not like it, and maybe even loath doing it, but like Geronimo said, they decided it that way and they are the ones who rule. **This means that if you want to get ahead with the boss, any boss, you have to suck up to them in any way possible.**

Most CEO's, bosses, etc., like most everyone, are suckers for a compliment, and ambitious underlings can gain an advantage if they are skilled at flattery, ingratiation and agreeing with everything the boss has to say. Compliments delivered to the boss, even disingenuous ones, are powerful and often cause them (**the bosses**) to feel the need to reciprocate with favoritism, even to employees that they don't like. **So brownnosing then is not only good for you, it is good for the company.**

And very good for you, since if you make the boss feel less insecure you will stay employed even in a bad economy. This is also great news for the lazy or incompetant, since how else are they going to keep their jobs. So, your mission then, should you choose to accept it, **(like mission impossible)** is to remain gainfully employed with as little hassle as possible for as long as possible.

If you want to get a promotion or a plumb assignment, it's probably best to lay it on thick. Just do it when only the boss can hear it, because even if the boss is succeptable to the compliment, co-workers will see that he is being manipulated by you. Gifts, compliments, dinner parties, golf outings, **anything**, will work.

Now, most CEO's or bosses are men, who are especially vulnerable to ingratiation by women. Women are way, **way** better at it because they are more subtle, more facile half-truth tellers and expert at knowing what to say to get others to like them. For women, getting the boss to feel good is a piece of cake. They don't even have to leave a half-promise of sexual favors, only let it sound that way. However, the reason that most women are not bosses is because most women are less likely to engage in sophisticated forms of ingratiation that can get them to the top.

I suggest that you practice it on subordinates or equals first, then move up to bosses. You will need to make it into an art form. Your equals will not detect brown nosing if you are kind and complimentary **(only with sincerity and only when well deserved)** to everybody. So whenever you see somebody, pay them a compliment,

"Ed, that's a cool new jacket! It looks good on you."

or

"Ed, great looking suit! Where did you get it?"

or

"Corrine, nice hairstyle!"

But say ANYTHING!!

You will become known as the most positive person in the office, which will soon translate into raises and promotions.

The road to success is a series of popularity contests. Don't believe them when **"they"** say that it is more important to be respected than liked. Raises and promotions are more apt to be awarded based on a workers' charisma than on his or hers academic background or qualifications.

And during even downturns, hiring and firing decisions are based on how well people are liked by their supervisors. Likeability, then is a skill that can be learned so that you can be likeable in the eyes of your boss.

So how do you do it? First, make a sincere effort to be open and greet everyone. Say

"Hi!"

to everyone you see in a day, even if it's 100 times a day. As you pass by someone, stop and say a little ditty so that they know that you are acknowledging them. Smile a lot and give off positive vibes such as have a twinkle in your eyes; i.e. have cheerful eyes.

Secondly, make contact with people, such as sitting close to them in a meeting or at an event. Don't stay in the back, away from everyone; get closer to the person. **Real close**! But don't make them feel threatened by how close you are to them. There is a certain distance from another person so that you are not in their "space". On this, you will have to play it by ear, as to how close is close.

Most people will relate better to you if you care about what they do, or what interests them. Say that you have done the same things or have gotten the same responses that they do; this way, it generates a feeling of mutual interests.

And then, the bottom line is can you meet the person's wants and desires. If you can, then this person will love you and know that you care about their needs, not only during work, but also emotionally. You want the person to have a positive impression of you and that contributes to your allure. Find a way to connect with this person's outside interests or what they are most passionate about. Everybody has emotional needs and if you respond to them they will always think highly of you.

Again, always try to see things from the other person's point of view. Become empathic to them and feel what they feel. They will believe that you are with them and are the same type of person. Thus you will become **"friendlier"** and your likeability will dramatically increase. So, in other words, when you make others feel good, they will tend to like you more.

You can become this type of person by maintaining a level of high enthusiasm, optimism, and energy during the entire workday. These type of people are as fresh at 10PM as they are at 8 AM.

You will never hear one of these type of people complain how late it is or that he or she is exhausted. That's because when these people talk about their jobs or their careers, they have a gleam in their eyes. You can develop your enthusiasm and optimism also by searching for the best or positive things in a given situation. And by evaluating your energy level does take a lot of work, but it is definitely worth doing it to become this type of person that everybody likes.

Again, so how do you do this. Having a mirror image of you is your rocket to the top.

Tape a picture of yourself next to your bathroom mirror to keep reminding yourself of you. Tomorrow morning, when you're in front of it, look closely at yourself. Do you see a quality person? I don't mean that you're rich, beautiful or famous, but a really quality person. That's what will catch your boss's eyes.

His or her confidence and trust in your operation directly relates to your success. It's not that easy to gain the confidence of the top guy or gal. These men and women receive a lot of different messages, see things in different perspective, are pushed and pulled in many different ways. There's really no one correct way to keep in closer touch with your boss. It takes more than sprucing up and looking good.

So set exact and do goals that are demanding. Challenge every person including yourself to exceed personal expectations. Demand as much as possible, but show by example what is attainable. It's not that hard to do, but it takes a lot of detail work to get to the top.

Look at those who make it to the top- they stand out from everybody else. They dress, talk and act differently. And they've acted this way long before they ever came to the top position. They were **"comers"** long ago.

Role playing is acting. You decide on a role, i.e. president of the company, and you act it out until **YOU ARE** president. I know that this sounds hard to believe, but you have to have a **"president"** personality, before you will actually be a president. The late prime minister of Great Britain, Sir Anthony Eden, took a picture of himself at 10 Downing Street, dressed the way he thought a prime minister should look, when he was **10 years old!!** And he kept that picture until he finally was made prime minister.

First take an acting course. Parade up and down in front of a mirror and practice. Practice delivery, timing, facial expressions – everything. To be successful, you must master it. To become extraordinary is the single most important thing that you will ever have to learn in your lifetime. Not manners, nor etiquette, not even toilet training is as important as is becoming extra ordinary. Basically, it just means going out of your way all the time to fool everybody with fancy footwork and constant maneuvering, so that you always come out on top and smelling like a rose. **Not hard!!** I know that it sounds hard, but it isn't.

However, to become extra ordinary, is not a game. It's a deadly serious method of attack and defense, lubricated with all manner of slick talking, that determines what sort of advancement you will make in life. And it's not a matter of choice whether or not you play this **"game"**. Because the **"game"** will go on playing you if you do not take a conscious and active role. So the question is not whether to play, it is simply **"how"** to play.

It's like being a car salesman. You have to be friendly and outgoing. You don't have to do this forever or even until you're found out that you're really a fraud. You only have to do it until you make the sale and then you move on to the next person up on your list.

B.s.ing is part of playing the **"game" (a large part!)**, and so are brownnosing and backstabbing. So are the abilities to lie, cheat and con. They are all important, the primary skills of the great player. Just realize that the **"game"** is putting into practice what you've already learned from this book.

First off, you have to see what works and what doesn't. If one line of b.s. doesn't work, then switch to another. Adapt your **"line"** to the person that you're talking to. For instance, you'll talk differently to a child than to an adult. You'll talk differently to a woman than to a man. Always be ready to change your **"line"** as you're talking. Just remember to keep track of what you said and to whom. It doesn't mean completely becoming an opportunistic slimeball, but that helps. Simply think fast on your feet and let words ooze out of you. So ready or not – **let's play!!**

Playing means always writing memos to cover your ass, and doing it as if your very life depended upon it. Believe me, **it does!!** So do this now; write two memos for each option on a given proposition – two in favor, two against. After six months, nobody remembers what position you took, so just pull out the memo with the appropriate approach and smugly say,

"I told you so!!"

If somebody senior to you in your office dies, Say,

"I got first dibs on his office."

And laugh as if you're joking, but you know that you're not. Then ask if you can move into that office **"temporarily"** so that your **"cold"** will improve. Say that you need the sun.

"Those rays of sun work wonders for a cold."

Now, here's exceptionally good advice. Some managers like to see a clean desk all of the time, while to others a cluttered desk is the sign of a busy person. The best way to handle this dilemma is to start off every morning with a clean desk and then pile stuff on it all day to make it look like that you're very busy. Then every night stay a few minutes late and clear off your desk again.

You need have absolutely nothing to do. All you have to do is to look busy is do the following: Heap your desk with blank sheets of paper, old magazines, obsolete company reports, etc. – it doesn't matter what . Also have several pencils and pens thrown around your desk. This completes the effect.

People rise up the ladder to success by first pretending that they are important. In other words, you pretend and make an exaggerated outward show, like being ostentatious. You buy an overly expensive suit or car, you show off your Lionel train collection to the Harvard Review, your name appears in the Guinness book of world records twice. No bragging, but you are more important. **(or at least show this to the world)**

Acting pretentious to get ahead is perfectly acceptable and it is usually characterized by an assumption of dignity or importance. You go overboard in everything. If everybody has fences, around their house or property, you hire a security guard as a gatekeeper.

Now that's acting pretentious!

Always keep up the air of

"I'm important. You definitely are not!"

Not being a snob, or even being thought of as an elitist, but using your God given right to **"act"** better than everybody else. First **"play-act"** the role that you want in life by pretending that you are a very important person.

So how do you do this? First have credentials, either real or imagined. Credentials are a guarantee to your success and advancement as is wearing the right clothes or in marrying the boss's daughter. You should strive every day to impress people with your credentials in the same way that you say good morning to them. **(you DO say good morning to EVERY one, don't you?)**

Credentials are important, not only to the personnel department, but as a selling tool for you or your company. If you've got 3 degrees from Harvard, then flaunt it. If your name appeared in Who's Who, yell till your throat is sore and if by chance you're related to royalty (**or a former President)** then show your crest or explain that you are next in line to the throne.

Don't let any opportunity pass without giving a 15 minute discourse on why you are so good at whatever it is that you do. Bend their ear a lot and talk them to death about that memo you circulated on attracting the right people to your company. (**like they did in hiring you!)**

Don't leave anything in your career to chance. Put together a profile of what your ideal career is and act on it. Don't wait for your employer to initiate discussions about job performance and expectation. Check in regularly so that your boss knows that your expectations are the same as his.

In other words, plant what your boss thinks of you, by telling him over and over again how great you are. But don't leave anything to chance. Tell co-workers to tell the boss what a great job you are doing. So the better that you get along with coworkers, the easier a time it will be for them to tell the boss what a great guy or gal you are.

There are certain tricks that you can use to make your way in the world, things that the average person wouldn't stoop to trying. And that's why they'll always remain just that – average.

First do this right now: just tell everybody that you are a great guy! Don't be shy, you can accomplish this easily. Keep telling yourself,

"I AM THE GREATEST!!"

Or

"I REALLY AM WONDERFUL!!"

Or anything else to boost your ego.

Imitate beautiful people when they primp themselves in front of a mirror. Mouth,

"I LOVE YOU!!"

At your reflection. And never let a mirror pass without checking out how you look. Also, smile and wink at yourself. Say aloud,

"YOU HANDSOME DEVIL YOU!!!"

Another point is your voice. A voice full of assurance and confidence commands attention, so listen to a local late-night stereo radio station for a full month. Start to talk like the disc jockey or like the announcer. Practice having this firm resonant voice with deep rich tones, and when you talk to others or talk on the phone, use this voice. Buy cassette tapes and practice this while recording yourself daily for one or two hours until you perfect it.

If you can, take a DJ course at a radio school. You may not be going for a career in communications, but it will set up a certain style in you.

Show all of the characteristics of voice that mark great showmen – warmth, softness, caressing tone, low pitch and modulation. For instance, hold the phone close to you and pretend that you are talking to your lover. Or sing the scales, do re me fa so la ti do, using different personality types. Make one type sound like a fast talker, one like a lover, another like a master of ceremonies. Practicing this daily will make it and you perfect.

But you've not only got to be able to talk well, you've also got to dress well.

Be slightly overdressed for whatever you're doing or wherever you'll be. Look at men's magazines, such as Playboy or Esquire, or the best, Gentlemen's Quarterly, for the latest in men's fashions. The New York Times Magazine spring and fall fashion supplements are also well worth looking at. Don't forget to see what all the rock stars are wearing to various awards shows.

If you can, wear the colors of a peacock, and you'll do fine. In other words, always be at the height of fashion and wear what's in style. Be color coordinated, with your shoes, **ALWAYS** shined and your hair combed so that not one strand is out of place. And again, never let a mirror pass without checking yourself out. You must say to yourself,

"LOOKING GOOD!!"

But say it aloud so that you can hear it too. You are also trying to impress yourself, and repetition of an idea will engrave it on your subconscious. And your conscious. And on anybody else who's listening.

Wear expensive clothes, such as $2000 wool or blend suits. If you can't afford $2000 suits, then buy $1000 or $500 suits, as long as the color and pattern are right (blue or grey suits or pinstripes of either color). Have a different suit for each day and one extra to change to. Don't wear the same suit twice in the same week. Buy two plain shirts for each suit and four dark ties for each suit. This way you've got a month's time before someone sees you in the same thing. But make sure that your shirts are lighter than the suit and the ties darker than the shirt.

You have to be the sharpest dresser there, no matter where **"there"** is. Always wear what's **"in"**. Be a little too flashy for whatever that you're doing, like working on your car or around the house. Tape about two month's worth of soap operas on TV and study them to dress like the actors do in them. **You should be fine!**

I would suggest that you also go without an overcoat on especially cold days to show that you are above all those **"average"** people who get cold or are susceptible to weather. Say,

"Nah, it doesn't bother me. I was at the South Pole in the Navy. I'm used to cold weather."

But if you must wear a coat, then buy a beige coat with a cashmere lining so that you can double it as an overcoat.

Excessive gold or jewelry is okay if you're a late night Casanova, but not if you're a b.s.artist. The only jewelry that you should wear is a good watch, one that is waterproof and has a calendar or date on it. I happen to like a good Omega, but if you can afford it, then buy a Rolex.

And always check the time every hour to show off your watch. Say something like,

"My is it five o'clock already? The time sure goes when you're having fun."

Buy several pairs of good expensive shoes. You should be able to see your reflection in the shine. Five minutes of hard polishing on each shoe will bring this about. I delegate Sunday nights, while watching TV, for shining shoes. I shine up all of the shoes that I'm going to wear that week. So in less than an hour, I'm all shined up.

Carry a nice-looking pen around with you that looks old-fashioned and expensive but isn't. I prefer the Parker "Big Red" series or Wearever types. Such pens look different from all those push-push ballpoint pens that everybody has. You have to take off the cap to write with the expensive kind.

You can execute this action with a flair and it make for a nice impression. For the few extra bucks, get the whole assortment of colors they have and color-coordinate your pen to the clothes that you're wearing each day. This will soon make an impression that people will recognize and look for. And when everybody is used to that, one day come in without the pen. Soon people will ask,

"How come no pen today?"

You want to be remembered. But if you want to be more conservative, then get a good gold or silver pen, a Cross or the equivalent.

The car that you drive is important, so be car conscious. But don't go for Cadillac, Mercedes, or such, since you want to show that you're unpretentious. I would recommend Buick Electra, Lincoln, Mercury Brouham, or such. It's not that I'm partial to any of these cars, it's just that most **"old money"** and senior management types seem to drive these cars.

You can quickly get into a conversation with these types if you have the same kind of car as they do. The color of their car is usually forest green (**the color of money**) or silver (**the color of coins**) or sometimes even a gold color (**the color of gold**), and their cars are kept scrupulously clean, with a copy of the Wall Street Journal lying prominently in the front seat.

Then, learn to walk deliberately; have an individual walk, a very definite walk. You don't have to sway or swagger a lot, but you should strive for individuality in your walk. It could be either ultra fast or very slow, or have a certain cadence to it, like John Travolta, in Saturday Night Fever. Walk like you're listening to music, the best that you ever heard. You can do this easily. Get a tape of your favorite music and play it as you practice walking. Just think of moving to the music in your own private dance. It doesn't matter whether it's rock or Beethoven, as long as it's **YOUR** type of music. After doing this for about two weeks, do it without the music; just keep remembering the tune.

Now here's a trick to use if you're rushing to get someplace or running to make an appointment. When you get there, and just before you go in –

STOP!!

Compose yourself, take a deep breath, and then calmly, coolly, walk in. If there's a bathroom around, use it. Comb your hair, straighten yourself up.

Look composed, as if you took your time getting there. If it was raining, look like the raindrops missed you. This also can be easily done. Carry a complete plastic rainwear set consisting of boots, hat and coat, that when folded up is no thicker than a wallet, all inside of your jacket pocket. This enables you to appear somewhere with not a drop of rain on you. It makes for a good impression, if, during a heavy rainstorm, when all others trudge in with umbrella, raincoat, galoshes, and hat, you walk in dry, unruffled, and seemingly without any place to hide cumbersome storm gear.

IT DOES WORK!!

And the cost of such rainwear is so negligible that you can throw it away after each use so you don't have to worry about folding up a wet raincoat.

You will have a better chance of getting ahead if you change your first name to one that is unusual. Now, I'm not talking about having an alias, but for some strange reason, most successful people have unusual first names. It must make them strive to get ahead further and faster, and it seems that unusual first names are a key to getting ahead.

You don't need a court order, so stop thinking that you have to get a lawyer. Instead, get a baby book of names and go through it. I am sure that you will find names there that are beyond the usual. Another great place to look for names is in the Social Register. There are more unusual names in there than anyplace in the world. Go through it and you'll find out what names constitute success.

Also copy down the first names of the officers of the nations top five hundred companies. Those officers didn't get there on looks and brains alone. It was their **"good name "**that got them where they are, even if they don't know the actual reason themselves (**and most do not**). Here are some examples for name changing:

If your name is John Smith, you'll have a better chance if you change it to Lamar Smith. Or Victory Jones from Steven Jones. And Judson Carpenter from Bill Carpenter.

See how easy it is!

Just schmalz it up. Also, go in for those first names that can be shortened to a nickname that people will remember: "Hub" for Hubbard, "Corn" for Cornelius, or "Cal" for Calvin. Try several out before you decide.

Here is a list of uncommon first names that were in the financial section of the newspaper one day in a column on people gaining promotions:

Curtis, Dwayne, Burton, General, Carlton, Anvil, Avery, Compton, Zachary, Bradley, Calvin, Dilbert. Notice that except for one or two, all of the names begin with the letters A to D. This should tell you something about which are of the alphabet to look in.

Now, if you don't want to change your first name, then change your **MIDDLE** name. This can also work for you if you don't have a middle name. Then just add one that you like for the effect it has. You can get the same effect by using a middle name for a first name.

Some examples of good names are: Lawrence Anvil Patterson, Jeffrey General Mcdonald, Zebediah Zachary Zane.

You could also change your middle name to a **NUMBER**. John Ten foster, Larry Seven Jones, Jim Twelve Harris.

Or change it to a **DAY**: Joseph Sunday James, Leonard Tuesday Love

Or how about to a **MONTH:** Robert January Jones, Horace July Foster, James October Kean

Or even to **WEATHER:** James Rain Carson, Rodney Hail Smith.

If it works, why not? Some stupid names have really gotten some people very far.

Next, you **MUST** maintain a file on just about everybody you know, with his full name, that of his spouse or girlfriend, of his children (with ages and sex and what school that they attend), and of course, of his secretary – with birthdays of all of them. You should also note, the person's interests, hobbies, pastimes, vices, and passions, and how you came to meet them.

You never know when you are going to need a favor or what you might need to know about someone important to tell to somebody else.

Every time that you have contact with a person on your list, you should use this information that you have gathered to your advantage. Do you owe him any favors, or does he owe you? Always try to make sure that he owes you a favor, but don't collect on it until that you really need to. Put down in the file when was the last time that you saw or spoke to him and keep the file up to date.

Also note your acquaintances home and business phone numbers, and any "**private**" phone numbers (such as those of mistresses or hideaways).

Next, you should always send cards to the people in your life, not only on Christmas but also on their birthdays. Include a personal note from you. Send an additional card once during the year to "**keep in** touch". Do the same for the person's wife, children or secretary. Keep this information in a card file, on a Rolodex, computer or locked in a safe. You should also have a list of the most influential people in politics, banking, law, etc. It should contain at least 6,000 names.

Have most of the information on your prime people memorized. This way if somebody asks if you know, "**so and so**" you say of course you do, and that you're his personal friend. (**Try to get the phone numbers of the Pope and the President of the United States as well**)

Now whether people send you Christmas cards or not, you must never let an occasions as important as this pass without sending them cards. Go right up the ladder from a boss to the president and chairman of the board of your company. But not only send them cards, send them small gifts via registered mail, to be given to the addressee only. That way you know that they are going to them, and not their secretaries.

The gifts should be something like a pocket weekly planning calendar with **YOUR** name imprinted on it, or a silver money clip with the person's name on it **ANYTHING!!!** the more expensive the gift the **better. Even a high-class hooker would be appreciated. I know that I would appreciate such a gift)**

To become extraordinary there are suggestions to improve your life.

For instance, if you wear glasses, get contact lenses. It frees up your face and people can see your eyes. And the eyes do have it; they are the windows to your soul. Also. Don't blink unnecessarily. Your eyes need to blink to wash them and prevent dry eye, but there are some people who constantly blink.

Control them!!

Look at a spot on the wall and try to hold your eyes still, without blinking for a count of ten. Increase daily until you can hold still to a count of 50 or 100.

Also, get a good hair styling that shows that you are up to date with the latest fashion in hair style. A word on the hair stylist that you pick. I have found that a stylist of the opposite sex does a better job on presenting you to the world. I have nothing against male barbers, but even male hair stylists do a better job on a woman than female stylists do.

And in addition to a good hair styling, get a hair coloring. For instance, if you show signs of graying, forget the do-it-you-self type of hair coloring that you get from a bottle. Grey hair always turns red from the hair coloring that you buy in the store, so do yourself a favor and get it professional colored. It will be worth whatever it costs to your career development.

Then there are several things that you can do to become extra ordinary that most people don't even think about. For instance, smile more frequently. Nothing lights up a room if you have an infectious smile. Not a leering smile, but a natural, I am so glad that you're here smile. It makes people feel at ease in your presence.

Don't make unnecessary hand gestures either. Don't talk with your hands, like some people do. Talk with your mouth, that's what you were given a mouth for, not with your hands. Try to hold your body still for five minutes or more at a time. Don't fidget, don't scratch your eyes or nose or your ass.

Also, hold a full glass of water and walk around the room. It is great practice on maintaining your control.

Also, don't let your voice crack.

Talk like a man!!

Talk in a range of several notes, starting with the lowest note on the scale until you feel comfortable with this voice. Sing up and down the scales and holding E-E-E for a few seconds.

You should rigidly control your thoughts so that you can think of one thing at a time. **Do not let thoughts control you!!**

Learn how to walk, stand, talk and project your magnetism to others.

Then never address your inferiors as if they are your inferiors. **This is never charming!!** Affect (**show, pretend)** great interest in others views, even if they are exactly opposite to yours**. But be shameless in your flattery, when you want a person's support.**

CHAPTER 20

HOW TO MAKE EXCUSES

Excuses come in so handy for every occasion that it should be one of the first steps you choose to take up in climbing the ladder to success. Making excuses is ingrained in our culture. We are not interested in results, only excuses.

And most people do make excuses. They make excuses about why their children didn't do well in school (**it's the teachers fault**!) or why they just missed out on a fantastic deal that is now worth millions (**Yeah, 20 years ago I could have bought the Brooklyn Bridge for a song!)** or even why they haven't gotten a raise. (**Nepotism! That's why!)**

Excuses are a required part of any job that you should always choose from each day. Use and choose them as you would select from the four basic food groups.

    a. **I didn't do it!**

    b. **Shift the blame to somebody else."It's Joe's fault because.......**"

    c. **Yes, but**.....

    d. **Accuse your attacker."You did it!"**

So for instance,

"**I didn't do it",**

you nullify your responsibility by shifting the blame to someone else. Denial of responsibility is a primitive technique but one that comes in handy a lot. Children use this as their favorite of all time.

We are taught from childhood to make excuses.

"You didn't **MEAN** to hit him?"

your mother said.

"Wasn't it an ACCIDENT?"

she said, and from this, every time a teacher or parent caught you in the act of hitting your brother, you said,

"He made me do it!"

This now sets the stage in your childhood for some real excuse making later in life.

Welcome to the alibi club!

And for shifting the blame to somebody else (**a personal favorite of mine!),** you constantly wriggle out of trouble by blaming someone else. You may not gain everyone's enmity, but you will put others on notice that you will not accept blame for their mistakes (**or perceived mistakes, or even what mistake you did**).

The "**Yes, but**"

excuse minimizes guilt by offering extenuating circumstances. This excuse offers a biased account in your favor which is highly favorable and recommended. And accusing your attacker

"**You did it!**" is still the best excuse of all. Shift the blame to them.

Men and women have different attitudes toward excuses. Men are more likely to try a boldface denial of guilt, while women are verbally more sophisticated and lean to an explanation.

Either way, you should set a standard for your excuse. For instance, if you're playing ball, before you even start, claim that you injured your arm (**leg, ankle**) and that way if you play badly, you have an excuse. If you do well, you're likely to get a lot of extra praise.

You should strive to become a chronic excuse maker, especially hard-luck excuses. These are that you habitually blame outside forces –traffic, weather, such as,

"It took me over 3-1/2 hours to get to work today. The weather and the bumper to bumper traffic was unbelievable!"

And then say,

"I have to leave early today also. I'm not going to spend another 3-1/2 hours trying to get home."

To become good at making excuses simply don't make any decisions **(especially if you don't know anything at all about the subject).** Always try to explain away our all too human goofs in order to maintain a good impression of ourselves.

Do this;

Constantly hide out!

Become very good at long lunches or sharpening pencils. Say,

"I'll get back to you." (and then never do!)

Delay decisions at work by also saying:

"I'm much too busy."

If they can't find you, then you can't be asked to make a decision, now can you? This is the gist of making excuses. It simply means to put up a defense by having an excuse-

ANY EXCUSE!

And never deviate from it. You just stick to whatever idea you have **(the world is square**) and nothing else exists. **(even if Christopher Columbus proved it round-He's an idiot!))** It doesn't matter whether it's right or wrong, as long as you believe it. You've talked to people like that, no matter what you say they won't budge. **DO THE SAME!!**

You should start by making a least one excuse a day, on any subject,

" The computer goofed again! These glitches are moneywasters!"
It wasn't you, it was the computer.

That's the attitude that you have to maintain, that it's never your fault, it's something or someone else's fault.

AND IT IS!

The best kind of worker is the one who is so busy defending their mistakes that they never learn a thing about how to avoid or correct them. **And why should you**? There are other people to do the correct job. You're job is to just make excuses.

REALLY!

You should have an excuse for everything. It's not only a need to bolster your ego, but if you persist in making excuses for why you didn't do something, the other person may eventually give up asking. You should automatically make an excuse when none is necessary. Such as,

"The bus was late."

or

"I forgot to take something out for dinner."

Women are great at making excuses, especially when it comes to sex. Or some women use their menstrual periods as a convenient excuse for everything. So never use an excuse in moderation,

USE IT CONTINUALLY!

Even hard-luck excuses are great. Such as, if you're playing racquetball, and you're losing, complain about the wind

(there is no wind, it's indoors!),

"They opened the door again! When will they learn to close the door when we're playing!!"

or the court is warped and that's why you're not playing well.

"Will you just look at this court! It's warped !They must have washed the floor. What idiot would wash a wooden floor!!"

To really become adept at making excuses you should try to blame someone else. In this way it does two things. First it boosts your ego (which boosts your confidence to make you more assertive) and it puts **THEM** on the defensive.

For example, always blame it (**what ever "it" is**) on somebody else.

"It's Joe's fault because I didn't have the proper information."

or

"Jim didn't make the schedule that we all agreed upon and that's why, but I tried, I really did."

Always move your feet with fancy steps. Get it off of your back and onto theirs.

If you're a cryer, everybody will feel sorry for you and leave you alone. Now think back, every time you ever met a cryer (someone who cries about **EVERYTHING**), they say,

"Oh isn't it terrible that such and such can't make it because...."

SO DO THE SAME!

Always cry. Whine and complain a lot, but only to the highest authority. Try to have people take pity on you.

The best way to become a chronic excuse maker is to study one in action. There is more than one in your office right now. Just follow their fine example and you'll do fine.

To be able to make excuses takes a bit of ingenuity because you always have to have all evidence and material that you need, either in front of you or close at hand. So always have a defense, a protection to hide behind. Let's say if someone calls you on the phone, like your boss, or a higher up, and starts to bend your ear on any details, fend them off but nicely,

"I'll answer your question just as soon as I get to my files,..."

And then get all the stuff you need out .Put tabs on each folder such as:

"EVIDENCE"

or

"PROOF"

or

"CYA"

or

"VERBAL RECORDINGS"

or

"EVERYDAY EXCUSES"

Etc., And keep them handy so that you can reach anything you need at a seconds notice. (**the secrets of the Universe or any project that you worked on in the past 30 years**)

Again, so if your boss asks why you didn't finish your project, always blame it on others

"I didn't have the information."

And if he says, how come? Say,

"Joe Blow never gave it to me."

Or if Joe Blow says,

"I gave it to you."

PROTEST LOUDLY!

"You never did Joe! I flew this idea up the flagpole and you said that we didn't need it to complete this project. I came over to you several times and each time you repeated that they didn't need it. "

Always make up excuses as to why your co-workers didn't give you the correct information. Make them look like a fool for not giving it to you in front of everybody, especially your boss.

And show the boss and this idiot what you saved on a tiny scrap of napkin that was talked about at lunch!

"See, I saved it because I knew that it was important."

Afterwards, go over to this co-worker and say,

"You know Joe, you're a FUCK! You had this information." (as you wave this piece of paper napkin with scribbling on it)**"You told me that we didn't need it!"**

And again, go over to your boss with your **"proof"** ,

"See, Joe Blow had this information all of the time. He told me that I didn't need it! I'll NEVER trust him again!"

Make sure that the boss nods and agrees with you every time that this happens.

And while you're making up your excuses folder, always give your co-workers the wrong information even if you have the correct info. (**but never e-mail this to them**) Only do it in passing them by conversations.

"Say Joe, you asked me about the Schmuck report? I put it in the" do nothing folder" You can get all of the information that you need in there."

Then quick like a bunny go back and **move this to another folder!** Especially where this co-worker can't find it, but is obvious to everyone else. **Hey, you've got to do what you got to do!**

The key ingredient here is you have to make up an excuse a day, every day, especially when it comes to your work. Any co-worker is fair game, especially those who are at the same level as you are. Because if you can get these co-workers to be doubted, to have supervisors question their work ethic and their capabilities, then you are well on your way to becoming **THEIR BOSS!!**

So to become good at making excuses again, simply don't make any decisions. (**especially if you don't know anything about the subject**)

Another part included in making excuses is do not daydream at work. Never sit back and relax, somebody can sneak up behind you. So always look busy. Try to make combackers to anything anybody says. If somebody says,

"I hope that you're not sleeping (or relaxing) on company time" say,

"No, I'm deep in thought trying to come up with a solution for this. Why are you interrupting me? I'm very busy!"

So always retort to somebody's snide comment if you are doing something. Never let it pass. If you can't think of anything, say something and then at every opportunity, attack them.

"I see that you did not finish your report. What? Do I now have to pick up your work too!"

Never let them get away with anything!

CHAPTER 21

HOW NOT TO MAKE OBSERVABLE MISTAKES

This is a hard subject to master but you can do it if you remember the number one thing of all time: Everybody and I mean everybody (**including me**) makes mistakes; (**okay, okay, so maybe I only make small ones**) you just have to make sure that you cover up your shortcomings.

How? I'm glad that you asked that question. First, assemble all sorts of documents (**especially any that put you at risk**) and then make this file disappear. **REALLY!! It's that easy!** It is great for having major files all of a sudden disappear and you can do this quite easily in this age of computers. Say,

"It was all on the hard drive."

Then follow up with,

"I don't know what happened. When I logged off for the night it was there, but in the morning it was gone. Crazy huh?"

Then, always make up phony but logical sounding reasons on why you could not do something.

"It rained so hard even the cats and dogs were afraid to go out. I couldn't take them out for a walk."

So never tell the truth.

"The Sun didn't come up, so how did you expect my rooster to cock-a-doodle-doo?

Sidestep issues.

"The right side up is wrong. But it all really depends on what is the right side."

Try to explain away a goof in order to maintain a good image both for yourselves and others.

"Our group did the estimate correctly, it's just that the client changed his mind over five thousand times."

Then, always have a grab bag of excuses from which to choose:

"I didn't do it."

or

"It wasn't so bad."

Or

"Yes, but…"

So you have to maintain your reasons to have a biased account that is highly favorable to you.

"I didn't do it. If I had done it, the world as we know it would not be here anymore! And since as you can see that we are all here, I made the right choice."

People lie to avoid making observable mistakes because lying is effective; it does give you an edge. You will compete within and across workplaces, so you always need to look better than you actually are, whether it is for clients or especially bosses.

Deception in the course of saving yourself from being found out in a mistake is perfectly acceptable. Especially if you have to respond quickly in a stressful situation or pressures to look good. And you have to look good always.

So deception is a tactic of survival. But you're not looking to merely to survive, you are looking to dominate. Which is why you need to fabricate just about anything, big or small in any form of communication available, whether it be e-mail, on the phone or face-to-face.

Now with the telephone, there isn't any paper trail, and no physical interaction (**like in a face to face meeting**) So by personally removing yourself from a certain type of a situation, you can distance yourself from the consequences of whatever happened. You didn't get the important meeting notice given by the President himself, so you claim that your Blackberry must've malfunctioned.

"I can't believe that my Blackberry must have malfunctioned and that's why I didn't get the meeting notice."

or that you missed work because of food poisoning.

"I had the worst case of food poisoning that anyone can imagine. I was throwing up for 26 hours straight. I couldn't even LOOK at my Blackberry to see if there were any important meeting notices."

You can argue that you're not only saving your hide, you're also being smart.

So always make yourself look better,

"I'm right on top of this! You know that you always can count on me to get this project out on time and under budget."

And if you're late for a meeting, this is what you should do to avoid embarrassment,

"I was late because of all of the construction on MARS!! Why don't they do all of the out-of-this world work at night instead of during the day!"

You can also say that you have weekly physical therapy appointment's and that's why you can't come into the office until late in the day.

"You remember that I got hurt at the company picnic playing softball. Well, the therapy sessions are only given in the mornings and that's why I can't come in until after lunch."

Strategic lying to not make observable mistakes, but to advance yourself up the ladder, again is perfectly acceptable. **Everybody does it, so why not you**? The best way to keep your job then, is to give an excuse, any excuse that you can think of at the moment for a failed project,

"Nobody knew that the 7 year locust was in reality the 30 year locust; and you know what they do. So that's why the best corn crop of the decade was decimated."

or give an excuse for a mistake that you made,

"I was given the wrong information by the IT department (always blame them!) and you know how slow they are, so I had to go on whatever information that I had at the moment."

or a deadline that you missed,

"I was told by their Vice-President that we didn't have to give it to them on Friday, and that we could wait until Monday."

The secret to not making observable mistakes is simple, it's really like gravity. **(remember Isaac Newton?)**What gets thrown up in the air **(like floating a crazy idea)**,or dropping an apple from a tree branch, must come down. However, before it comes down you have to make up a logical sounding reason for it not doing what you want it to do. You must be willing to lie like you're pants are on fire!

"I have found a new type of wave called the hyper wave, I can demonstrate it, but we have to wait until a black hole appears in the sky before we can test out my theory. It is light years before Einstein's Theory of Relativity."

Make sure that you forget to tell them that the next black hole to appear is 300 years in the future.

Don't be afraid or be worried of what people will think. Because if you do, that is from having a low self-esteem. To be a success at not making observable mistakes you have to raise your self-esteem and think that you are perfect; **(You are!!)** you do not make mistakes- others do.

So do this now. Write memos to your boss telling him what you did was so great **(inventing hyper waves)** and how great this project is or how great this chore came out.

"Yeah, I saved 14 sheets of paper, by not crunching them up in little balls and throwing them out. "

Now if someone should question what you did, or what you said without documentation, hold a meeting. These are really great places to put the blame on others and get them off your back and onto theirs.

"I didn't authorize that!"

to somebody wanting to know who let you work on a top secret project. Or if you do hold a meeting, then cancel it at the last minute. You can do wonderful things like closing the door to the meeting room and putting a sign on the door directing them to another office. This way you can sleep in piece, or offload decisions and also feel important.

The practical alternative to work is holding a meeting a day for maybe 7 hours. This way you don't have to make any decisions period so you won't make any mistakes.

Then, always have others assemble stuff for you, so you do not have to make a decision, and if they are wrong, you can always blame them. Say,

"Jim, can you just give me your opinion on this. I really value your insight on this subject." (the world coming to an end)

and if it doesn't, you can say,

"See, Jim said this and it just isn't true!!"

You can always say that you were not aware of the data because it was not part of your job or that you didn't review the other parts of the project not related to your part. (**like the rest of the Universe**)

And if they press you for an answer, say,

"I'll have to take it under advisement and get back to you."

Or

"I'll get back to you." (AND NEVER DO!)

The secret to not making observable mistakes are self-preservation first and foremost as well and being excused in the name of a higher truth. (**your job!**) So the order of not making observable mistakes comes down to this order:

1. **Self- protection**
2. **Greed**

3.   **Self-aggrandizement**
4.   **Political ambition**
5.   **Erotic pleasure**

You can also add to your list of not making observable mistakes those that are promulgated out of compassion and tact. But try not to do that since you want to be seen as someone who is exact and not someone who is a wimp or one who looks too simple-minded. But basically, professions have been built around their prevalence.

Making mistakes is unavoidable, so you just might as well learn to deal with it. The world is unavoidably full of hucksters and liars who hide their mistakes, i.e. The Emperor's new clothes, for example.

"Oh isn't it nice and isn't it fine and isn't it beautiful."

But you have to make a decision to make a statement and never deviate from it. Say,

"I'm not going to talk about it."

So always know your liabilities, understand what is needed to prove to people and prove it.

"I told you that the world was going to say that I am the greatest, AND I AM!"

Do not make any other statements except like the above. Just enforce this the rhetoric about your leadership and that you don't make mistakes (**OTHERS DO!!**) and that everybody should just take you on faith. (**like the Emperor's new clothes**) If somebody says that's not going to happen, just say,

"Get SERIOUS!!"

And then walk away. Even if that offends everyone in your office, just keep up the myth of your invincibility.

Then you have to be exact and correct when you give someone information. Because if it's not correct **"they"** will try to cut your heart out. Say anything on the spur of the moment.

"I gave Jim the information that I had at the moment. My back-up is in my files, which I told you was lost when the server crashed last week. Ask IT if they can recover it."

Never leave a conversation until **"they"** do. Be like sticky gum,**"** **I'm stuck on you."** Because the first one who leaves first- **LOSES!!** Be like the last one to leave shuts out the lights. Even if they caught up with you on the way to the bathroom, stay put. Even if you have to pee in your pants don't leave the scene of this until they do.

So become a very likeable character. Be affable, amiable, show a lot of enthusiasm. So always listen to what somebody has to say and give them time to speak, never interrupt them.

You need to assume whatever attitude or positions are needed to survive. Instead of trying to get work done, you have to keep covering your ass. Make sure that you document everything, to the point where you might have to have a pocket tape recorder at meetings. (**Always a good idea!**)

So again, look at those who survived massive lay-offs. It's not the one who was the smartest or the brightest, or even the one who did the most work, it's the one who covered their ass every single time and documented what was said 6 months or a year ago, that now is coming out.

Also, count the number of mistakes that not only you make but what others make. **THIS IS VERY IMPORTANT!!**

Keep a chart with all of the people in your department or company and what was either **"real"** mistakes, or **"perceived"** mistakes. It doesn't really matter if it was real or perceived. Upper management thinks that all mistakes are

"TERRIBLE!!"

and that it really doesn't matter to them if you were rushed to make a decision or were given the wrong information. It only boils down to what **"they"** think is a grievous mistake.

So say to your boss,

"Just for your information, Jim has already made 14,568 (always give an actual number) mistakes this week and I have not made any. This has cost the company million of dollars!"

And then circulate this chart of mistakes to **EVERYBODY!!**

Of course, if you have made any mistakes, you definitely should not report it on this chart **(even if found out!)** Again,, you want to circulate and have an air about you of invincibility and that you are perfect and that you don't make mistakes, only others do.

"Bury" your mistakes and selectively tout **(your occasional wins)** for self-promotion. You have to be bombastic solely to garner attention. Yell and scream your way **(which is the ONLY way)** to tout what you have done.

Be like the pundits on TV and in the press. They make all sorts of predictions and they **NEVER** come true and **NOBODY** says to them that they made a mistake.

DO THE SAME!!

IGNORE! IGNORE! IGNORE!!

If someone says that it was you who made a mistake,

SAY IT ISN'T SO!

"No, it is not true."

Say that you were right 99% of the time and that it's only 1% that could possibly be blamed on statistical evidence and **NOT YOU!**

Again, say that you are perfect and you don't make mistakes, it never happened.

So remember, the first one who gives in loses. So don't be the one who gives in.

DENY! DENY! DENY!

Remember? Keep repeating this.

However, what happens if **"they"** absolutely can prove that it was you. You made a mistake. And it was terrible, and how can you have done such a stupid thing. Simple. **LIE!!**

Again, say it wasn't you, but somebody else in the company with the same name **(that's always a good one)** Or say that you acknowledge that there might have been a mistake, but it definitely was not you.

It was somebody who looked like you, and people are always saying that you must have a twin working here.

SPIN! SPIN! SPIN!

Never stop putting the blame on someone but you, even if they positively corner you with pictures of you doing it, or your signature, or a memo saying to do this "**terrible**" mistake.

As I stated earlier, the first one who gives in loses, so don't lose, just refuse to accept any responsibility for the mistake. It wasn't you. Keep repeating this all day long, as long as it takes, until people stop blaming you for the mistake.

And as always, add spin that clearly shows you not to be at fault, what took place, and show how more of the same mistakes will lead to more problems. Most important, don't just cast blame (**JIM DID IT!!**) recommend a solution and ask for action. Attach a copy of your original memo requesting the help that never came. Send copies to everyone who has even the slightest connection to the issue. Even if the mistake was sudden and there's only one memo, you are covered.

Always say to yourself,

"Am I covered?"

The answer had always better be yes.

CHAPTER 22

MANIPULATING PEOPLE

If you don't try to manipulate people to your way of thinking, others will try to do it to you. That's why you have to do it first

BEFORE!

They even get a chance to do it to you. For example, the next time that the boss wants you to sit in on a meeting or take on a new assignment, don't say that you can't because you're loaded down with work, or you're headed home or out to lunch. Instead, tell him you'd be happy to help, but doing so would interfere with something else that you are already tackling

FOR HIS BOSS!!

And say that it was he who told you to help **HIS** boss out by giving you this priority.

"Mr. Jones, you told me to give Mr. Right my absolute commitment to getting his project done ASAP. Should I interrupt HIS priority for this?"

Spin, and don't be timid about it.

"Mr. Right said that the client was very clear about ensuring the delivery of this today."

Emphasize to him the dangers of postponing what **HIS** boss wants and let him make the choice. I am sure that he will say,

"No, no, that's okay. You can do this after you finish Mr. Right's project."

It's hard to say no to the boss, but use him as your scapegoat when saying no to everyone else.

"Mr. Jones has me on a rush project for Mr. Right."

Simply tell others, that you'd love to help, but that your boss has buried you under tons of work that has to be finished immediately.

"Jerry, I'd really love to help you out, but I'm up to my eyeballs in rush projects that Mr. Jones has me on."

Now, let's suppose you have your back against the wall with all of these priorities, and other people come to you for help. Everyday (**unless you live on Jupiter**) there are always crisis's that appear and demand immediate attention.

"Len, this problem in the field just came in and you have to work on this immediately."

It doesn't matter if you're under the gun and working on 27 other priorities, things like this happen daily. Usually, under most circumstances, you'll never get anything done if you continually allow daily interruptions to take priority over what should be your top priority. And what is your top priority? (**in actual order of priority**)

Keeping your job!

Pleasing the boss!

Advancing your career!

Other than doing these 3 major items, don't drop everything and try to help what others want. Say,

"I'm sorry Bill, I can't do it now. Can you wait until next year?"

You should make up a daily list of priorities and keep telling anyone who comes over to you.

"Would you just look at this list of priorities I have that Mr. Jones and Mr. Right have me on! I'll have to work right thru Christmas and

New Year's and maybe by July 4th, I'll be able to get my head above water."

Again, you first have to protect **YOUR interests and YOUR priorities.** Nothing else matters, even protecting yourself from other bosses on what you are doing.

"Mr. Wrong, Mr. Right has me on this super priority. Can you check with him first. Thanks, I appreciate it."

You should also hide from co-workers and even other bosses what you feel is the true priority. And what is that?

KEEPING YOUR JOB!

PLEASING THE BOSS!

ADVANCING YOUR CAREER!

You first have to protect your interests no matter what.

Then, don't put up with co-workers or underlings who are difficult or not helpful or even antagonistic, especially when you have gone to great lengths to help them. You must start to take action against them at once if there is any sign of trouble. If you don't do this, it will show that you are a pushover, and they will gladly do it every time that they see you.

This comes about primarily at meetings. So, use meetings to identify people that you want to manipulate. Don't use meetings to listen to others babble on and on. And they do if you let them. Make use of the time wasted by others during meetings. Most meetings drag on for hours. Don't believe them when they say it's from 10AM to 11AM- it'll keep on going till past 3PM if you let them. Volunteer to make the minutes,

"I'll take the minutes."

Then at 11:30 AM, say,

"I have another meeting at 12."

But if your boss is in the meeting, never leave the meeting before him. Watch your boss.. Sit across from him and a little bit off to the side of him. See what upsets him, what kinds of statements and comments turn him off. And above all, see who says those things. Also, see what pleases your boss.

What did that person say to him that made him look pleased. Try to emulate that pattern in future meetings.

You must also plan your time to allow for unforeseen meetings and other interruptions that come up every day. Always allow extra time to get things done.

Now, if a person forgot to bring you something that you needed to get the job done, write a memo on it. Make it clear who was at fault,

"He Was!!"

for the schedule delay, and also make damn sure that the person wasn't you. Add to this memo that you were not at fault, what actually took place, and say that if that person doesn't get it right the next time it will lead to bigger problems. Also, bring this problem to the boss and say that you are only bringing this problem to him, because you know his priorities and that you have a plan for correcting it making certain that his priorities are met.

In manipulating people, you need to develop a plan. And the first one that you have to manipulate is your boss. Don't say that you can't do this – **you most certainly can!** You have to develop a plan and see if your boss is reacting to the way that you want him to.

Purposely tell others untruths and then try to get them into trouble. For example, take pictures or document something that someone did wrong and circulate it to the higher ups. Say,

"See, This is proof that engineering did not know what they were doing. If Maintenance had been given the opportunity, this goof-up would not have happened!"

Now if you are in Engineering, you can say the same exact thing about Maintenance that they did.

Once you get to know your boss, you should look for signs that you can tell whether or not your are succeeding. If he has nice things to say,

"That was a great job you did Len."

Then you know that you are succeeding. If he doesn't say anything, ask him how you did after you did your job. So always be good, don't be wrong – at least try to give that impression.

Also, if you get something good (a new update of a computer version) say it aloud and show it off.

"See what I just got! I am special!!"

Do this especially if you are the only one in the office to get it. In addition always have an excuse,

"Oh, it's lunchtime." (like you are going out to lunch)

or

"It's quitting time."

Anything not to do something to delay or not meet a schedule.

If you give someone something to do that you did 99% of the work and you ask them for help, blame them for any mistakes in it, especially if it's yours.

"This is all fucked up!!"

and say to the person directly,

"You fucked this up. What I gave you was perfect, and all that I asked you to do was finish just one small part of it."

Again, try to be as loud as possible so that all eyes are on you.

The, always explain why you couldn't do something and just do this all day long.

"I didn't have the information."

or

"I was rushed into making a decision."

Then always defend yourself. Say that you were working on another job and that's why you couldn't do something **(even if you're just sitting around doing your usual nothing)**

Here's another always. Always whine and complain about why you can't start or can't finish the work. Always act like an infant, uttering aloud any comment. Also, use what kids say, like,

"Cool!"

to anything good.

You should also pick up on something that someone did.

"This is not right!"

Even if 99% of it is correct and there is a missed comma, pounce on it.

"Can't you get anything right! There is a comma missing! What else is missing?"

Make them feel that you are in charge of everything and are checking everybody's work.

Even as you talk to someone, always look around and see who's watching you. Then also talk to them or make a comment on what just happened.

"I can't believe the idiots that we have here!"

You can also add (**but say it aloud**)

"I don't want anybody bothering me or talking to me today! I AM SO BUSY!!"

Also, when you are overworked always mention to your boss and everybody else around you,

I'M LOSING MY MIND! I'M SO BUSY!!"

So always complain and whine that your co-worker is holding you up and that's why you can't get the job done.

"Jim is holding me up. I can't get my work done because of him!"
ATTACK AND BLAME!!

Don't let them get to you first. If someone say,

"Where's the Schmuck file?"

You say,

"I don't have it."

And then **ATTACK,**

"You probably took it. You were the last one to have it."

If you are in a meeting, always start the meeting by saying that the other guys are not giving you the right information and that they are holding you up from doing your job.

"I can't do my work until Mechanical gives me all of the correct loads. I can't proceed with anything because of this."

Then, don't do any work. Especially when there is something that you don't know how to do. Delay it and delay it for as long as you can. Look like you're working on it but don't ask a co-worker or the boss. A good tactic here is to take off sick the day that it's due. Call your boss and say that you're sorry that you got sick and you know that it's due and ask him if there was someone else who could do it for you. And joy of joys, if he assigns someone who **DOES** know how to do it and it's not exactly right, tell the boss that they messed it up. That if you hadn't gotten sick, you would've had it out on time and correct. Make sure that you always blame others for you getting work or even extra work to do.

"Jim left at 4:30 and I had to wind up doing HIS work. That's bullshit! I have my own work to finish."

Again, always ask a co-worker how you would do something **(that you don't know how)** and then privately go over to the boss and say,

"Mr. Schmuck, how does this look?"

If he says that it's shit, tell him that your co-worker told you to do it. However, if he says that it's great, say that **you did it!**

In a joking manner to him, say,

"Just look at this work that I'm doing- it's fantastic! Don't you think that I really do great work!"

And then laugh, like you're joking **(but you mean it!)** Every time that you see your boss, even if it is a thousand times a day, always have this big smile on your face **(like a big stupid grin)** that you are happy to see him. And when you see him, always talk about others to your boss **(you are, aren't you?)**

"Did you see that Jim is reading the paper until 10 in the morning and I'M BUSTING MY ASS!! What's going on here? Where's the justice?"

You also need to cover up your shortcomings. Again if you do not know how to do something, say to your boss,

"Mr. Reid, I'm SOOOOOO busy with the Schmuck project, can Jim do the (fill-in anything here) so I can concentrate on getting it out." (but never do it!)

Each day, like it's by rote, stop by and blatantly brown-nose your boss. (keep in his good graces) Always ask,

"I'm going to the (store, coffee shop, etc.). Can I bring you back something?"

Then another good one is to copy anything that is useless **information** (especially useless-the time of day in China, etc.) and show this to your boss,

"Can you use this? It shows all of the time zones in China as well as Outer Mongolia. It's good if we get work there."

Or

Always make up standard details that your type of business uses (charts, graphs, whatever) and circulate it to others, especially your boss and say,

"Do you want a copy of this? It's really a great time saver."

Or if you have something of interest in your field, a shortcut to do something, always ask your boss,

"Do you want a copy of this?"

Or if you have standard details that everybody in the world uses, say,

"Here's a copy of the TV channel guide. It saves time when you're trying to find something quickly."

Then, when you see your boss late in the day, say,

"Hi, how is your day going so far?"

And don't just say good night to your boss when you leave, say,

"I hope that you have a pleasant evening. I'll see you in the morning."

And then in the morning, when you first see your boss, make a general statement about nonsense,

"Good morning Mr. Jones. The program guide that you got us is so cool."

And another thing about saying good morning to your boss. As soon as you see him, say good morning to him, even if you have to shout from across the room or across the floor or across the state,

"GOOD MORNING MR. JONES!"

Next, try to become the filing place for your boss. If something is done (a **transmittal, folder,e-mail, a napkin from last night's dinner!**) say,

"Do you want me to hold on to it for you?"

And always try to make standards that make it save time. A train schedule with the times that it is pulling into the closest station, the dates of the new and full moon when vampires come out, **ANYTHING**- when dental check-ups are due. Show the boss; tell him that you are working on it on **YOUR OWN TIME** to make it easier, not only for you, but for him and for everybody else. Even if you see your boss or a higher up in the bathroom, always say something to them,

"We've got to stop meeting like this." And then laugh, or say anything to bend their ear that is non-threatening,

"The weather is crazy for this time of year."

Also, keep track of the number of tasks that you do. And always keep reminding your boss or higher ups of all that you did.

"Remember, 2 weeks ago, I did 53 PROJECTS IN ONE DAY!!" (WOW, WHAT A MAN)

Then say aloud, **VERY LOUD**,

"I AM GOOD! I AM SO GOOD!!"

Every time that you finish something ordinary, like stapling pages together or making copies, always tell your boss,

"Mr. Jones, I'm taking care of you."

And then nod your head and smile very broadly. Make a statement that you saw something in error wherever you go in the company, especially if it's not even in your field of expertise. Go over to your boss and say,

"Yeah, those heating guys really fucked it up royally. Do you know what I saw them do?"

And proceed to tell him in infinite detail what you witnessed.

"The Sun is supposed to shine directly over your office so that you look good, and they changed the direction of the Sun!!"

And by chance if somebody makes an error **(say if something was delivered to the wrong place)** say aloud,

"OOOOH, look what they did! Can't they get anything straight!"

And then go over to your boss and again say this with a disgusted perturbed look,

"The (heating) department can't get anything right. They need a whole new shake-up from top to bottom."

Next, ask someone on your team or on your job or a co-worker,

"How are you doing with this?"

This sets up that **YOU** are controlling the project or what they are working on. And next, go directly over to your boss and say,

"Damn heating department. They are always holding us up." Then say aloud,

"We've (or better I've) got so much to do!!!"

You should always try to interrupt somebody who is doing something so you can get your job out first. Let's say that somebody is using the copy machine, you say,

"Jim, this is a RUSH! Can I break in?"

or

"C'MON! Use some other machine – I have a SUPER RUSH job here!"

Then, if someone doesn't do something that you needed, always pounce on them and talk about it with glee to your boss or those higher up,

"He totally missed it!"

Also, you should look for back-up in talking to your boss or higher ups when you can't answer a question. Ask a co-worker or your boss,

"Help me out here Jim."

For information or an answer that you have no clue about. Or if you make a statement to a higher up, always say to your boss,

"Isn't that right?"

People (co-workers, bosses, higher ups) are constantly trying to second guess you. Even if you had the proof dead to rights, they'll say,

"Well, you should have thought of that."

So prepare for everything that could possibly go wrong and even if you do,they will always ask you,

"Why did you spend so much time on this?"

Tell your boss or higher ups,

"Well, I had soo much work to do and you know that Jim messed it all up. So I had to re-do whatever he did and that's why it took more time than usual. But I tried to get it out as fast as possible. I really did."

Save your own skin and try to ingratiate yourself with the people that can do you some good. Also, and this is very important to manipulating people, do not have a grasp on what it takes to be a nice person. If your boss come over to a co-workers desk, looking for something, always ask,

"Are you looking for something particular? Maybe I can help."

Then always show and tell your boss everything (**especially if it's old**) like you are discovering a new way to take a piss.

"Hey Mr. Reid, did you see that tuna is now coming in a can. Wow! What will they think of next."

First and foremost, find out what your boss's or supervisor's favorite food is, then buy an extra one at lunch or breakfast and say,

"I know how much you like (whatever- banana chip muffins), so I got an extra one for you. I love them too."

Again**, petty but effective**. Always get the brownie points in.

You have to be exact and correct when you give someone information. If it's not correct **"they"** will try to cut your heart out. Never say anything on the spur of the moment. Always say that you don't have all of the information required to give an answer, and that you'll get back to them. Then, never make any decisions, and always have back-up.

Actually, you should have others assemble stuff for you so you don't have to make a decision. And if they are wrong, you can always blame them. Say,

"Jim, can you just give me your opinion on this? (is the world coming to an end)

and if it doesn't, you can proudly say,

"See. Jim said this and it isn't true!"

Also, if you don't want to do something that is beneath you **(like doing something that you don't know how to do)** say to a co-worker,

"Jim, could you do this? I have to be in Tibet in the morning and I don't want to get my hands dirty with the ink."

And again, don't make any decisions. **(especially, if you don't know anything about the subject)** So do this now: constantly hide out. Become very good at long lunches and sharpening pencils. Because of the way that most organizations are structured, pass the buck to someone else. Just don't comment on it, approve or reject it. If you want to advance quickly, try to offend no one and also give the appearance of doing a great job. Say to no one in particular, but so that everybody in the office,

"I am doing such a great job, I'm surprised that I haven't gotten a promotion yet."

So you have to look credible in appearance and appear self-assured and in control. Then you really need to have incredible arrogance. Continually avoid any conversation that is related to the meat of the matter. Do everything that you can to avoid talking about whatever the conversation is about. So always try to put down somebody with a funny or cutting comment especially if you don't know anything about the subject.

"Hey Jim, the sun is coming up. You said it wasn't going to happen because of the solar eclipse. I guess you got that wrong."

Before doing something or taking on something, **THINK,** can someone make a wisecrack about this? If possible, wait until no one is watching what you are doing.

You can always say that you were not aware of the data because it was not part of your job or that you didn't review the other parts of the project not related to your job. But a lot of times, **"they"** will say you should have known this and looked at **ALL** parts of the project, not just your part. You should then say,

"I'm not the project manager or the supervisor who's responsibility is to review all parts of the project for correctness before it goes out. My part was very minor - just to dot the I's and cross the t's."

Also, always try to see what errors and omissions others have done, even if you have no business in questioning it. **DO IT!!** This way you can look like you're looking out for the company or your department.

But, you don't have to be the source of all information in the company. If somebody should ask you,

"How come Joe Schmuck isn't in today?"

Just don't give an answer whether or not you know – **LIE!** Or make up a blank response.

"Joe Schmuck's not in? I didn't notice. Gee, it's just that I'm so busy."

Always be foxy, cagey, don't give them the real answer even if you know it.

Also, generate a lot of paperwork daily – especially on nonsense. Your boss and those higher up should see a memo or something initiated by you **EVERY DAY!** And if you transmit copies of stuff that you send out, make sure that you have different times and different dates on them. Make sure that there are too many in a day and that they can comment on it. Spread the work out so that you look like you work on different things daily.

Then, if somebody makes a comment about where your work is (**status**), you say,

"You're talking to the Engineering Department. We are way ahead of deadline."

Make sure that your boss hears this and then say it so that your boss can hear it,

"Isn't that right, Mr. Reed?"

And of course, he will say,

"You tell them Len!"

So be specific to a boss or higher up. Give a number.

"I worked on 23 drawings last week and this week I'm working on 32 projects with a combined total of 564 drawings."

Also, always say that you had so much work to do last week and worked six million hours overtime to get it out. (**which you did not get paid for**) And because it backed up all of the other projects that you're working on so you now have to work 20 million **MORE** hours of overtime this week, and it will delay getting the 347,000 drawings that you are working on.

So if somebody asks how's it going, say,

"It's like a 5 alarm fire with fatalities, is better then what's going on!!"

Finally, always try to find shortcuts to doing something and then impress your boss with it.

"Yeah, I just found a shortcut to China by digging straight down!" and then say,

"Pretty cool,huh?"

CHAPTER 23

NETWORKING

To expand your career, you have to expand yourself. It's more than **"It's not what you know, but who you know that counts."**

Contacts are very important. Only those who aren't ambitious are bitter enough to accuse those who are better connected or more widely well thought of, receive a promotion or a new job. Networking is the real secret and the real strength.

When you have others that you can count on, you can look up to help you and guide you then, that's networking. In building a network, you have to take some bold actions, but not too bold. You must first prove yourself by working hard on your ambition and making it known. (**but not too well known**) You must first prove yourself and earn the trust of your colleagues.

There are still two types of networks –"old boy" and "new girl". They are composed of men or women who all went to the same school or belong to the same country or tennis club.

The premise behind networking, it is the practice of contacting everyone that you know, and everyone that they know to ask for their advice and support. Sometimes it works and sometimes it doesn't, so don't believe all of the hype that it is the greatest thing since sex, it isn't. But most of the time it does work and can help you. So to do this, you call people that you know and meet people who want to help you. You need to tap your network of friends, family members, acquaintances, and anyone else who would help you. But the question here is why would they help you? So, if they need a favor you would help them. It's really an old item.

"It's , You scratch my back and I'll scratch yours."

This has always gone on from the time of the ancient Greeks to now. Trying to find a better job by calling people you don't know and asking them for help sounds dreadful, but cold calling can sometimes help also. But, if you have friends and colleagues who can help you to find a job, it still is,

" what can you do for me."

An effective networking relationship helps. The people you contact talk about themselves and what is going on in their career. If these contacts can match you and your new employer a favor, they hope it will be returned one day. You are taking information from that person now and you hope to give it back sometime at a later date.

So, make a list of people who might have information on available jobs, or better yet, who know other people who might be helpful. Even though many of these people may never hear about job openings, they are important because of the many friends and contacts to whom they'll refer you to.

Linkedin, Facebook, and Twitter all will help. And even Monster and Career Builder can help sometimes.

Decide what you'll say when you reach people that you've contacted. If the person responds that they don't know of any job openings, all you say is that what you really want now is their opinion of the hiring market and the names of colleagues and friends who might know of openings. People in every field will at least know something from the grapevine of what they heard is going on.

If you get a name or two, thank them and give the contact when you call these names. Continue to contact the person every month or so and ask for new leads. Don't become a pest, but you need to be relentless in using your network contacts.

So set networking goals. Determine whom you want to meet and what you want to find out from each person. Make a listing and evaluate the types of people who are the most helpful and try to contact others who share their same personality. You should devote at least 30 minutes each day to your network schedule for it to get results. Frankly, I do 30 minutes before starting work and 30 minutes after starting work, so before I leave for the day I've met or talked to at least 1 hour's worth of people, whether they can help me now or not.

Most often, people you like and with whom you share common interests likely will become your most valued contacts over time. So, when you network, develop a friendship other than getting something from them. If they like you, they will probably think of you when an opening comes up. Firms are always looking for good help, and they will always ask their employees, **"say, do you know someone who does.....?"**

Say, of course you do and give names whether they are available or not.

You should also become active in professional or community organizations. Again, networking isn't easy, and a lot of times you will come up empty, but it is an effective strategy that you need to employ whether it helps you or not. Just overcome your reluctance to take advantage of others and try to network.

Networking then, is basically a means to meet people in a setting that easily carries over from the office environment. It's the most comfortable way to meet peers these days. So, instead of trying to make connections just as exclusive clubs, on golf courses and a women or men only functions, try the following:

1. **Social events, such as dinner parties.**
2. **Health Clubs**
3. **Tennis Courts (or Racquetball Courts)**
4. **Church Clubs**
5. **Professional Organizations**

6. **Alumni Organizations of all types of schools, not just Ivy League Universities**
7. **Community Affairs**
8. **Charity functions**
9. **Ski Clubs (even if you don't know how to ski)**
10. **Running Clubs (even if you never ran in your life)**
11. **Gym's**
12. **Vacation Places where the rich and famous hang out such as Martha's Vineyard, St. Bart's, etc.**

Also, look in the daily newspaper or on-line to find out what's going on in your town and just go there. Most people come to these places because they are interested in friendship, which has a business and a social aspect. Women have taken their cues from men and have capitalized on what men have done for years. They are doing it in a very professional manner. It is a great networking system as respect of one professional to another. But women, also go because they are more interested in romance than in business deals or new jobs. **That's the nature of women.**

Make a list of your business and professional associates and resolve to have some lunches or phone catch-ups with the people who make or break you.

"Jerry, what are you doing for lunch? I need to catch up on things."

Compliment a peer or a subordinate each day for one week.

"Martha, kudos on putting that report together. The client called and said it was great. Good Work!!"

Maybe the club you are interested in joining doesn't meet during the summer, but be ready for the first meeting in the fall.

"Say John, Not only do I want to join the club, I want to give a presentation at the first meeting on my ideas for several informal meetings during the year."

Don't pass up the chance to represent your company in trade-association activity. So don't look down on such functions and resist any temptation to be too busy**; Go to these association functions**. You'll come back knowing people who work for your competitors. If they're high level and impressed with you, they be a source of a career opportunity.

But speaking from personal experience, some of this is actually b.s. Sure, they'll tell you that they want you to join their company and when push comes to shove, and you call them and say that they offered you a job, they'll say,

"Well, that was before. I only hinted that it might be a good idea."

PURE BULLSHIT!!

It's nice to go to these things, and you'll meet a lot of people, but don't put all your hopes on these **"promises"**. They never really come to pass.

Also, never pass up an invitation to appear in forums or panel discussions **(the merits of salt or no salt in a Margerita)** They can be a quick way to become known in your industry. Don't wait for the President of the association,write or phone them and say that you just discovered a new way to have sex **(that should get their attention!)** or some other great idea that you have which will interest the membership. Most people do not volunteer or even go to most meetings, so if you can offer something new on an old idea **(sex in a moving car!)** – why not? They are always looking for ways to gain exposure.

Then never pass up an invitation to play in a company or other company's golf or fishing trip, so that you can get to know other people.

"I wouldn't miss the free beer."

It doesn't matter if you don't play golf or have ever gone fishing – pretend **(nobody is going to say that you don't even play to handicap or have to catch the limit.)**

And don't try to work out alone at the gym. Try to learn racquetball or basketball whenever you can. You will get to know other people from different fields and you may never know who can help you or get you contacts.

"Say, Phil, I know that you're a printer – can you tell me who does your billing?"

But there really are fundamental rules of networking that is effective. If you can, try to get people to have a private lunch or dinner with you. Try to be known as someone who knows others and whom others consider worth knowing. **One guy that I know has 6000 contacts**! Now that's networking!!

Networking is one sure way to build relationships, and reinforce client connections. It can also build your career. However, I have to keep saying that even if you have 6 million contacts, it may not help when you really need it. People will say, "Yeah, I'll do it "and **they never do**! But even still, try to market the professional services to people who either know who you are, or even if they haven't a clue. For instance, at corporate events, take the opportunity to improve your name recognition and perception of who you are and what company you work for.

I've always felt that time is measured in 3 ways professionally. If you're early, then you're on-time, if you're on time, then you're late, and if you're late, then you're useless as a business contact.

So show up early; and look like a professional, that means bring plenty of business cards.

"Here's my card, can I have yours?"

Eat early, so that you can work the crowd. (**Do not eat to dullness**)

You should target prospects, so know who's going to be there and what you need to bring with you to outline your ideas.

"I just invented hyper-waves; it will take you to another dimension – want to try it?"

Let the other person talk first –what do they do? Then, in a few seconds, tell them what you do.

"I'm a lobbyist for the S and M Group. I know it's a tough subject to talk about, but have you ever tried it?"

If you are standing next to another person, bring them into the conversation, especially if you know them.

"Bill, this is John Smith – he works for the Puritanical party. You should ask him what he did at Salem. What a witch hunt!"

You should try to walk around the room at least 2 or three times, stopping at each person and get some face to face time with each. Try to make them laugh. Most people want to do business with confident and enjoyable people.

Always stay until the end. Remember, the first one who leaves early **LOSES!** The later you leave, the more contacts that you will make.

Remember what President Kennedy said," Ask not what your country can do for you, ask what you can do for your country." You can network your way thru life, asking for stuff with no action on your part. But, that is not the way to network. **Always ask what you can do for your contacts and not what they can do for you.**

You must also have the guts to complete the networking. It's not just e-mailing them on Lindedin or Facebook, but if you want to meet a mayor, governor, senator or president of a company, you must go do it. Make the necessary visits or phone calls e-mails to their office. Especially camp out in their waiting room, and tell the receptionist that you are not leaving until you see them. **(however, if they call Security, I would leave)**

You should make a listing of the influential people that you can keep on your computer. These lists can be categorized by occupation, city, state, etc. You never know when you might need a lawyer, doctor, banker, or politician. I also keep phone numbers of cops that I know, **(you never know when you may need a ticket fixed)** local hospitals, fire fighters, etc. One of the easiest ways to build a large name file is by using the friend of a friend concept. Each of your friends can give you contacts who can help you in the long run. Get them in your debt and then collect over time who owes you and only collect on them when you have to.

Also, every time you promise to do something, jot down on your hand held device or on a card or paper napkin, the exact thing that you promised and what needs to be followed up. It does work. One of the most important reputation building qualities you can develop is to follow through on what you promise regardless of how minor it is. People will remember that you are reliable.

People that you know are not just the connections to help you get a job. A lot of times, they may try but cannot help in that regard. That doesn't mean that you should forget them, just because they didn't come to your rescue. But, take it with a grain of salt –if they can help you, fine –but don't put all your eggs in that one basket, because you will find that all the eggs are broken.

CHAPTER 24

ADD STRENGTH TO YOUR DEMEANOR

Adding strength to your demeanor means building your self-esteem. Higher self-esteem makes us better at seeing opportunities and pursuing them, and even makes people want to be around us. These are the ones who say,

"You can trust me and depend upon me."

You need to project an image that tells others what your desire is. This image is more of an attitude and a manner than just dress. You have to look like you know what you are doing. You move and act purposely, deliberately, even when just walking. You have to be observant, noticing and recording things mentally, not just gazing abstractedly into the distance. Your attire should not call attention to yourself and you should have an absence of wrinkles and a very proper fit to your clothes.

Your demeanor must show an air of energy and vitality. Successful people have an image that sets them apart from others. It's not because of their accomplishments, but because of their image that they portray. This perception becomes a self-fulfilling prophecy. Successful people are expected to do well, and when they do achieve something, it is noted and applauded. They are encouraged by their successes and the recognition they receive and they continue to act in ways that they know are approved. **Image becomes reality.**

The first step then, is to acknowledge the importance of image and to understand why it is so important. Your message must be like I stated earlier, **"You can trust me and depend upon me. I am like you. I share your values and understand what it takes to be successful."**

Corporations look for the persons who fit their style because such individuals provide the security of the familiar. So the answer is not just a matter of ability or technical competence, but of the image that you project. So then what is the image that you should strive for, and how is that image portrayed? There are six specific items that you must project:

1. **Appearance**
2. **Purposeful**
3. **Competant**
4. **Analytical**
5. **Decisive**
6. **Confident**

So, **for appearance**, you dress one level up than your peers. And you must keep your physical weight down.

For **purposeful**, you stand and sit straight, you walk briskly, you look people directly in the eye and you know where you are going and how to get there.

For **competent,** you stay calm, you organize your thoughts before speaking, you do not appear rushed or harried, and you are brief, simple, specific and direct.

And for **analytical,** you do not accept generalities, you do more asking then telling, and you listen to the answers and respond to them.

For **decisive**, you always talk straight, state the problem and then give a decision, and you do not waste time.

So, for **confident,** you know the art of small talk, and you aren't tense with superiors, and you talk about challenges and not obstacles.

You can achieve all of these traits and they can be easily acquired. However, an improvement in your image will not happen overnight or because you just want to. You must make it happen consciously working to alter those aspects of your image that needs improvement. Persistence is the essential element in your program of change. These are human behaviors that you are changing and that only occurs in small steps, not overnight.

Start with one element of your image that is most in need of change. Focus only on this image. When you are satisfied with your improvement, choose one more. In a few months you'll see a distinct improvement in your image and in the way that others react to you.

Personal demeanor improvement is like physical exercise – you have to start and proceed as if your demeanor was out of shape instead of your body. Some people favor doing affirmations or goals that are important to them and reviewing them daily. They write their affirmation in a notebook or a journal and use these to put a fresh face on. I usually feel that what I want my inner self knows and as long as I repeat it to myself, I am guided to these traits that I want to possess.

If you commit to a program of positive change, you exert strength and will accomplish more. You will be happier than you thought possible. When your personal demeanor dominates your thinking, you will have the kind of power that makes the right things happen.

Voice quality contributes to your demeanor. A pleasant voice contributes to your standing in the world of business and whatever you want it to be. To improve your voice quality, try some of these techniques:

Listen to your voice on tape recorder, videocassette or voice mail. Keep repeating the same message until you are satisfied that you sound like a confident and magnetic person. If you find some voice problems like a monotonous tone, squakiness, too thick accent, mumbling, or talking too fast, identify them and try to get rid of them.

HOW?

PRACTICE! PRACTICE! PRACTICE!!!

Practice speaking to others using the voice quality that you think will convey the impression that you are a personally magnetic person. If you have to, consult a speech therapist or voice coach to help you identify any parts of your voice that detracts from the image that you are trying to project.

But changing the quality of your voice so dramatically can take years unless you are willing to do this daily. But by just modifying a few of your worst habits you will to able to make some noticeable improvements. Often more significance gives to the **WAY** something is said than to **WHAT** is said. A voice which includes a consistant tone denotes power, control and confidence thus contributing to your demeanor.

With self-discipline and practice, you can take on many of the traits, characteristics and actions of people who demonstrate strength in their demeanor. You can prod yourself to engage in some of the types of people who you admire that have a great deal of strength in their demeanor. You need to have a warmth and playfulness about you that people, both men and women, find comforting. You need to smile frequently, and make reassuring gestures with your eyes, face and hands. Speak in a low tone that soothes and reassures. Your presence must project emotional support, understanding and strength. People will tend to gravitate toward someone who has these qualities and you can develop them too.

The correct way to smile is also very important. Do what Asian airlines teach their female attendants how to smile correctly. You hold a chopstick in your mouth so that just the correct amount of teeth and smile is showing.

Remembering the names of people is a prerequisite for adding strength to your demeanor. Leaders have a superb ability to remember names, and if you want to become a leader, then you must do this also. And it's really quite easy. When you meet someone for the first time, carefully listen to the person's name and then repeat it several times to yourself. Concentrate when you hear the name. Ask for the person's business card and make an association with the person and his name.

You have to become a special sort of person. When you walk into a room, you want people to take notice. You need to have a striking presence. You also need to have a look in your eyes that you are ready to accept contact with whomever you may encounter. You have to look comfortably into another person's eyes and look right into them as if you are speaking to them from somewhere deep within you to a similar place.

You also need to hear people out and never rush someone to make your point or steal their thunder. And when you smile, your whole face should smile and from a place within you, a contagious form of laughter. Your presence must emanate from deep within you, reflecting the deep confidence that comes with self-acceptance. And because of that self-acceptance, you are "**all there**". You have the personal integrity to know that life is good. This is called the wellspring of confidence.

In adding strength to your demeanor you should be as lavish as possible with invitations. Always put your key business contact on every guest list that you are involved with. When any of the organizations has a special event, send out an invitation to or business contacts who might be interested. And never let a pair of tickets for anything go unused. If you are too busy to attend, send them to someone you thing might enjoy the event.

When sending out Christmas cards you your demeanor in there. Have the envelopes hand addressed and sign your name, don't just put a printed card in thee. Also add a few words of greeting.

To add strength to your demeanor, means to just suck it up and do it.

You have to show that you are outspoken, confident and persistant.

CHAPTER 25

JOIN THE COMPANY'S SOCIAL ACTIVITIES

Nothing gets a person advanced or promoted quickly as much as joining the company's social activities. Whether it's physical activities like softball, bowling, volleyball, soccer, touch football or going out for an after work drink or coffee or picnic or Christmas party.

Whatever!

Whatever it is, just by joining your co-worker's and better, even your supervisors, you can get a leg up in the company's social order. Social means extending yourself to be with other people, and not just being by yourself. So that means that you stay late just to be with your other co-workers, or you learn to play golf because your boss or boss's play golf. You learn to play tennis or racquetball because everybody in your workplace does. It doesn't matter if you enjoy it or not, you just have to do what everybody else does.

In fact, if it was me, I would organize other social activities, such as different Holiday parties. St. Patrick's day and go out for drinks and fun after work; Halloween, and have everybody dress up in costumes, July 4th, and have a barbeque (at your place or at a park); even on holidays that most people don't celebrate like Flag Day (and have everyone bring a flag). Also, you can organize a fishing trip, hunting trip, bird watching trip, **anything!!** So, not only will you become known as the company's social director, you will have people and boss's remember your name as a person who organizes and plans the company's activities.

Now, once you get better at planning the company's social activities, ask to start going to seminars or business conferences where you can mingle with the boss's. This way you can be alone with senior management even after work, and they can see what a team player you are. You will be able to bond better with your boss, his boss and others who would normally go to these business get-togethers. It's been my experience that when you are out of town at these conferences, boss's get to know you and vice versa, in a more relaxed atmosphere.

Company picnics can nourish a budding career. And a no-show will make no points with the boss. So if you've thought of skipping your company's annual picnic because you find such outings boring and artificial, **think again!** Your absence may be noted and frowned upon by management.

"I see that Jim didn't show. He's really doesn't seem to be a team player."

Your boss's boss may say to him. So to make sure that this can never happen, always go to the company picnic. No matter if you have to skip your family's functions that are on the same day, even at the same time, or in another time zone. In the larger scheme of things, they aren't important,

BUT THIS IS!!!!

The company outing still is as much a part of the summertime landscape as the July 4th fireworks. And at most companies, it's the only family-oriented social event of the year.

YOU CAN'T AFFORD TO MISS IT!!

Activities vary from company to company. Some like to have an old fashioned ranch barbecue (**hee haw!**) each year for their employees at their headquarters, while some like to hire a place and have their party at an amusement park or other place like a farm.

One of the places that I worked at liked to hire a very well known place in the country known for its Great Gatsby motif, and hire famous actors and musicians to liven up their party. It was great, and I got to meet some famous people as well as see my supervisor's let their hair down. Everybody could pose for pictures with their favorite stars and we would talk about it for months afterward and look forward to next year's.

If you know of any talent agents or people on TV or the movies, ask them if they would be able to supply actors, actresses, musicians, comedians, **anybody!** Even if you can't make it happen, at least let your bosses know that you tried to do it.

"I almost had the President of the United States come to our picnic, but he was too busy."

And then tell them who you were able to get instead,

"I know this guy who knows this guy, and guess what, the President's butler will stand in for him at our party!"

You should always try to get somebody to come, even if it's the janitor or cleaning lady and make a fuss that it was almost impossible to get them, but because you are a really special person and the world knows it, they will come because **YOU** asked them to!

The picnic is one way companies attempt "to create organizational cohesiveness"and a sense of extended family. By attending, it shows that you care about your co-workers, your supervisor and your company. So this is all a **MUST-DO!!**

And don't neglect spouses or guests. Volunteer to act as a host or social director, or even distribute name tags. Before hand, tell your spouse and other guests about the people they will meet and what to do, what their interests are and to make talking easier with them. Then, go ahead and point them out.

Always introduce your spouse or guest to these people first, as soon as you see them.

You should talk to children ahead of time also. Let them know how they're expected to behave. If they get out of hand, take them aside for a quiet but firm talk. Tell them that this is your boss and your company and they have to behave.

Then, you should wear clothes that are clean comfortable, colorful and neat. Don't stray too far from the dress norms of your company. The employee picnic is not a place for a ladies man or a femme fatale. It is a place to see and be seen. So wear nice clothes but don't overcompensate to impress them with what you're wearing.

Since it's a dress down sort of event, wear comfortable clothes – jeans, etc. but with a nice pressed shirt and jacket. Look like you've just come out from of one of those magazine pictures that feature clothes of the best dressed people. You don't have to be one of them, but try for the **"look"** of it. It will make you blend in and again look like you came right out of the magazine.

Then, hang out by the food place or the bar or where the coffee machine is. Say,

"Oh, you're having the B-B-Q ribs too? They are really great!"

This one place that I worked at, had a pig roasting over a slow fire for days and they cut the food right to your order in front of you. Ribs, or pork roast; it was mouth watering!

or

"This glass of wine has some bouquet –don't you think?"

It gives you a topic to talk about with your boss or another supervisor. This is better than walking coldly up them and start talking about some nonsense about the job. At least if it's a topic that you both can relate to (**food, drink, etc.**) it starts to set up some sort of liking the same things, that can equate to future dealings back in the office.

(We are the same. We like the same things)

If your boss's and co-workers go out for lunch or after work, **YOU MUST DO THE SAME!!!**

No matter how much it costs **(the national debt).** If you go out, it builds a commraderie which will help you if a lay-off is planned. The bosses will say,

"No, we can't lay off Len – He's too valuable."

Or something to that effect. But never forget to go out. Even if your bring lunch from home or go to the gym after work, forget that stuff. **This is so much more important to your future than even your health**! You can always say, that you are on a diet and that's why you aren't eating lunch or having a glass of wine. But, you'll just have a little bite with them or a glass of water to show that you want to mingle with them.

At these functions, be aggressive in your socializing but not too aggressive. Try to know everybody as if you were already acquainted. Always seem to say the right thing. Know everybody or let it seem to be. And have no shame about making sure that your business cards get pressed into as many palms as possible.

If this behavior strikes you as a bit barracuda-like, **you're absolutely right**! And that's the way it should be. Maybe you've had more than a few encounters with a pushy, loud mouthed glad-hander who makes a fool of himself by hitting on everybody in the room for something, be it business leads or mating possibilities. But you have to do it in a way that doesn't look like a pushy, loud-mouth glad-hander way.

Knowing how to effectively socialize is only the first in a series of steps that can lead to limitless possibilities. It is an exercise in an ongoing activity. This socializing doesn't promise instant gratification, because it is designed to bring new people into your life that you can socialize with. It requires a long term view. Not only does it mean knowing how to find the right place to go, the right people to talk to when you get there, it also means that you take the primary responsibility for the development of the relationship over the months and years that follow the first contact.

Again, becoming part of the company's social activities is to talk to everyone, everywhere about everything. It's a part of a sense of belonging to the company, their work culture, their entire being. So, in order to do this, you have to listen in on other people's conversations and then break in on other people's conversations.

You do this to tell **YOUR DESIRES** and not theirs. So this way, you speak with confidence and you take care of yourself before taking care of others.

CHAPTER 26

THE BULLSHIT POLICE

Everybody will try to cut you down if you are on the way up. I call them the **"bullshit police"**. It's whenever you go to try to get ahead, there is some asshole that wants to give you grief or stand in your way. So you must make up logical sounding responses for getting ahead. No matter what **"they"** say,

"I heard that you work for a real jerk."

Answer: **"No, Mr. Jones is a vibrant, exciting individual that realizes my potential and has made me his assistant. I'm really happy to work for him."**

Or

"No. Where did you hear that? Mr. Jones is one of the best bosses here in the company. I really love working for him. Your boss should be as good as he is."

So who are these scoundrels? They are your bosses, your co-workers, in fact everybody who tries to undercut you. They should be at the top of your **"hit"** list.

Other are so jealous of your talents that they lie to force you out. How easy it is to divert blame. **Scapegoating feels good**! But it doesn't add a dime to your salary.

Neither does it help you get a new job. So just jump from situation to situation, and look narrowly at each as if it has no meaning past the isolated circumstances in which it occurs.

The biggest challenge you have to do is to find out who these bullshit police players are. They do not wear a sign that says'

"PIG"

or

"LIAR"

or my personal favorite,

"SCUM OF THE EARTH!"

CHAPTER 27

BEING A BOSS

There was a commercial for wine recently in which the person said what I have found out to be true. I've worked for short bosses, tall bosses, fat bosses, skinny bosses, good bosses, bad bosses, terrible bosses and now that I am a boss, I have learned a few things. What I've learned is never forget about small inconsequential items, because if you do, they will become big items. Most bosses that I know scream and yell about the tiniest items because **THEIR** boss is watching them or they think that their boss is watching them and they don't want their boss watching them.

You have to get people to feel safe with you and trust you, whether they are underlings or big bosses. Each big boss has an agenda; theirs was to get 6 million projects out on time and under budget and without errors. A monumental task that never happens in any field, but I tried, even without the proper amount of staff and what staff that I had was inexperienced. My boss would always proudly tell project managers that I could do their job with both hands tied behind my back and do it in less than 1 second. This because I made a monumental mistake – take on 30 jobs at once and get them out on time and under budget with minimal staff. Take my advice – **DON'T DO IT!!!**

Because if you miss one minute item on any job it will come back to haunt you. And your boss will never say that you had too much on your plate. He will cover his ass and will say that you screwed up monumentally, even if it was one of your people.

You have to remember that every boss you ever had is your only source of income. So you have to look at them like they are your God. **THEY ARE**!! They control your destiny in the company. **Listen to them and to their agenda!** Never feel that they don't talk to you because you never listen to what they say. This is a very simple idea. When talking to your boss, always steer your conversations to them and to what they want to hear. Not only in business, but what their interests are after work. Ask about their families, school ties, hobbies, sports, **anything!**

The main thing here is to make your boss, any boss. Feel safe with you and trust you. Even if it's 30 times a day that they call on you. Always make them feel safe with you and that you have control over their problem.

"Jim, I have it under control. The project will go out tonight. You can trust me to get it done."

And once you get it to go out, **ALWAYS** copy them. And not only them, anyone connected with that project. His boss, the client, your coworkers, the man in the moon – **ANYONE!**

Because if you can get your boss to feel that you did the project that he assigned to you, and that it was gotten out on time without any mistakes, he will take care of you. And that is the main thing to saving your job.

Now, even if you do all of this, some time from now, whether it's 5 minutes, or 1 week , or 3 months or even a year from now, some asshole who received your **"perfect"** job, will call and say what kind of idiot you were that you didn't sign the proper paperwork, or that one "t "or "i "wasn't crossed and he will tear into your boss for having such an idiot on staff. Your boss will then either run over to you or call you into his office and say that the client or contractor called and said that you fucked up royally.

STOP!!!

Don't go crazy. Assure your boss that there is some sort of simple explanation. That you'll take a look at the problem immediately and get back to him within a few minutes. Assure him that you followed all of the proper procedures and had it checked over by several people including you, and that the person making the call must not have the proper information.

Then, as soon as your boss walks away, **RUN**, do not walk, over to the people who helped you on the project and say,

"We got a problem here! Get out all of the information on the Schmuck file that you did for me (last year or 6 months ago) and we've got to talk about it RIGHT NOW!!! The client called screaming his head off and we've got to defuse the situation."

Now, if it was just you who did this project or report, go thru all project files and CYA stuff on this **(remember, I told you to keep a file on everything to save your hide!)** Hopefully, you will still have this. Go thru all this file, looking for any mistake that you or others might have made.

Most of the time the person calling your boss is an idiot, and did not look at all of the items correctly. This is especially true of contractors or civil service employees who never look at everything closely, but try to put the blame on you because of their shortcomings and then call your boss or those higher up screaming about some sort of minor or major error.

Once you have gone thru all of your papers and calculations, go over to your boss and say that this person who called is an idiot and that see, everything is correct. Then have both you and your boss call this person and assure them that everything is correct.

However, if something is not correct, try to sweep it under the table. Say that you didn't have the right information, that the file was lost and can't find it or make up some sort of crazy apology. But try to assure the client and your boss that it was a minor error and you can correct it immediately and that it won't happen again.

I remember being at a public agency and overhearing their boss say to them,

"We are not interested in good work. We are only interested in errors and omissions that others have made. That's is your only job – to find errors and to jump all over the people that made them."

So that is what you are up against. Especially, if you are dealing with public agencies or contractors or clients. They have one agenda and you and your boss have another. You save your boss's hide and he will save yours.

The problem is that this happens on a daily basis. You will get calls continually if you are a boss or a supervisor. You or your boss will get calls from higher ups or clients on why you didn't do something or why something wasn't exactly correct.

You have to stand and deliver and tell them that they are wrong and then you have to go and prove it.

And even if you prove it, **"they"** clients, contractors, bosses will quickly forget that what you did was right and they will say **"okay"**. No apology for cursing you out, no apology for making you spend countless hours, back doing research on what you did. To them it never happened. And guess what? In a day or two, they will do it again. Mark my words. They will do it again and again, causing you and your bosses stress and more stress. But, it's part of business and you have to put up with it, especially if you want to be a boss.

And your boss always may want to give approval on everything that you do. This is the custom in most companies, is to consult with the boss before proceeding on a task. Again, most bosses don't want someone who is headstrong **(like you!)**, or someone who is looking to make a name for himself **(like you!)**, and even possibly a threat who is not only out to take his job, his bonus or profit or even both. **(you are!)**

You just have to keep calm and again, allay his fears that he has something to fear in you **(he does!!)** But don't let him see this in you.

"Nah, I'm just a small fish here. I'm just here to make you look good."

Don't forget that you are his go-to guy, the one he has to call if he has a problem. **(and being a boss, he will!)**

Typically, your boss will give you one specific project that probably can be completed in a couple of days or weeks. And if that project turns out okay, without any problems, he'll ask you to take on a second project. When that is done he'll give you a third project and so on. He may call you in and ask how each project is being done, and you'll say,

"It's going great! No problems, and I should be finished this Friday."

And that's all he wants to hear. After he gets comfortable with you, he'll let his hair down with you. He'll discuss the problems that he is facing on a daily basis, or inside dirt on his bosses in the company or even tell you stories to make your hair stand up on projects that went wrong, before you came along.

However, you have to just listen to this crap and nod accordingly. The bottom line here is that you have to take shit all the time because you want to keep this job. You will have to take shit from your boss, his boss, whomever, just so you can keep your job. But eventually, this shit that you are taking will become second nature to you. And you won't care about the shit that you are taking every day, because, shit happens, and you are so accustomed to it, it will become second nature to you. So forget about shit happening; once it will become second nature to you that you won't care about shit happening, and at that time, you will become a boss. I know that this sounds crazy, but it is true.

It took me years to wise up to how and why things happen in the world of working people. Shit happens, and it is how you respond to how shit happens every day, as to when you are noticed. By higher ups. **REALLY!!**

The trick here is to move forward in any direction, whether it is sideways, or up or around, but forward. Whatever happens, don't collapse, don't fall apart, and above all ,**don't leave!** You will be better off if you move one foot at time, one step at a time, one right after the other, rather than jumping from place to place.

So here's what to do on those days, when it all feels like just too much. Check out these tips before you do anything rash. And believe me, I feel for you. I've been there, working for bastards and idiot bosses who don't know a hydrant from a horse:

1. Don't promise what you can't deliver.
2. Learn to manage your emotions, instead of them letting them control you.
3. Cultivate a sense of humor.
4. Resist perfectionism.
5. Resist micromanaging of yourself and others.
6. Make some friends or allies at work.
7. Vary your routine.
8. Stop trying to multitask
9. Learn to say "no"
10. Avoid negative people as much as possible **(this may not be possible if you work with idiots)**

CHAPTER 28

NOTHING SACRED (SANDBAGGING)

There is nothing sacred –**NOTHING!!**

Whatever you've been thru in this life so far is **B.S.** You have to set people up (sandbag them) before they do it to you. If you don't want to become a verbal punching bag then let loose on anyone who gets in your way. This is also called **"blindsiding"**.

Always try to blindside someone so that you have the upper hand. To be blindsided is to be attacked from a direction other than that in which you are looking. This is why people are surprised; they are so wrapped up in their work that they don't see this coming. Survival requires nothing less than an all-out effort. Your job may be chaotic and nonstop, and you may have to run from one activity to another. You may have to defend yourself against people who seek your job or have the same goals as you have and will leap at the first chance to take advantage of you. So even though you have to respond to the pressure of unreasonable demands by bosses and everyone else, you have to always watch your back, because someone wants to sandbag you.

And this is usually co-workers who sabotage you by their lack of cooperation and ability. What you should do is blow up at them and also your subordinates for giving you no support and then demand unreasonable rewards in return. Go after these to show that you know what they are doing and that you will not take it anymore.

Your peers probably blocked your view so that you couldn't see what was happening and take corrective action. If change occurs from others, you should be able to change your plan or tactics accordingly.

So corner someone and blame them and erupt like a volcano or overflow the banks with emotion (**hence the term sandbagging!**). It's terrible if it's done to you but can be a lot of fun if you do it to someone else. There is a male adage concerning females,

"If it moves fuck it! If you can't fuck it, leave it alone."

That applies here. Every successful person that I hae ever heard of is in one word – relentless about sandbagging. They do not stop for a minute, for a second, for a millisecond in order to achieve what they want.

So convince yourself that you are above all others. (**AND YOU ARE!!**)

Never be sentimental. Never consider others, never fight for others behalf. Only consider and fight for yourself. All the rest is weakness. Plan ahead; only a fool is careless and doesn't know what the odds are before you act. Don't be content until at least one person knows how dangerous you are. So be honest only when it is in your own interest. The less people know about you the less harm can be done to you. Do don't be polite when there is no reason to be.

CHAPTER 29

BECOMING AN INTEGRAL PART OF THE COMPANY'S WORK CULTURE

In every company there is a work culture. For instance, everyone wears a suit and tie or in another company, nobody wears anything but dress down clothes. In still another, people hang around the water cooler or coffee pot. But the culture of each individual company is like your individuality. But to become an integral part of the company's work culture you have to stand out or you are going to be overlooked.

This said, winning is the ultimate result of ambition. Winning then is all. It doesn't matter how you win, even if you lie, cheat, or steal to win. Since winning is everything, **anything is acceptable.** So to get ahead, use anything that can help you. A mentor, a name, a school chum, a lunch date – anyone and anything.

That's the ticket to win – anyone and everything. You have to assume whatever position or attitude that is needed to win. Instead of trying to get work done, you need to constantly cover your ass. You must make sure that you document everything. Always show yourself in a **"correct"** light. So always win! That means be cautious; wait and observe what reaction takes place. If it's a good reaction, then say,

"Actually…..I thought of it first, way before anybody else did." (no one can prove that you didn't)

And then go all out championing the idea as your own. Everybody will just assume that you came up with the idea. But, you are probably thinking how does winning become an integral part of the company's work culture?

BECAUSE IT IS EVERYTHING!!!

Do not leave the elite of the company to themselves for a moment. Keep after them, impose yourself on them and make yourself indispensable to them. Convince them of the merit of your abilities and the purity of your will; conquer them, court them, win them, match wits with every candidate among them who shows a disposition to challenge you. Give the impression that you alone are in control of yourself.

You have to think ahead to save your job. Like everyone else, you want security. You have to focus on your goals instead of focusing on your fears and see every risk as a needless risk. To gain the right perspective on risks always preface everything by this simple formula:

What can I do to make certain that I don't get eaten alive.

What can I do if something goes wrong.

And most important – what are the weaknesses if something was overlooked.

Can I be thinking all wrong about this?

Whenever you join a new company, no matter what the level, spend some time observing what its politics are. Find out about the career successes and failures that have occurred there, and why. Every company has a political environment that builds on itself. Guidelines are established that must be followed. For instance, if you are a dedicated family man you had better think twice about joining a company whose executives routinely go out for drinks at the end of the day. These company men may applaud you for your devotion to your family, and when they say have a good night, they will make some important decisions in your absence. **(and it could be about you!!)** In today's work culture, you fall in behind your boss. This means that you have to learn what your boss's mission is, how he planned to achieve it and how could you help him do it.

Being observant can also reveal what's acceptable behavior and what's not, because top management always send out such signals that establish the parameters of proper conduct in that office. Also, watch those managers who are always testing the limits of acceptable behavior in that office. Every company has them. Those who test too often – or go beyond the norms – will either be forced out or pout in a **"penalty box"**. Office politics often spins around certain personalities, so make sure that yours mixes with your peers. If the chemistry between you and another manager is bad, it may be due to a clash of conflicting styles. There is nothing wrong with working toward success, provided that the tactics are aboveboard, and there's nothing wrong with declaring your aspirations as long as you do it diplomatically.

You shouldn't zigzag from one lateral move to another. Talent is really not enough. Only about 50% of the people in any company recognize this. Really, nobody wins at corporate politics without connecting mentors, a career plan, colleagues and company acquaintances. Properly spun, you can weave a web that snares visibility, influence and access to information. The higher you climb in the company, the more intense the political game becomes. Most co-workers are not at all bashful about saying that they can handle your job better. And they will say thing like,

"If only Jim had done this, and not that, we could have made a lot more money."

That's why I always say, you must become a career b.s. artist in order to survive in a company, any company.

So, you should always look for a mentor. A mentor can be a marvelous help in many ways. He can act as your defender if trouble arises, he can be an advisor to any question that you can't answer, and he can do other things in a company environment to help you along the way.

There are certain things in a company's work culture that you need to do. First, cultivate networks, maintain visibility. The time to cultivate your network is before you need it, not after. Therefore, you've got to work at being known to others in your profession. Participate in volunteer activities, that will increase exposure to those who might someday help you. Second, develop talents and skills that will increase your value for other employers, maybe through formal education, seminars or special projects. Avoid overspecialization, maintain generality. In anything, never cite anything specific, but limit yourself to vague remarks, follow it up with a comment that can be summed up by saying,

"Clarify and resubmit."

That's always a good one.

CHAPTER 30

BECOMING A SOCIAL BUTTERFLY

Everyone in a company likes the social butterfly because they don't offend anyone and drift from one person (**flower**) to another, picking up little bits of information (**pollen**) and disseminating it on others. They never do any work, all they do all day long is to flutter here and flutter there, b.s.ing all day long. But to do this you need not only to become a smooth talker, you have to be well versed and well-read in just about everything. You don't have to read the newspaper or listen to the 11PM news, but listen to a channel or radio or TV station that gives you glimpses of what is going on in the nation and the world.

So you can always talk about the weather, especially if thee was some sort of natural even that just happened. You can talk about the movies, music, books, etc. Talk about the concert that you just went to or your favorite stars in movies and music. Especially talk about sports, even if you don't like sports, since a lot of people, including women are into sporting events. Pick one sport that you are interested in and bone up on the key players and movies. Then you can talk about your hobbies (**do you have any except for work?)** Some supervisors like to fly kites, collect things or build things**. If they do, then you should too.**

Everybody likes to talk about travel. Whether you just visited someplace or not talk about it. Or even talk about the place that you'd like to travel to.

Everybody eats food, so talk about what you love to eat or cook. Talk about the restaurant you just tried or the place that you'd love to try. Talk about where you're from and where you live now and what are the differences. Maybe someone that you're talking to knows someone from the same city or someone that went to the same college as you. Talk about your family but not to the extent that you talk about who is getting divorced or who just died. You can also talk about pets if you have them, but be cautious, since if you say you hate cats, the person that you're talking to loves cats.

If you wear glasses, you should get contact lenses. Also, getting a good hair styling will help, and if you're showing grey hairs, then get a hair coloring. (**don't do it yourself since it looks like you did it yourself!**) Make people feel at ease in your presence. So, don't let your voice crack; **talk like a man**! Talk in a range of several notes, starting with your lowest note on the scale until you feel comfortable with that. Then, don't blink unnecessarily. Also, don't make unnecessary hand gestures. Hold your body still for 5 minutes or more at a time. Try holding a full glass of water and walk about the room. This should get you focused on not spilling a drop.

Next, observe what is hot right now, what is being talked about and capitalize on that. The first key rule and **the ONLY RULE** to becoming a social butterfly is to tell stories. Just tell stories to get your point across. Don't give a power point presentation or bore the person with figures or numbers, just tell a story.

"When I was in Antartica last month, the penguin parade was just fantastic to watch."

Don't feel that you have to expand on the story unless they ask you to. **(which they will!)**

And in order to be successful at becoming a social butterfly, you have to change the way that you talk to people. You have to **"walk the floor"** a minimum of 3 or 4 times a day, stopping at every person to chat. **Don't use the phone!! Don't stay in your cubicle or office! And especially DON'T DO ANY WORK!!** Just go down and meet people. That's the ticket. People will forgive you if they like you and the way for people to like you is to see them every few minutes. All day long, say something aloud to draw somebody into a conversation even if it is the most common thing.

"The ice is really frozen solid."

Or

"The Sun is really shining."

Or

"It's really dark out at night."

Then impress everybody with your knowledge. **(however limited it is!!)**

"Did you know that the Brooklyn Bridge wasn't called a bridge when it was built. It was called an erection!!"

Always pick someone close by to a conversation and say,

"Isn't that right, Hubie?"

or

"Right, Hubie?"

As if asking for agreement even though you don't necessarily want it.

Also, make statements and noise aloud on nothingness to anyone that you see just passing you by.

"You starting trouble Hubie?"

or

"Big Ray!"

or

"Doo, doo, doo!"

To anyone or no one. Again, you're just making a statement or a noise to attract attention and people. So make a big deal of talking aloud about something, i.e. The Super Bowl score or the World Series as soon as you come into work – nothing else matters, not work, nothing except what you are talking about.

"Wow!! What a last quarter!!"

or

"Did you see that play?"

Try to get involved in minor company things, like a coffee club, where you contribute or even if you don't. Buy milk and cookies out of your pocket; or do it even if you are reimbursed. Soon everybody will think that you are doing it all of the time and they will expect you to do it. Like filling the copy machine with paper. Always make sure that everybody knows that you filled the copy machine with paper.

"See everyone, I filled the copy machine with paper."

Or fill the towel holder in the bathroom with paper towels or whatever.

"Hey, everyone – I filled the towel paper holder in the bathroom with paper."

Make sure that everybody knows it was you and you alone was the one who did it.

"I'm the only one here who does anything!"

Even filling the coffee cup dispenser with cups.

"I filled the coffee cups. You all can now have coffee."

The say aloud what you do, even if it is meaningless.

"I do such beautiful work!!"

And then say in an aside to anyone nearby,

"Isn't this good?"

The one basic approach to becoming a social butterfly is humor. But humor is not your ultimate goal here; it's just a tool to help you make your point or in this case endear people to you in your quest to become a social butterfly. Used properly, humor can be a powerful aid. It accomplishes several things:

1. It gives you likeability and respect
2. It makes people that you're talking to, listen more attentively to you.
3. It helps whomever is near to you to remember what you are saying even if it's garbage **(especially if it's garbage!!)**

Doing this will get people to respect you and like you because it will make them think that you are one of them. **(YOU ARE AREN"T YOU?)**

And anyone who wants the respect and admiration of who is listening to him. Getting people to listen to you is not always easy work; it requires concentration and it **IS** work.

So always give **"ALL"** secretaries and mail room people gifts for Christmas and such, as the following"

1. Single layer of cookies
2. Double layer of cookies.
3. Finger candy bowls
4. Etc.

Then, have at least two people, one from each sex, check you out each day. Say,

"How do I look?"

So, no loose strands on clothing showing, tie and collar straight, hair combed so that not one strand is out of place, even if it looks casual.

Your car doesn't have to be special, but it has to attract attention, like a late- night Casanova. The tires should have white raised lettering and a candy apple red color or a sports car with the same colors.

Wherever you go, say to a bank to cash your check, or make a withdrawal, tell a girl teller, while she is counting money,

"You are FAST!!"

Maybe she'll goof up and give you more money.

"It's a pleasure to watch you work!!"

Smiling is a necessary part of being a social butterfly. For some reason, people with a lot of teeth smile. Adopt this tactic. However don't have a faceless smile that you turn on and off. It should come out naturally; let it ooze out of you like melted butter.

Here's how to learn to have the perfect smile. Hold chopsticks in your mouth. **Seriously!** That's how China trains attendants on how to learn the perfect smile. Not too big, not to small, just right. You can keep this type of smile on all day long, **try it!**

However your conversation should not stay in negative territory and then smile. Always do a positive take, since you don't want to frighten somebody. It's a delicate twist but you have to learn it if you want to become a social butterfly.

So to start a conversation or drag somebody into a conversation, say (**as you're passing by them**),

"Ask Jim, he knows all about it." (why the world turns on its axis!)

And as always, never stop talking. Be like a woman who never shut up. They can talk for hours on nothingness. So, don't be like a man and say one word answers, talk like a woman and speak for 120 minutes with each person. If they try to walk away to get back to work, say,

"One more thing, did they ever catch Billy the Kid?"

To become a social butterfly has to include a combination of extraordinary leadership traits. Your personal qualities has to enable you to form friendships with men and women who may have originally opposed you.

"How about that Jets game huh?"

You have to repair injured feelings,

"That didn't hurt so bad, did it?" And laugh. Because you don't want these injured feelings to escalate into permanent hostility. And most of all you have to take full responsibility for the mistakes of subordinates, and to find and give credit to anybody and to learn from your mistakes.

Everything that I've described is a means to an end. And what's the end?

This is.

THE END

ABOUT THE AUTHOR

Leonard Love Matlick is an engineer and a personal success and confidence trainer.

www.ingramcontent.com/pod-product-compliance
Lightning Source LLC
Chambersburg PA
CBHW060543200326
41521CB00007B/466